THE STORY OF LABRADOR

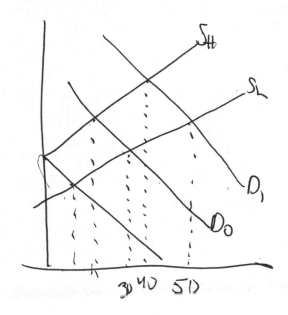

The Story of Labrador

BILL ROMPKEY

McGill-Queen's University Press
Montreal & Kingston · London · Ithaca

© McGill-Queen's University Press 2003
ISBN 0-7735-2574-2 (cloth)
ISBN 0-7735-2995-0 (paper)

Legal deposit third quarter 2003
Bibliothèque nationale du Québec

Printed in Canada on acid-free paper.
Reprinted 2003
First paperback edition 2005

McGill-Queen's University Press acknowledges the support of the
Canada Council for the Arts for our publishing program. We also
acknowledge the financial support of the Government of Canada
through the Book Publishing Industry Development Program (BPIDP)
for our publishing activities.

**National Library of Canada Cataloguing
in Publication Data**

Rompkey, William, 1936–
    The story of Labrador / by Bill Rompkey.
    Includes bibliographical references and index.
    ISBN 0-7735-2574-2 (bnd)
    ISBN 0-7735-2995-0 (pbk)
    1. Labrador (Nfld.) – History. I. Title.
    FC2193.4.R64 2003   971.8′2   C2003-901574-2
    F1137.R64 2003

Typeset in Palatino 10/12
by Caractéra inc., Quebec City

For Carolyn, Hilary, and Peter

Contents

The Pageant

When I was principal of Yale School in North West River, one of the joys of the year was the Christmas concert. It was a time-honoured custom in those days, and it was watched and enjoyed by the whole community. Each class, young and old, put on a performance. It might be simply the nativity scene, or it might be a skit or singing or tumbling or a play. The children had the right to choose the performance and they did. It was theirs. They were proud of it, and it was applauded by the whole community.

It seems to me that the story of Labrador is like this. Over the centuries different peoples have appeared on her stage. Some stayed; some did not. Some retreated to the rear of the stage for a while, though we were still very much aware of their presence and waited for them to emerge once again in the full glare of the lights. Some learned from others, competed with others, or learned to work together. Some fought. Some tried to dominate and did. Some cared for and protected others and helped them make the best of their lives. Some moved. In the midst of the events that helped shape their lives and their land, whatever their role, they gave their performance, and we have witnessed it and reflected on it and assessed it. Those who are still there obviously are staying. They have made it their place. They cannot go home because the big land is their home.

What they have in common is the place, Labrador, where they have lived and moved and had their being. A big beautiful land, sometimes bitter, sometimes challenging, always varied, always stimulating and attractive, a land that grips you and won't let go – the forger of lifelong friendships. Not everyone has seen it this way, but the people who haven't are mostly those who have never lived there or spent enough time there.

What follows is an examination of the various people who have trod, sailed, paddled, and flown the Labrador, both groups and individuals, and who, whether lasting or temporary, in spite of or because of the tides of history have left an imprint. This was their place. Those who were born there had a very strong sense of place; but even those who came from away have grown to appreciate the identity of Labrador and see themselves as Labradorians.

Jacques Cartier, who assembled his fleet at Chateau Bay in 1534, called Labrador "the land God gave to Cain." In Hebrew, Cain means "smith," a worker with metals, and this is indeed the story of those who over the centuries have worked with metals and stone – with Ramah chert, iron ore, and latterly anorthosite, silica, and nickel. For this is the story of how old economies have been replaced by new.

It is also an examination of how Labradorians were governed and how they tried more and more to govern themselves. Although both the Inuit and the Innu had their own forms of governance, for some time after the coming of the Europeans there was really no government at all. Then there was government by non-governmental organizations. Finally, the government governed. But how and for whom? The fact is that Newfoundland and Labrador have been like two uneasy stepsisters who have left the house of their mother and tried to share a common place. Each with its own strong identity has sustained the relationship because of mutual dependence or because there was no clearly identified alternative. But the relationship, in the way of siblings, has been thorny and prickly from time to time. Only recently have there been signs that it is changing.

Acknowledgments

I am very grateful for the help of a number of people. First of all, Peter Neary encouraged me from the beginning and made some very helpful comments and suggestions. George Perlin was also very supportive. Peter Steele was enthusiastic from the start. I am indebted to David Clarke, an excellent researcher, and to Janice Marshall for finding important details and helping with the indexing. Ron Rompkey was always there as a sounding board and adviser. Michael Staveley helped me with the section on the boundary decision. Stephen Loring reviewed and suggested revisions to the first part. Sean Dutton made helpful suggestions. Because of his unique background, the comments of Edward Roberts were very useful. Carlotta Lemieux, an excellent editor, pointed out my sins of commission and omission, and saved me from the abyss of historical inaccuracy.

A number of Labrador residents, past and present, gave generously of their time for interviews and I am grateful for their important contributions: Gordon Manstan, Dick and Barbara Budgell, Ed Montague, Ed Hearn, Dorice Marcil, Joe Smith, Hank and Bella Shouse, Charles Devine, Lester (Ghandi) Coombs, Art Rendell, Edward Blake, Mac Moss, Andy Chatwood, Len Leyte, Alphonse Rudkowski, Max Short, Peter Roberts, Adelard O'Brien, and Doug and Marie House.

I am deeply indebted to my son-in-law, Joel Trojanowski, for his great skill and patience in drawing my map.

The staff at the Parliamentary Library, the Center for Newfoundland Studies at Memorial University, the Provincial Archives of Newfoundland and Labrador, and the Archives of the Anglican Church in St John's, as well as Burton Janes of the Pentecostal Assemblies, were unfailingly kind. So were the staff of the Labrador City Library. Gill Brown of *Them Days* kindly assisted.

Finally, my deepest gratitude to my wife Carolyn, who has lived Labrador with me for forty years and who still patiently made those cups of tea every time I emerged from the basement computer to seek her advice. This is a story I have wanted to write for a long time, and she is a part of it in so many ways.

Inukshuk at Okak
Photo: Government of Newfoundland and Labrador

The Viking Wonderstrand, a fifty-mile stretch of golden, sandy beach just north of Cartwright
Photo: W. Rompkey

The Torngat Mountains rival the Norwegian fjords in their awesome
beauty.
Photo: W. Rompkey

Recognized for its prime fishing rooms since the eighteenth century, and
an early Grenfell and communications post, today Battle Harbour is
a tourist mecca.
Photo: George Way

Grand Falls, renamed Hamilton and then Churchill, had,
as A.P. Low said, "a stunning effect ... heard for miles away as a
deep, booming sound."
Photo: W. Rompkey

Dr Harry Paddon, who not only
pioneered health and education in
Labrador but was a spokesperson for
Labradorians who had no other
Photo: *Them Days*

Joe Retty and Mathieu Gregoire, his Innu guide,
on their way to the iron ore find of the 1930s
Photographer unknown

William Martin checks his traps in Sandwich Bay, c. 1910.
Photo: *Them Days*

The Voisey family in 1910. Today their bay is the site of the world's
richest nickel mine.
Photo: *Them Days*

Bach chorales brought by the early Moravians were still sung by
the Nain Choir in the 1960s.
Photo: Government of Newfoundland and Labrador

Inuit occupied Hopedale (Avertok) from the 1500s. The Moravian
buildings include one that dates from the early nineteenth century.
Photo: Government of Canada

North West River in 1935
From a painting by Isobel Watts

The Moravians brought prefabricated buildings from Germany in the
eighteenth century, such as these at Hebron.
Photo: W. Rompkey

As MP I met often with the founder of the Combined Councils of Labrador, Bill Andersen of Makkovik, whose sons, Toby and Chesley, are leading land claims negotiators for the Labrador Inuit.
Photo: Government of Canada

Kate Hettasch, the daughter of "Dr" Paul, was an outstanding educator on the north coast.
Photo: W. Rompkey

Jack Watts, with his wife, Annie Baikie, provided strong support for two generations of Paddons at North West River.
Photo: W. Rompkey

As late as the mid-twentieth century, Newfoundland fishermen still depended on the coastal boats for their summer sojourn to Labrador.
Photo: W. Rompkey

The Ski-Doo has replaced the dog team, but modern Labradorians still travel the ice surface to reach trout and seal holes.
Photo: W. Rompkey

A Grenfell wop carries an Inuit child from the air ambulance at North West River; at far left is Rev. Carl Major, himself a pilot.
Photo: W. Rompkey

Hon. Wally Andersen, LIA, Peter Penashue, president of the Innu Nation, and Sheshatshiu Band Chief Paul Rich join the award-winning team at the Labrador Winter Games.
Photo: Michelle Baikie

The *Northern Ranger*, the latest and most modern of the Labrador vessels
that have been the lifeline for the coast since the nineteenth century
Photo: W. Rompkey

The Quebec North Shore and Labrador Railway, built through rugged
but spectacular country, brings iron ore from Labrador West to Sept-Îles
and Pointe-Noire.
Photo: Government of Newfoundland and Labrador

Huge trucks extract iron ore from an open pit in Labrador West.
Photo: David Turner

Labrador West has excellent downhill and cross-country trails which the
Canadian National Team has used for training.
Photo: Government of Newfoundland and Labrador

Carved out of the wilderness, Labrador City rivals any town its size for amenities and quality of life.
Photo: Iron Ore Company

Military jets from Britain, Germany, and Italy are still the economic mainstay of Goose Bay.
Photo: Institute for Environmental Monitoring and Research

The historic lighthouse at Point Amour, now a site for whale watchers, has guided many a ship through the Strait of Belle Isle.
Photo: Government of Newfoundland and Labrador

L'Anse-au-Loup, where a successful fishermen's coop, the Labrador
Shrimp Company, has its headquarters
Photo: W. Rompkey

Some of the best black spruce in the world piled on the dock at Goose,
which became the most important Labrador port when construction of
the base began in 1941
Photo: Government of Canada

A portion of the Trans-Labrador Highway, which opened up the territory for people and trade
Photo: W. Rompkey

The dog team, so vital to early Labradorians, now stars in international races like this one in Labrador West.
Photo: W. Rompkey

Woodward's new ferry, the *Apollo*, has plenty of room for vehicles and passengers crossing the Strait of Belle Isle.
Photo: W. Rompkey

With the Arctic ice melting rapidly, more and more icebergs cruise the Labrador coast.
Photo: W. Rompkey

The George River caribou herd is still among the largest herd in the world.
Photo: Institute for Environmental Monitoring and Research

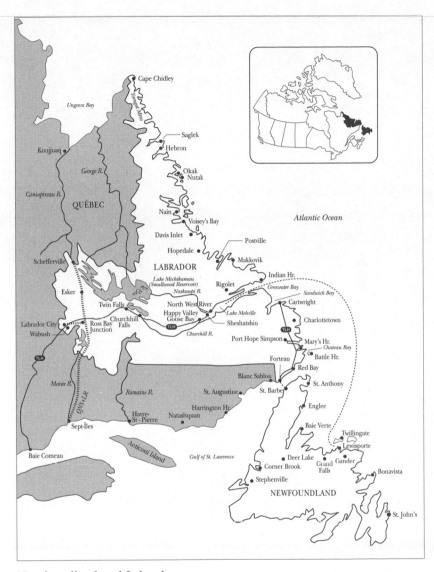

Newfoundland and Labrador

THE STORY OF LABRADOR

What Is Labrador?

Oh you wilderness land of cold, clean distance, you pitiless Labrador of winter twilight, we shall love you forever, yes, forever with the love of children and savages, you land too strong to be spoiled by men, you land of fathomless beauty.

Elliot Merrick, *True North*

Indeed there is in this wild land a silent happiness which many a man and woman in England might envy: solitude without absolute loneliness, days of ease without care, nights of pleasure without parade.

Lambert de Boilieu, *Recollections of Labrador Life*

For our purposes, Labrador is the east coast of the Ungava Peninsula, 300,000 square kilometres, or more than twice the size of its half-sister, the island of Newfoundland. Although in earlier times the name referred to a larger area, including most of Ungava, it is now as the Judicial Committee of the British Privy Council defined it in 1927: extending due north from Blanc Sablon on the Quebec North Shore to the fifty-second parallel of latitude, then due west to the Romaine River, and then meandering north "along the crest of the watershed of the rivers flowing into the Atlantic Ocean to Cape Chidley." The boundary was still largely unsurveyed in 1991, mostly because Quebec did not consider the question of jurisdiction settled even though it had negotiated iron ore and hydro agreements as if the boundary were in place. On Killinek Island, at the northern tip, Labrador has a short boundary with its new neighbour, Nunavut.

Geographically, Labrador is part of the Canadian Shield, some of the oldest rock in the world. Formed 800 million years ago by forces deep within the earth, Labrador has through millions of years been shorn and torn by wind, rain and ice. It has been submerged under the sea and wrenched by continental drift. Ice has shaped its character. Glaciers moved across it, scouring and scraping the land and carving its surface into majestic mountains and rocks, leaving it a land of endless variety. The glaciers dug trenches and ravines that filled with water to form lakes and river valleys. The Churchill River, 335 kilometres long, drains a watershed of 77,700 square kilometres. It drops 1600 metres in a 26-kilometre stretch. Out on the coast, the ice dug even larger valleys, so that when it melted and the sea level rose, deep fiords such as Saglek and Hebron appeared, rivalling those of Norway. The glaciers pushed Labrador's surface into the earth so that when the ice finally passed and the land lifted again, fossilized shells appeared on the surface. In time, tundra shrub and forests offered a habitat for wild game, as well as fuel and shelter for the humans who found their way there.

Mountains, sometimes stretching all the way to the sea, dominate the north coast. The Torngat Mountains, named for the Inuit spirit, stretch along the coast from Port Manvers to Cape Chidley, with coastal elevations as high as 1524 metres north of Nachvak Bay. Here Mount Caubvick, called Mont D'Iberville in Quebec (it is on the Quebec-Labrador border), rises 1652 metres, the highest peak in Canada east of the Rockies. To the south, the Kaumajet and Kiglapait mountain ranges, containing seventy small glaciers (the most southerly in North America), extend 400 kilometres south almost to Nain. Arctic vegetation is found only in the valleys. Lower elevations south of the fifty-eighth parallel, roughly the edge of the treeline, support an abundance of wildlife in forests mainly of spruce, fir, and larch. Farther south the mountains are softer and less forbidding as the boreal forest covers the mid section of Labrador south to the Gulf of St Lawrence.

The first comprehensive account of the geography of the region by Tanner in 1944 described the "endless wooded solitudes of the central part of the peninsula" as well as "a great plain, strewn with a strange multitude of lakes and a veritable labyrinth of ponds, alternating with very extensive swamps and bogs."[1] The Labrador coast, mostly bare rock and windswept barrens, has myriad bays, fiords, and islands. The greatest cleavage in this lengthy coastline is Hamilton Inlet, its shores heavily forested, which extends some 240 kilometres in from the sea. Near its mouth a glacier has deposited a vast stretch of sandy beach, the Wonderstrand of the Viking sagas. Although much of Labrador south of Cape Harrison consists of rolling hills, there are mountain ranges such as the Mealies on the south side of Hamilton Inlet, where Parks Canada has plans to establish a national park. Here, as elsewhere in Labrador, grow some of the best black spruce in the world.

Not everyone has been effusive in praise of Labrador's interior. In 1833 the naturalist John J. Audubon described it thus: "From the top of a high rock I had a fine view of the most extensive and dreariest wilderness I have ever beheld. It chilled the heart to gaze on these barren lands of Labrador."[2] But Audubon visited only part of the south coast for about a month, recording and making portraits of the birds he saw: puffins, gannets, gulls, guillemots, ducks, terns, geese, swallows, cormorants, and ptarmigan. Had he gone farther north, his heart would no doubt have soared as high as the eagle nests that he certainly would have encountered. Nor could he have experienced the pulsating and shimmering hues of silvery gold as the northern lights dance across a clear arctic night. At moments like that, "dreary" is the last word that leaps to the mind.

In the interior are numerous lakes fed and drained by a multitude of streams and rivers. The province's largest and longest is the Churchill River, formerly known as the Hamilton and before that the Grand. Others running into Hamilton Inlet are the Kenamu, Kenemish, and Naskaupi. The White Bear, Eagle, and Paradise rivers flow into Sandwich Bay, while the Pinware ends at the Strait of Belle Isle. The largest of Labrador lakes, Michikamau – at times home to both the Innu and the settler trappers of Lake Melville – in the 1960s became part of the 5698 square-kilometre Smallwood Reservoir above the Churchill River. The interior, like the coast, is a breeding ground for a variety of animals, birds, and fish. Labrador may still be relatively unexplored because of the flies spawned on its vast expanses of water.

The flies – just the beginning of the Labrador food chain – are consumed by dragonflies, which in turn provide food for the baby speckled trout, themselves prey for the majestic osprey wheeling menacingly overhead. On the other hand, a deadly germ can decimate the snowshoe hare and the lynx that feeds on it. The weasel searches for voles and lemmings under the snow. Foxes and martens listen intently for their movements as well. And if the vole comes out at night, that is when the great horned owl is most alert.

Perhaps the caribou is the most prominent and important land animal in Labrador, providing sustenance for the Innu and Inuit as well as for many settlers. There are herds in various parts of Labrador – the Red Wine Mountains, the Mealies, the Torngats, Lac Joseph – but the George River herd is the largest in the world, with perhaps over 600,000 animals at present. Spectacular bands, both large and small, sometimes in the hundreds or even thousands, roam from the George River area in northern Quebec to northern Labrador, their southern perimeter lately extending as far south as Lake Melville. In the late winter and early spring, small groups of females calve in the tundra east of the George River before moving to summer feeding grounds near the coast. In August and September the herd moves west again to the George River area and south towards Lakes Mistinibi and Mistastin.

Along with the flies, a predator of the caribou is the wolf. Like the caribou, the wolf travels in packs of eight to ten. Lambert de Boilieu described them in action in the nineteenth century:

They march just like the front rank of a company of soldiers with their leader a little forward on the left; they keep two feet apart, and when a herd of deer is sighted, at a given signal they break up into detached skirmishing order. In a short space of time, however, you will observe the whole of the skirmishers in a close circle round the deer, fast closing to the center, where the conflict, being so unequal – for the wolf is immeasurably stronger than the deer – soon terminates in the wolves sitting in banquet over the bodies of the conquered.[3]

Berries on bushes and on the ground sprinkle the hills and valleys with splashes of colour. In autumn, when the land is ripe with blueberries, redberries (partridgeberries in some parts of Labrador), and bakeapples, both women and men make an outing for the day with their pans and baskets to harvest a winter supply for pies and puddings and jams.

Labrador's trees are all below the fifty-eighth parallel. The south is thick with several excellent timber stands, the colours more delicate than those of central Canada; but the trees thin and gradually disappear farther north around Napartok Bay. The black spruce dominates, a hardy tree that draws its life slowly, even from the permafrost, and takes up to a hundred years to grow. Yet it is this very tight weave that gives it great strength, making it the best in the world for the manufacture of cardboard boxes. But groves of sprightly birch are not uncommon. Other trees, such as balsam fir, try to survive. North of the treeline only the hardiest plants are found.

Majestic icebergs break free of the northern glaciers (doing so more and more frequently of late) and are carried south by the cold Labrador Current. They bring with them the plant, animal, and marine life that lives in that cold habitat. For in spite of its fierce storms and chilling cold, Labrador has provided a rich and bountiful supply of fish and game for those who have trod its shores and sailed its waters over the centuries. The black bear is prized for its furry coat, though not as highly as the great white polar bear. There is also a variety of seabirds, including an island full of gannets; and ducks of different hues make Labrador their home for part of the year.

The Labrador Current with its load of ice makes navigation almost impossible from December to June. It heads east to meet the warmth of the Gulf Stream, and the happy meeting produces waters replete with plankton on which feed capelin, herring, haddock, mackerel, halibut, and the most famous fish of all – cod. As well, the waters are home to the seal, so fundamental to the culture of the Inuit; it has sustained them and others since humans first arrived on the shores of Labrador. But it was the whale that drew the early Basques, searching for oil for the lamps of Europe, just as today drill ships seek out oil for the modern industrial machine, exploring the seabed with its huge untapped fields of gas and oil. Also in these waters is the Atlantic salmon, whose homing instinct underlines the magnetic draw that Labrador has had, and still has, on so many. The salmon shares the great Labrador rivers with the highly prized arctic char and the trout.

In the Labrador Straits fog comes and goes, sometimes with astonishing rapidity, creating a menace for navigators. Many a plucky mariner has sailed with great caution through the Strait of Belle Isle, and many a ship has found a watery grave beneath its waters. Military divers are still examining the wreck of HMS *Raleigh*, which impaled itself on the rocks off Point Amour. Still, the strait is the gateway to the St Lawrence and to the centre of the continent, and on a clear day, if you are sitting near the old lighthouse at Point Amour, you may see a giant ship escorted by a gambolling pod of whales.

CHAPTER ONE

The Originals

The big men with clever fingers
Who had no dogs and hauled their sleds
Over the frozen northern oceans
Awkward giants
   Killers of seals...

Al Purdy, *Lament for the Dorsets*

The hunting tradition that we have been taught by our families we regard as part of our lives ... We have kept these traditions and cultures from our fathers ... We are a proud people, a proud nation.

Michael Pasteen

MARITIME ARCHAIC

In 1973 James Tuck and Robert McGhee, two archaeologists from Memorial University of Newfoundland, discovered a strange mound of rocks on a high sandy beach at L'Anse-Amour in the Strait of Belle Isle at the point closest to Newfoundland. Digging below the rocks they were astonished to unearth the grave of a young man. Twelve or thirteen years old, he had been buried face down, wrapped in animal skins tinted with red ochre. A large stone lay in the middle of his back, ostensibly ensuring that he would not come back to haunt the living. Radiocarbon dating has revealed that the grave had been dug 7000 to 7500 years ago, in an age when no people in North America were burying their dead in such a ceremonial fashion (a period 2000 years before the building of the pyramids of Egypt). Yet here were a people with customs and traditions, who by means of this burial were stating clearly that this was their land and this was their way.

Paleo-Indians had moved into Canada as the glacial ice retreated almost 12,000 years ago, but in Labrador archaeologists have yet to uncover any remains of these early people. Sometime between 8000 and 9000 years ago, early Maritime Archaic people came to the land now called Labrador. The oldest sites currently known appear to be about one kilometre from Pinware, where artifacts have been found that include leaf-shaped and oval knives made of local quartzite and small thumbnail scrapers of quartz and quartz crystal. There are also battered stone wedges, possibly used for woodworking. These people were supplanted by the later Maritime Archaic, one of whom was the twelve-year-old boy. They moved north as the ice sheet retreated and the warming climate provided them with vegetation, mammals, birds, and fish. Their occupation of the coast was extensive, with campsites dotting the interior as well as the coast, and they maintained contact with one another for wood and other essential supplies. Some 7000 years ago they had reached Okak Bay, about 80 kilometres north of today's Nain, and 6000 years ago they reached the Saglek area. In the same general area, where recently two Newfoundland prospectors found the richest nickel mine in the world, the Maritime Archaic people found what for their time was an equally rich substance: Ramah chert, a grey silicate with a grainy texture. It was a new technology for them, easily flaked into tools and thin symmetrical weapons.

Living in large communal houses, hunting walrus and seals, the Maritime Archaic people had a rich and bountiful life. We know from their burial sites that they practised elaborate rituals, and we know from the Ramah chert found in Newfoundland, the Maritimes, and Quebec that they participated in long-distance exchange and communications networks by means of oceangoing boats.

Like those who came after them, they chased the caribou in winter and hunted for seals and other marine life in summer. There is evidence that they used some of the same hunting methods as their successors, the Innu, herding the caribou to a hill or stream, where the animals could be killed as they plunged into one depression or the other. Also like their successors, they killed caribou for food and clothing, and believed that possessing a portion of a bird or animal would give them certain desirable powers belonging to that creature or make it easier to hunt successfully. But while they used the land and what it provided, they were primarily a maritime people. Along the Labrador coast from Hamilton Inlet to Saglek are found traces of their tent rings and hunting blinds. As well, the foundations of their longhouses are visible – long heaped-up rows of boulders and gravel enclosing two to four small rooms, each with its own outside cache. Bill Fitzhugh of the Smithsonian Institution discovered a series of

campsites near today's town of North West River that were first
occupied more than 3500 years ago, around the time the Maritime
Archaic people disappeared from the coast.

PALEO-ESKIMOS

About 4000 years ago a people racially, culturally, and linguistically
different made their appearance on the Labrador coast. They were
the Paleo-Eskimos, or Pre-Dorsets, who occupied the coast from
Saglek to Hopedale and even south to Hamilton Inlet. They lived
year-round on the coast, and while they took advantage of the bounty
of the sea, they were terrestrial hunters as well, particularly of
muskox and caribou. We know little about their dress, art, ornamen-
tation, or spiritual beliefs, though they resembled today's Inuit in
appearance. They were people of the High Arctic who gradually
moved south at the expense of the Maritime Archaic people, who
retreated before them.

These early Inuit brought a new technology, a colourful fine-
grained chert that was different from that used by the Maritime
Archaic people. Their kit included burins for slotting or carving bone,
ivory, and wood, along with arrows and scrapers. Spear points made
by the Maritime Archaic have been found in Pre-Dorset sites, which
suggests that there was some form of contact between the two peoples. How they managed their coexistence in Labrador for five hundred years is still a mystery. They probably avoided each other as
much as possible.

DORSETS

About 2500 years ago the Paleo-Eskimos were replaced by the
Dorsets. Dorset sites have been found all the way from the northern
Labrador coast to the Quebec North Shore and also along the coast
of Newfoundland. Tent rings, rectangular sod houses, and above-
ground meat caches found along the outer coast show that they
occupied this territory until about 1200 years ago. They, too, lived
mainly on the coast, hunting seals and walruses. Like their predecessors and successors, they hunted seals at breathing holes, but they
also collected nesting gulls on the cliffs and caught fish in the ponds
and char in the river mouths. All this was available to them as well
as berries, shellfish, bears, foxes, partridges, and whales. With them,
whalebone made its first appearance on the runners of sleds, a practice that continued well into the twentieth century by Inuit and non-
Inuit alike, until whalebone was replaced by iron and eventually

plastic. Like their successors, they used soapstone bowls and had lamps (kudliks) in their dwellings for heat and light. They had a strong belief in the ability of spirits to influence both nature and humans – their sites have yielded tiny amulets, figurines, and carvings. At Saglek, carved soapstone images of owls, bears, and people were found. They include a couple in an obvious sexual embrace and human faces on miniature pot and lamp fragments.

The Dorsets shared the Labrador coast with the Groswater Eskimos (who had evolved in Labrador from the Pre-Dorsets) and with Intermediate and Point Revenge Indians, the probable ancestors of today's Innu. By about the time of Christ the Dorsets had spread onto the island of Newfoundland, where they survived beside the ancestors of the Beothuk for the next thousand years. They were amazing artists, these Dorsets, as displays in the Newfoundland Museum will testify. Their demise remains a mystery, but we know that within a century or two of their arrival in Labrador the Thule Inuit had completely replaced them and spread as far south as Hamilton Inlet. Some of the Dorsets may have retreated to Ungava, while others may have been absorbed into the Thule community. By the end of the fifteenth century the Late Dorsets had disappeared. Yet they remain in the memory and tales of the Inuit as the Tunit – strong but peaceful giants.

INTERMEDIATE CULTURE

We have no idea what happened to the Maritime Archaic people or their way of life after about 4000 years ago. The culture that replaced them lasted for 2300 years. Nobody is sure where the Intermediate Indians came from, but traces of them have been found around Sheshatshiu and in Groswater Bay, as well as on the Labrador coast between Hopedale and Hebron and as far south as the Strait of Belle Isle.

Their use of Ramah chert was minimal, and burial sites like those of the Maritime Archaic have not been found. More importantly, they lived mostly in the forests and away from the sea, perhaps because of the presence of the Pre-Dorsets on the coast. They visited the coast only in summer and only for short periods. The relationship between the Intermediate people and the Pre–Dorsets is the earliest evidence of competition and conflict between two peoples in Labrador, and it must have been responsible for the retreat of the Intermediates, who moved southward and inland to avoid contact with the Inuit. The people of the Intermediate period were likely the first who came to this area to escape starvation and persecution and to find a new life, just as the Innu later did and just as settlers from the Orkney Islands and Scotland would also do.

LATER PERIOD

After the Intermediate period a new people inhabited Labrador. Their culture dates from about 1200 years ago, and they were likely the immediate ancestors of today's Innu. This period in Labrador can be divided between the Daniel Rattle Complex (AD200–1000) and the Point Revenge Complex (AD1000–1500). Both groups used Ramah chert, though the shape and size of their tools and weapons differ. Stephen Loring of the Smithsonian Institution contends that Ramah chert had considerable spiritual significance, for although the people of Labrador had to go a long way north to the territory of the Dorsets to acquire it, they sought it in spite of the fact that there were substitutes. Furthermore, their tools were sometimes ritually "killed" by burning. Of course, they might have acquired the chert by trade, as part of a complex trading network through which this mineral found its way as far south as New England and as far west as James Bay.

These people were not primarily caribou hunters. Although they undoubtedly did foray into the interior to hunt caribou, they were primarily a coastal people drawing their living from the resources of the sea. Yet caribou were important to their way of life. The women turned caribou hide inside out to make coats, hoods, pants, and leggings, as the Innu later did. And like the Innu they used caribou hides along with birchbark as a tent covering.

They occupied most of the Labrador coast south of Saglek Bay and probably most of the interior of the Labrador Peninsula until 500 years ago, when the Thule Eskimos arrived and pushed them from the coast. Skirmishes with the Inuit are still remembered in the Innu oral tradition. As a result of such attacks, these predecessors of the Innu were, for the most part, confined to the interior, where the Inuit did not go. They turned more and more to caribou, though they did travel to the coast from time to time, and thus came into contact with Europeans.

INNU

Before the coming of the Europeans, the Innu inhabited the Labrador Peninsula, including portions that are now parts of both Quebec and Labrador. They called their territory Nitassinan, "our land," as they still do today. Recent archaeological excavations appear to support the contention that the Innu are the descendants of almost two thousand years of uninterrupted Algonkian presence in Labrador. The Daniel Rattle Complex of sites shows that the Innu's ancestors were fully established in central Labrador by AD200, and similarities in more than thirty prehistoric sites and twenty-two radiocarbon dates suggest a continuous cultural tradition from Daniel Rattle to Point Revenge to the small scattered Innu bands encountered by Europeans in the sixteenth century. Today, not far from Daniel Rattle, the new village of Natuashish (people from Davis Inlet) is arising.

But it is from the records of the Europeans they encountered that we discover the Innu, and perhaps it is best for us to see their later development in relation to those European nations. Jacques Cartier described the people (probably Innu) whom he encountered as follows:

There are people in the said land who are well enough in body, but they are wild and savage folks. They have their hair tied upon their heads in the fashion of a fistful of hay trussed up and a nail or some other thing passed through it, and therein they stick some feathers of birds. They clothe themselves with skins of beasts, both men and women, but the women are closer – and tighter in the said skins and girded about the body. They paint themselves with certain tawny colours. They have boats, in which they go by the sea, which are made of bark of the birch trees, wherewith they fish a good many seals. Since having seen them I am sure this is not their abode, and that they come from warmer lands in order to take the said seals and other things for their living."[1]

It was the ever-increasing presence of Europeans such as Cartier and the expansion of the Thule Eskimos along the coast of Labrador that forced the Innu to move more and more into the interior. When the herds were plentiful, the Innu were self-sufficient and there was little need for European goods. But the coming of the fur traders had a profound effect on their lives. Hunters who had previously tracked caribou were now enticed to trap sufficient beaver to satisfy the demands of the European fur market.

To the early Europeans the New World was undiscovered virgin land, where the original inhabitants were simply waiting for an end to their primitive existence. Many Europeans viewed the native people not only as members of a conquered nation but as inferior. For the native people themselves, the reality was very different. They resisted the loss of their unique identity and their assimilation into white society. Not until the late twentieth century did white society, through its courts, acknowledge the rights of aboriginal people and slowly begin to change its attitudes and policies.

The raiding and trading between the Inuit and Europeans deprived the Innu of their access to the coast and the social networks they had previously enjoyed. Although small groups of Innu attached themselves seasonally to European and Canadian posts, over time most of them continued to tie their fate to that of the caribou. We shall

meet the Innu again after the arrival of the Europeans, who had –
and still have – such a profound effect on them and their way of life.

THULE AND INUIT

The Thule Eskimos, ancestors of today's Inuit, arrived in northern
Labrador about seven hundred years ago. Three hundred years earlier, they had begun their migration east across the Arctic from northern Alaska to eastern Baffin Island and Greenland. Caches discovered
at the west end of Saglek Fiord indicate contact between the late
Dorsets and early Thule. The Thule learned much from the Dorsets
in technology, hunting, and religion. They arrived with dog-drawn
sleds, large skin boats (umiaks), and kayaks, all of which enabled
them to traverse whatever mountains, ice, snow, and water lay in
their path. They were well prepared for the harvest of both sea and
land, with their toggling harpoons, bows and arrows, dogs, and
spears. Not since the Maritime Archaic people had there been such
whale hunters. Remains of their sod houses tell us they lived in partly
submerged structures of sod, wood, stone, and whalebone, which
were divided into kitchens, sleeping areas, and entrance passages.
Three to five families might occupy a typical settlement, living in
rock-walled houses of hide in the warmer months and moving into
sod houses in late fall. They brought with them soapstone and slate.

The Thule lived relatively close to the Innu, who by this time had
confined themselves to the interior. Clearly the two peoples met from
time to time, and although relations between them were hostile, they
may on the whole have practised avoidance rather than warfare. The
Thule hunted bowhead and white whales, walrus, seals, and birds,
all of which were numerous around the outer islands. The hunting
was a cooperative effort like that of the Innu. Indeed, in summer their
caribou hunt resembled that of the Innu with the use of fences and
drives for herding the animals.

The coming of Europeans changed their lives. If the aboriginal
people encountered by the Vikings were Inuit, their next known
contact was in the sixteenth century. Evidence of a meeting between
Europeans and the Labrador Inuit is contained in two handbills
printed in Augsberg and Nuremberg in 1567, and they may have
encountered Martin Frobisher in the 1570s. Over time, the influence
of the Europeans grew. The Inuit continued to hunt marine mammals;
their houses did not change, nor did their treatment of the dead, but
the cumulative impact was great. European goods became objects of
great prestige, and some Inuit went to great lengths to acquire them.
Outstanding hunters and leaders in the communities became traders

for European wares, and Inuit middlemen established their own trading networks.

Gradually the Inuit moved farther and farther south along the coast, drawn either by a greater supply of wood and food and the milder climate or by easier access to European goods. By the late 1500s three sod houses had been established in what is now Hopedale, and around 1600 a settlement was begun at Eskimo Island in the narrows of Hamilton Inlet. By the seventeenth century there were Inuit settlements all along the Labrador coast from Killinek to Hamilton Inlet.

Now the Inuit were in regular contact with Europeans. Slate and soapstone were replaced by iron, and skin boats by wooden whalers. By the eighteenth century they had abandoned the outer islands for settlements on shore, where they could exploit more resources, for by then many had started to rely on fish and caribou to supplement their diet. At this time Inuit settlements were reported all the way from the Button Islands to Cape Charles in the south. Arvertok, later the village of Hopedale, was the largest settlement of Inuit in the central part of the Labrador coast. They travelled inland too, hunters sometimes crossing the height of land to the banks of the George River. By this time, a house could contain as many as twenty people. While the nuclear family was the basic social unit, men often had two or three wives all living under the same roof. The father or husband, the authority figure, might own an umiak and perhaps a wooden whaleboat or sloop for travelling, whaling, and trading.

We know the names and histories of some of these eighteenth-century Inuit. Mitsuk, a name extant on the coast today, was a man from Okak who owned two boats and whose household consisted of thirty-seven people. Tuglavina, another name still found in Labrador, was a trader and shaman from Nain. He owned a two-masted sloop and traded from Nain to the Strait of Belle Isle. Karpik, whose descendants also live in Labrador, was a shaman and leader among the Hopedale people and a major force opposing the Moravian missionaries. Semigak is another whose name still lives.

Baleen, oil, ivory, and sealskins were traded farther and farther south, and European goods were traded farther and farther north, becoming more costly the farther they went, as is the case today. Of course the Inuit were a people who practised communal sharing, a people unfamiliar with the ownership practices of the Europeans and the procedures of Western trade. They are reported to have "stolen" what they could not obtain by trade, though it is a matter of interpretation whether taking what they needed from what they perceived to be a communal stock was stealing. Nevertheless, when they were caught "stealing," the Europeans retaliated with the harshest of measures – taking their lives. Relations between the two became characterized by hostility and treachery. Who started it? No matter who fired the first shot, as Gwynne Dyer has said in *Full Circle: First Contact*, it is not unusual for two people wishing to occupy the same territory to be at odds with each other.

These were the earliest peoples of Labrador, each succeeding wave displacing another to some degree. And more waves were gathering across the ocean. Over the centuries they would wash onto the shores of Labrador, submerging some in their path and carrying others with them. One way or another, they profoundly and irreversibly influenced aboriginal life, an influence that persists to the present day.

CHAPTER TWO

The Europeans

From a social or economic or religious view, no matter what you think of it, the Viking period was a kind of hinge in European history ... It was the time from which you went from early history and classical civilization into what we know as modern Europe and a modern world, in which people are exchanging ideas and moving around rapidly and exploring new frontiers, looking for new resources and new connections.

Bill Fitzhugh, *Globe and Mail*, 20 May 2000

In a way the Viking long ship was the Internet of the year 1000, connecting places and people who themselves could not even imagine what lay beyond that wide sea or that mountain range.

Hillary Clinton

THE VIKINGS

Who were the people the Vikings encountered during their stay in northern Newfoundland? The Vikings called them "skraelings" (people who wore the skins of animals) but it is difficult to say exactly who they were because the early writers did not differentiate between Indians and Inuit. Whoever they were, the eventual relationship was not peaceful. But we will never know who fired the first shot or why.

While the eighth-century Irish had sailed close to North America in their leather boats, there is no record of their landing. The Vikings are the first Europeans proved to have trod the soil of what is now the Province of Newfoundland and Labrador. Bjarni Herjólfsson sailed from Iceland to Greenland in 986 but was blown off course, sighting the coasts of Labrador and Newfoundland before making his way to his original destination. Leif Ericsson, who followed him, sailed past what is now Nunavut (which he named Helluland) and then proceeded south, going ashore in Labrador: "This country was flat and wooded with white sandy beaches wherever they went; and the land sloped gently down to the sea," recorded the Greenland saga.

"Leif said, 'This country shall be called Markland' [Woodland]."[1] At
a point on the Labrador coast just south of Hamilton Inlet at Cape
Porcupine, there are healthy stands of some of the best black spruce
in the world. More than fifty kilometres of white sandy beaches – the
only ones in the region – stretch before a dark forest. If there is any
part of the Greenland Saga that echoes actual geographic features,
this is it: the Wonderstrand.

Leif continued south and spent the winter at a place he named
Vinland. For years there was speculation about the actual location of
Vinland. It was W.A.Munn, a Newfoundlander, who in 1914 first
pointed out the place – L'Anse aux Meadows – on the tip of the Great
Northern Peninsula:

About 200 miles from Cape Porcupine brings us to the Straits of Belle Isle. I
believe when Leif started to come in towards the land, he was just south of
Belle Isle at the break of day, and when he came to land the island mentioned
is the Sacred Island just to the north of Cape Onion. They went ashore at
Lancey Meadows, as it is called today, where there is plenty of grass ... If a
careful search was made of the area I am certain that interesting relics would
be found.[2]

And indeed they were, in 1960, by the Norwegian scholar Helge
Ingstad and his wife, the archaeologist Anne Stine Ingstad, with the
help of a local fisherman, George Decker.

The Viking record tells us that Thorvald Ericsson later sailed north
from Vinland to Markland. Dropping anchor and going ashore, his
men discovered three canoes under which nine aboriginal people
were hiding. The Vikings killed all but one of these "skraelings," but
the one survivor must have told his camp about the massacre because
later there was a counterattack. Several of the Vikings were killed,
including Thorvald. His burial site is believed to be somewhere near
the mouth of English River on Lake Melville.

The Vikings continued to visit Labrador for another hundred years
in search of wood. What further contact there was with the skraelings
we do not know. But the Vikings had proved that transatlantic voyages
were possible and that there were rewards of various kinds at the
end of the voyage. They had also left an impression on the aboriginal
inhabitants of Labrador.

THE BASQUES

Basques were on the Labrador coast very early, possibly by the beginning of the fifteenth century, and likely had people working there
before Columbus and Cabot crossed the Atlantic. We know from the

archival records uncovered in 1976 by Selma Barkham, a British historian, and by subsequent archaeological work by Jim Tuck of Memorial University and Robert Grenier of Parks Canada, that there was extensive Basque whaling at Red Bay in the Labrador straits from the 1530s on. The Basques harvested oil from the whales to light the windows of Europe. And with the blessing of the Catholic Church, the whale meat they collected helped satisfy European appetites.

Their relationship with the Innu was amicable. Indeed, native people helped them process the whale oil. Witnesses of the time refer to trading with the Innu at Brest and Grand Bay. The trading of furs for iron tools continued for most of the century. A Basque historian referred to the *montaneses* (Montagnais), who had learned some Basque and helped prepare the fish on shore in exchange for a little bread, biscuit, and cider. By contrast, the Inuit encountered on the coast at this time were described as hostile to the fishermen, attacking them with bows and arrows. But all these records are difficult to interpret accurately because the Europeans often confused the Innu with the Inuit. In any case, the large number of Basques likely prevented attack; between 1545 and 1585 there appear to have been well over a thousand of them living and working at various harbours for at least six months of the year. There were probably more than six hundred in Red Bay alone, while there may have been another five hundred in Chateau Bay, with smaller numbers in Carrolls Cove, Pinware Bay, Schooner Cove, and Middle Bay.

In the 1580s the Basque industry in the Strait of Belle Isle declined, partly because they had overharvested the whale population and partly because their ships were being diverted by the Spanish for the war against England. The final blow to the Basque whaling enterprise in Labrador came when the Spitzbergen whale population was discovered and the British and Dutch began whaling. Nevertheless, whaling in Labrador continued into the eighteenth century, with as many as three hundred vessels reported as late as 1766. In fact, the English and Dutch employed Basques because they had the best whaling technology and skill. The Basque whaler – the only original of which above water is in the Parks Canada museum in Red Bay – was never bettered for seaworthiness. Hence, the lifeboats of the Royal Navy and Royal Canadian Navy are still known as whalers.

THE DUTCH

Independent Dutch traders taking baleen, skins, and ivory were present on the Labrador coast in the early seventeenth century. Although they did not establish settlements, they did meet aboriginal people. In fact, the oldest description of Labrador Innu by a European is recorded in a book published in 1720 by a Dutch whaling skipper. It not only gives remarkable details of the Innu culture at that time but also clearly shows that the Innu were used to Europeans and had traded with them. They had axes, knives, and even French caps. Their arrowheads were metal rather than stone, and they seem to have had the habit of trading skins and meat. They even used the word *capitaina*, which is of Basque origin. Obviously, they were not meeting Europeans for the first time.

THE PORTUGUESE

On 12 May 1500 King Manuel of Portugal issued letters patent to Gaspar Corte-Real, who subsequently made voyages in 1500 and 1501 that took him past Labrador. Corte-Real followed the shore southward, exploring Hamilton Inlet as far as the Narrows and perhaps Hawke Bay and the Gilbert and Alexis rivers. He took the Strait of Belle Isle for an inlet but probably landed, for he captured about sixty Innu on his first voyage and took them back to Lisbon: "Men, women and children ... they resemble gypsies in colour, stature, features and aspect ... are very shy and gentle but well-formed ... The sailors have brought from there a piece of broken gilt sword ... One of the boys was wearing in his ear two silver rings ... They were excellent for labour and the best slaves that have hitherto been obtained."

It was a Portuguese who gave Labrador its name. João Fernandes, a farmer or landowner (*lavrador* in Portuguese) of the Azores, was one of those granted letters patent by King Manuel. In the summer of 1500 he sighted land that he called Tierra del Lavrador, land of the landowner. Yet in nearly all the maps of the first half of the sixteenth century, including the Weimar map of 1534, Greenland is called Labrador. It was a century before the name was shifted west to its present area, which was previously known as Terra Corterealis. The explorer and geographer A.P. Low claims that Labrador is derived from the Portuguese for "labourer" and was given to the coast because Corte-Real brought home a cargo of natives. But it is more likely to come from "farmer" or "landowner." On the Wolfenbuttel map of 1534, along the coast of Greenland are the words: "Country of Labrador, which was discovered by the English of the port of Bristol, and because he who first gave notice of seeing it was a farmer from the Azores, this name became attached to it."

SEARCHING FOR THE NORTHWEST PASSAGE

"A land of stones and rocks, frightful and ill-shaped, for in all the said north coast I did not find a cartful of earth though I landed in many places ... In short, I deem ... that it is the land that God gave Cain." In spite of the fact that this overused and erroneous description by Jacques Cartier has stuck to Labrador for centuries, Cartier was not the only person to eschew the charms of Labrador. A Spanish map of 1529 claimed, "Labrador was discovered by the English. There is nothing there of importance." (Of course, this may have been a feint to keep other adventurers away.) In 1577 the British explorer Martin Frobisher expressed similar sentiments: "Foure days coasting along this land we found no sign of habitation ... All along this coast yce lieth, as a continued bulwarke, and so defendeth the country, that those that would land there, incur great danger."

Like Frobisher, other British explorers sailed these shores searching for the Northwest Passage, a water route through the Arctic. In 1586 John Davis spent a month on the Labrador coast searching for the passage, sailing into, among other places, Davis Inlet and Hamilton Inlet. He named Cape Chidley after his neighbour at home. Eight leagues south of Hamilton Inlet, perhaps in Sandwich Bay, he was attacked by "brutish people" with bows and arrows. Captain George Weymouth investigated Hamilton Inlet in 1602, and in 1606 John Knight arrived on the coast:

In latitude 57 degrees 25 minutes, but was caught in the ice and drifted south to latitude 56 degrees 48 minutes. Finding his ship badly damaged, he decided to put into a small cove to effect repairs if possible. While exploring the neighbourhood, looking for a suitable place to careen his vessel, he [John Knight], his brother, Edward Gorrill the mate and another man were set upon by the savage Eskimos and slain. The rest of the ship's company were left in a sore plight ... continually attacked by the Eskimos, whom they described as "little people, tawney coloured, thick-haired, little or no beard, flat nosed, and are man eaters.[3]

Eight years later, a Captain Gibbons was icebound for twenty weeks in a Labrador bay, probably Nain Bay. In 1610 Henry Hudson passed through Hudson Strait to Hudson Bay, and the following year Thomas Button entered Hudson Strait by a narrow channel, leaving his name on the Button Islands. In 1632 Thomas James was in the bay that bears his name.

The first of the journeys north to Labrador from Canada was that of Jean Bourdon in 1657, who travelled from Quebec to what is now Cape Harrison. Like John Davis he experienced an apparently unprovoked attack by Inuit. In 1682 Pierre Radisson and Médard Chouart Des Groseilliers sailed up the Labrador coast on their way to Hudson Bay. They went ashore in the vicinity of Okak and remained there two days to trade with the Inuit. On their return journey they weathered a storm in "the most favourable harbour in the world" but gave no indication of where it was.

THE FRENCH

After the Basques, the French were the next Europeans to establish a presence. By the early 1500s, French fishermen were regularly going ashore to get water and to trade with the native people. The initial relationship between the French and Innu seems to have been friendly. The Innu welcomed Samuel de Champlain to their shores, and for his part Champlain would not have been able to survive without their knowledge of the country. It was he who named them Montagnais after the mountains surrounding the area where he met them at the mouth of the Saguenay River in 1603.[4] They supported his plan to build at a location farther up the St Lawrence at what was to become Quebec City, for they hoped that the French would be a buffer between them and the five nations of Iroquois who lived just south of the St Lawrence River. The Iroquois had been staging raids on Innu settlements in an attempt to gain control of the fur trade. Sometime after 1570 increasing attacks by one Iroquois nation, the Mohawk, had drawn the Innu and several other Algonquian-speaking nations into a military alliance, which the French supported, believing that it would ensure them a regular supply of furs.

By 1623 European goods had made life easier for the Innu. Those living near the French fur-trading settlements of Tadoussac and Quebec were using copper kettles and iron axes and wearing European-style garments. But now a serious threat occurred to their position as middlemen in the fur trade. The Huron to the west had begun to act as middlemen between the French and the hunting peoples of the Ottawa Valley. In addition, Innu trappers had by this time depleted the beaver population in the area between Quebec and Tadoussac. Moose and elk had declined as well. Unable to acquire meat from their usual sources, the Innu became increasingly dependent on the food supplied by the French. At the same time, an outbreak of infectious diseases from which they had no natural immunity killed thousands of them. Their declining numbers made them vulnerable to the Mohawk, who renewed their raids, often joined by two other Iroquois nations, the Oneida and Onondaga. In 1661 the Iroquois burned the Innu settlement at Tadoussac to the ground. Further raids forced them to retreat eastward, pushing back the Inuit, who two centuries earlier had been spread all along the north shore of the St Lawrence. The Innu were becoming marginalized, confined more and more to North America's eastern extremity.

The French traders had not come alone. The church, first the Recollets and then the Jesuits, were part of the French attempt at colonization. Both orders advocated "civilizing" the Innu, though they realized they could not interfere with the Innu's role in the fur trade. In those days the French government provided no money for the running of its colony; the fur trade was the sole source of support in New France. So whatever the priests may have preferred, they had to give way to the demands of commerce.

In 1627 the French created a system of land grants known as seigneuries. In an attempt to promote colonization, French merchants, bureaucrats, and military men, called seigneurs, were awarded tracts of land, which were given for life and could be passed on to heirs. Some came with rights from the state to trade with the native people, and many trading posts sprang up in Innu territory. In 1661 François Bissot was granted the Isle aux Œufs, together with trading, hunting, and fishing rights over nearly the whole of the North Shore of the St. Lawrence River to Sept-Îles "and in the Grand Anse, toward the country of the Eskimo where the Spaniards usually come to fish." This became known as the Seigneury of Mingan.

Bissot was a Norman immigrant who had come to Canada sometime between 1641 and 1647. He was a man of enterprise and ideas, the first in New France to begin the tanning of leather, and he carried on fishing, sealing, and trading on the Labrador with great success. But perhaps his greatest claim to fame is that his daughter Claire married Louis Jolliet, subsequently royal hydrographer at Quebec under appointment by King Louis XIV and the first European to see the Mississippi River. In 1679, after Bissot's death, Jolliet became one of the seigneurs of Mingan, about 160 kilometres east of Sept-Îles. He traded as far north as Lac Naskapis, the present-day Ashuanipi, where Fort Naskapis was established as early as 1696. As a reward for his "discovery" of the Mississippi, he was granted the island of Anticosti as a seigneury.

By this time, the British had formed the Hudson's Bay Company and established trading forts on the bay. Jolliet realized how detrimental it would be for his trade if the skins gathered by the aboriginal people were taken to the great northern sea rather than to the St Lawrence. In 1679 he made his first voyage to the mouth of the Rupert River, recording a rather sparse account of what he encountered on the Labrador coast. In 1694 he made a second voyage, leaving fuller notes about his journey. This time he took five and a half months to get as far north as Zoar and recorded details of the country, the navigation, the Inuit, and their customs. He explored and named Baye St-Louis (St Lewis Bay) and St Francis Harbour, which he named after his ship and in honour of Sieur François Pachot, who had provided for his undertaking. He appears to have named St Michael's Bay on his previous voyage. Beyond St Michael's Bay he sighted a group of islands which he named St Thomas. Heading north past Cape Harrison, he landed about sixteen kilometres north of present-day Hopedale, and still farther north he named a bay Pachot. Jolliet's journal gives the earliest detailed survey of the Labrador coast from the Strait of Belle Isle north to Zoar.

In 1702 Augustin Le Gardeur de Courtemanche established a fishing and trading concession in southern Labrador stretching from the Kegaska River on the North Shore of the St Lawrence to the Kessessakiou River (Churchill), and built Fort Pontchartrain at Brador, where he employed about thirty Innu families. In 1697 Courtemanche had married the widow of Pierre Gratien Martel de Brouague. She was the granddaughter of old François Bissot, and therefore family ties drew Courtemanche east, as they had Jolliet. Courtemanche died in 1717, and his place as commandant of the coast was taken by François Martel de Brouague, who held the post until the British conquest in 1759–60.

Until 1763, when the Treaty of Paris ended the Seven Years War and the land was ceded to the British, the French controlled the Labrador trade by a series of posts and forts along the coast at L'Anse-au-Loup, Chateau Bay, Forteau Bay, Red Bay, Cape Charles, Pinware, West St Modeste, Brador, Isle aux Bois. and L'Anse-au-Clair. In 1736 Louis Bazil was given the right to catch seals and to hunt, fish, and trade with the Inuit at Chateau Bay, and in 1737 he formed a partnership with François Havy and Louis Fornel. The concession of Sieur Antoine Marsal at Cape Charles, established in the early 1730s, was the northernmost of the French establishments in the Straits. Hamilton Inlet was granted at different times to traders and merchants after a French memoir of 1715 recommended that a post be established at "Baie de Kessalaki."

In 1743 Louis Fornel, in a bold attempt to expand French fishing stations, led an expedition north along the coast. He met groups of Inuit and traded extensively with them. Fornel explored Hamilton Inlet, encountering both Inuit and Innu, and took formal possession of it for the French crown. He established trading posts at North West River and Rigolet, leaving there a group that included what are believed to be the first Europeans to winter in Labrador – a man named Pilote and his son, with Innu guides. Fornel's diary is one of the early records of life in the area.

Even after the Treaty of Paris officially ceded control of New France to the British, the French still maintained a presence; French and

British firms would argue over claims to Labrador posts for the next forty years. Cape Charles, for example, was first used as a whaling, sealing, and fishing site by the French from the time of Marsal's initial grant in 1735; thereafter, Nicholas Darby and the eminent British trader George Cartwright both had operations there. In 1788 Pierre Marcoux and Louis Marchand established a trading post at the far end of a bay which the Inuit called Ivuctoke ("place having many walruses") but was known to early British traders as Cross Water or Gross Water Bay. They called their post Rigoulette after the narrow channel that separated the bay from Lake Melville. The entire inlet had earlier been known as Esquimaux Bay.[5] In the channel between the two bodies of water was Eskimo Island. Here the Inuit acted as middlemen for the French in their trade for cod, salmon, and seals. Ideally located midway between Saglek in the north and the Strait of Belle Isle, prominent Inuit acted as wholesalers for the Inuit population in both directions, trading iron implements, fishing equipment, and wooden boats for whale baleen, seal oil, fur pelts, and walrus ivory as well as fish.

But those Inuit in the south had encroached on the territory of the Innu, and the animosity and bloodshed between the two groups spilled over at Eskimo Island about the time that Governor Palliser of Newfoundland made his peace with the Inuit in the 1760s. Thereafter, most of the Inuit confined themselves to the north coast, while the Innu clung to the forests and the rivers of the interior. Nevertheless, the animosity remained. Winston White has said that his mother, Judy Pauline White, an Inuk born in Nain Bay in the early years of the twentieth century, often singled out a cliff south of Nain where Inuit had reportedly been attacked by the Innu. In retaliation, the Inuit had hidden themselves in the face of the cliff and pushed boulders down on the unsuspecting Innu in their canoes.[6] The hostility ended over a hundred years ago when starving Innu arrived at Zoar, about sixty-five kilometres south of Nain, and were cared for by the Inuit. Over time relations between the two improved, particularly when overlapping land claims and negotiations with governments and large multinational companies brought them a common cause in the latter part of the twentieth century.

The trader Pierre Marcoux, who managed a major fishing station at Chateau Bay, was a friend of the Inuit and was known to them as Makko. In 1790 he established an outpost in the north at a bay called Marrovik or Maggovik (today's Makkovik), and he planned to build another station in an adjacent bay called Kippokak. The Europeans still depended on aboriginal people for the success of their trading endeavours, and this commercial interdependence brought them

① So economic activity joins, + it divides, it leads to abandonment of the old + adoption of the new

① closer socially. Carol Brice-Bennett, a preeminent Labrador historian, in her recent book with Paulus Maggo, tells us: "Marcoux and British traders, notably George Cartwright, who had premises in nearby Sandwich Bay, depended on alliances with Inuit families to support their trade activities. Marcoux's native associates may have adopted his name because some Inuit residing in the Rigolet area subsequently became known by the surname Mucko, who Paulus Maggo suspected were related to his ancestors."[7]

Throughout the eighteenth century the French continued to trade for cod, seal, and salmon at numerous posts in Quebec Labrador, which for French purposes extended all the way to Hamilton Inlet. Sealing was particularly important, for it supplied the oil used to light Canadian homes and was used for dressing hides in Europe. There are still traces of the French presence on the Labrador coast today, particularly in the place names that dot the south coast.

THE ENGLISH

Two acts of the British government in 1763 were to have a profound effect on Labrador. One was the Royal Proclamation that is so fundamental today to the aboriginal people in their land claims negotiations. It was the first legal document in which native people were assured their rights and was one of a number of proclamations attempting to stop the escalating conflict between aboriginal people and British subjects over the right to occupy land.

The Proclamation of 1763 ruled that all lands not already ceded to or purchased by Britain, and which formed part of British North America, were to be considered "reserved lands" for aboriginal people. Secondly, only the British crown could alienate those lands; individuals were no longer able to purchase land directly from native people, a practice that had led to so much unrest. The British, recognizing that the unjust occupation of native hunting grounds had spurred the 1763 uprising led by the Ottawa chief Pontiac, were apprehensive of a full-blown war. Their main concern was to keep the peace so that their commercial empire could flourish. Protecting land rights was a means to that end. The crown, in its move to respect aboriginal title, was referring to occupancy and use, not actual ownership (fee simple). It was assumed that Britain held the underlying title, as the 1763 wording indicates. It was "our dominions" that were being reserved for the native people and to which the crown was extending its protection. Not all native people have accepted the Proclamation. The Innu in Labrador and Quebec have never believed that their rights were affected either by the Proclamation or by the present "occupation" of non-aboriginals.

The other act of the British government in 1763 had implications that reached even further. It was the signing of the Treaty of Paris, which ended the Seven Years War and was the beginning of British hegemony on the Labrador coast. From then on, the intent of the English was to limit the French fishery in the North Atlantic and to save the area for the mercantile fleets of Britain. Nevertheless, there had to be some compromise, and the final agreement extended the French rights to catch and dry fish on the French Shore – the stretch of coastline between Cape Bonavista and Cape Race, circling the northern tip of the island of Newfoundland. The treaty also placed Labrador under the jurisdiction of the Newfoundland governor, Sir Hugh Palliser. His instructions not to disturb the French fishery caused more and more of the Newfoundland fishermen who had formerly fished around the French Shore to move to Labrador for their fishing.

But permanent settlement in Labrador was not what the British government wanted. Like the Newfoundland fishery, the fishing in Labrador waters was to be for the fleets of Dorset and Devon and was to be governed by fishing admirals. The establishment of shore-based fisheries was discouraged because it would continue the historic struggle between those who sailed from English ports and those who tried to establish fishing stations on shore. Palliser applied for naval reinforcements as he strove energetically to carry out the regulations. He built Fort York in Chateau Bay and garrisoned it with an officer and twenty men. But his measures were in vain; the Inuit destroyed the fort. He continued to encounter opposition not only from the English and French Canadian settlers on the coast but also from American fishermen, who were excluded from the fishery.

The British protectionist policy angered the New England fishermen, who had fished off Labrador since 1645. Indeed, their exclusion from the Labrador fishery was one of the lesser causes of the American War of Independence. After the peace treaty of 1763, they knew that Labrador was in reality ungoverned, and they violated Palliser's policy at every opportunity. He complained to the British Admiralty that between two and three hundred American whaling vessels had reached Labrador ahead of the British, illegally fishing for cod, selling to the French, destroying the British shore facilities, killing and plundering the natives people, setting fire to the woods, and doing everything in their power to obstruct the British fishery. Although legal control of Labrador passed from Newfoundland back to Quebec in

1774, the War of Independence that began the following year served to legitimize such behaviour for American privateers.

Anarchy continued on the southern Labrador coast. At the Treaty of Versailles in 1783 the Americans were conceded the right to fish the inshore waters and to process fish in uninhabited areas of Labrador. But the Americans from Newburyport, Gloucester, Provincetown, and Boston went beyond the bounds of the treaty. They traded illegally with Labrador residents, offering tea, rum, and tobacco more cheaply than local merchants did and paying higher prices for fish. In a few years their trade blossomed so that they very nearly ruined the Newfoundland fish trade in the early 1800s. But they were a source of comfort and support to the early resident fishermen, who were bound to the merchants by debt and faced a lifetime of dependence.

Chief Justice Reeves complained to the British House of Commons in 1793: "In truth there is no government whatsoever on the Coast of Labrador ... It is very much to be wished that some plan be devised for affording to that deserted coast something like the effect of civil government." In 1807 Newfoundland Governor John Holloway advised the British Privy Council that the reannexation of Labrador to Newfoundland was "the most effectual mode of suppressing the illicit trade carried on by the Americans who fished Labrador." In 1809 the privy council accepted this advice and returned Labrador to Newfoundland jurisdiction.

Meanwhile, the British authorities had realized that some wintering over was necessary to maximize salmon and seal fisheries, and in 1773 they had relaxed Palliser's regulations, though they still tried to confine the privilege of wintering over to the British. There was a rapid response. By 1808 the Labrador Company, headed by Mathew Lymburner, had acquired nearly the whole coast from Mingan to Brador Bay, as well as operations at Pinware and Hamilton Inlet. Captain Nicholas Darby of Bristol, father of the famous actress Perdita, set up near Cape Charles, reviving the Marsal post from the Quebec partnership of Bayne and Brymer. Noble and Pinson, already well known on the coast, were doing business at Temple Bay, later setting up sealing and fishing operations at L'Anse-au-Loup, Fox Harbour (St Lewis), and Sandwich Bay. Others, such as John Slade and Company and Jeremiah Coghlan, were already north of the Strait of Belle Isle in 1765, trading in seals, fish, and furs. Farther south, De Quetteville and Boutilier brought over former Bretons from the Channel Islands, some of whom stayed. Joseph Bird began trading at Forteau in the 1790s.

By 1772 Slade had displaced Noble and Pinson at Seal Island and soon established a fishing station at Battle Harbour. By 1775 this windswept island in the North Atlantic, headquarters of the Slade operation, had become the "capital" of Labrador, and it remained so throughout the greater part of the nineteenth century. At times, it is said, there were so many schooners at Battle Harbour that you could walk across the tickle on their decks. The Slades traded there until 1871, and Slade employees populated the coast, as they do to this day: the Acremans, Blakes, Broomfields, Browns, Buckles, Coombs, Davises, Dickers, Fords, Lanes, Martins, Olivers, Painters, Peytons, Phippards, Rumbolts, and Wolfreys. Later these families were joined by the Groves, Snooks, Saunders, Burdens, Pikes, and Yetmans. Farther north, English traders had begun moving into Hamilton Inlet in the 1770s. The first two white settlers were William Phippard and John Newhook, whose arrival was described by Lydia Campbell:

They was landed hear [sic] by some people looking for a place I think and gave these two people provisions and promised to come after them next year, but they never came back for 3 years; so my Father told us for he saw them when he came from England a prentice boy few years after. Well they went to a place to live in which there was a river and plenty woods, and that river was called English River to this day. The Indians, mountaineers, and Equimaux (for they was plentiful at this time) and got seal skin clothes from them, and meat to eat. About this time people began to settle, one after another, mostly French people, few English, for everything was plentiful at that time.[8]

Newfoundland-based ships that had operated in the Strait of Belle Isle had to concentrate ever more on the Labrador coast. Some of these crews came just for the summer, but others stayed on and settled there. So it was that the Joneses, Chubbs, Belbins, Trimms, Roberts, Davises, and Pikes arrived from Trinity and Conception bays, the Hancocks from Englee, and the Barneys, Cabots, Earles, Linsteads, Normores, and Rylands from England by way of Newfoundland. Other coastal names, including the Lettos and Dumaresques, date back to those who came to the Straits from the Channel Islands.

Caretakers for the European firms that did business in the Straits gradually acquired more and more independence. In 1834 a man named Buckle became one of the first planters in the area, with his own gear and his own account, for British firms had begun to realize that there could be more profit and less financial risk if settlers took on more of the operations of the fishery. But the settlers were still at the mercy of the merchants who provided them with supplies.

Patricia Thornton, in an article on settlement in the Straits, calls the period 1850–80 the "Newfoundland Phase." More than 80 per cent of those who arrived were from the Island. Some Irish families, led by the O'Dells of Carbonear, settled at Pinware in the early 1800s and grew large enough to deserve the first Roman Catholic church in the area in 1887. The British who arrived later were mostly from Jersey. In fact, when the Banque Union of Jersey crashed in 1873, it destroyed all the Jersey firms in Labrador. Most of them sold out to Job Brothers of Newfoundland, who went on to dominate the shore fishery in the Straits.

But the population of the Straits continued to be vulnerable. Well into the 1800s the French were so active in the fishery that Britain and France considered signing a fisheries convention in 1857 giving the French certain rights in the Straits area. During the hearings of the Newfoundland legislature, the deal was fiercely opposed by Newfoundland fishing interests on the grounds that the French, with their superior gear and superior subsidies, would severely cripple the Newfoundland effort. Even the bishops of the Roman Catholic and Anglican churches opposed the convention. As a result of the combined lobby, the British government desisted and the proposed fisheries convention was withdrawn. It was clear that the Newfoundland legislature was powerful and that fisheries policy could not be created without its consent. It was also clear that this power was used on behalf of the fishermen and fishing interests from the Island and not necessarily on behalf of the settlers in the Straits, who had profited by selling to the French and buying from the French. The interests of the merchants on the Island and the people in the Straits were not the same.

Conflict between Newfoundland and Labrador was not new. C.J. Poole, in *Catucto*, has commented on the conflict for fishing berths that had earlier taken place farther north: "Some very bitter disputes have occurred between the local fishermen and the fishing crews, both planters and floaters from Newfoundland. Berth locations are very critical in the salmon fishery as the way the salmon run along the shore in certain locations can make a great difference in the catch."[9] Disputes about fishing berths persisted over the decades and, together with other grievances, helped form the attitude of resentment of some Labradorians (who had settled) towards Newfoundlanders (who were just visitors).

Cartwright

George Cartwright was certainly not the first British trader to set up on the lower Labrador coast, but he has become the most prominent, largely because of the journal he kept and published. He was born in Marnham, England, in 1739 to a well-known English family. Two of his brothers were prominent: John, a naval officer, reformer, and patriot, and Edmund, a poet, philanthropist, and the inventor of the power loom. A captain in the British army, George Cartwright was drawn to Labrador after his visits to the island of Newfoundland with John, who was first lieutenant of HMS *Guernsey*, which brought Governor Sir Hugh Palliser to Newfoundland.

Disappointed in not receiving an expected promotion in his regiment, by 1770 Cartwright had quit his position in the army. Having an "insatiable propensity for shooting" and hearing that Labrador was practically virgin country, he was irresistibly drawn to the wild, free, adventurous life of a settler on the coast. He entered into a partnership with Francis Lucas, a naval officer and merchant trader, and Thomas Perkins and Jeremiah Coghlan, both of Bristol, to trap, hunt, fish, and trade with the Inuit of Labrador. The first post established was at Cape Charles, where Nicholas Darby had earlier abandoned his whaling enterprise because of Inuit attacks. Nearby, Cartwright built a house for himself, Ranger Lodge, in what is now Lodge Bay.

His greatest contribution to Labrador was perhaps the journal he kept. Entitled *Journal of Transactions and Events, during a Residence of Nearly Sixteen Years on the Coast of Labrador* and published in 1792, it is three quarto volumes full of what the poet Robert Southey, among others, found to be interesting insights:

I saw Major Cartwright (the sportsman, not the patriot) in 1791. I was visiting with the Lambs, at Hampstead, in Kent, at the house of the Hodges, his brother-in-law; we had nearly finished dinner when he came in. He desired the servant to cut him a plate of beef from the sideboard. I thought the footman meant to insult him: the plate was piled to a height which no ploughboy after a hard day's fasting could have levelled; but the moment he took up his knife and fork, and arranged the plate, I saw this was no common man. A second and third supply soon vanished. Mr. and Mrs. Lamb, who had never before seen him, glanced at each other, but Tom and I, with schoolboys' privilege, kept our eyes riveted upon him ...

This man had strength and perseverance charactered in every muscle ... He was good humoured and communicative; his long residence on the Labrador coast made his conversation as instructive as interesting. I had never before seen so extraordinary a man ...

I read his book in 1793, and, strange as it may seem, actually read through the three quartos. At that time, I was a verbatim reader of indefatigable patience, but the odd simplicity of the book amused me – the importance he attached to his traps delighted me, it was so unlike a book written for the world – the solace of a solitary evening in Labrador. I fancied him blockaded by the snows, rising from a meal upon the old, tough, high-flavoured, hard-sinewed wolf, and sitting down like Robinson Crusoe to his Journal ... I saw plain truth and the heart in Cartwright's book, and in what history could I look for this? ... Coleridge took up the volume one day, and was delighted with its strange simplicity.[10]

It is not an easy read, which Cartwright excuses by explaining that "the transactions of the day were generally entered at the close of the same, and were written for no other purpose than to serve as a memorandum for my own use and personal reference." Nevertheless, its pages give a vivid and minute account of life on the Labrador at that time.

Cartwright was a tough administrator: "I gave McCarthy 27 lashes with a small dog whip on his bare back, and intended to have made up the number 29." But he was religious too: "I read prayers to my family both in the forenoon and afternoon." He was a man of honour: when he failed in business, he refused to go into bankruptcy, preferring to carry his debt in the hope of paying it off. Wilfred Grenfell, who admired Cartwright while acknowledging his less attractive qualities, says in his introduction to C.W. Townsend's *Captain Cartwright's and His Labrador Journal:* "This book does not conventionally portray the life of a saint, but faithfully depicts that of a sinner ... being more interesting and therefore more likely to reach further. The Journals are a concise illustration of the enterprise, pluck, perseverance, self-reliance and stoicism of the old English stock."[11]

Cartwright's observations on the natural history of the country are particularly valuable, as is his account of the Inuit, with whom he had good relations. His partner Francis Lucas had learned Inuktitut from Mikak, whom he had brought to England a few years earlier. Consequently, Cartwright was able to persuade the large family of Attuiock to settle near his company of a dozen or so men at Charles River. Some of Cartwright's employees took Inuit women for their mates, and Cartwright treated all with respect and courtesy. Where his predecessor was forced to abandon the post because of Inuit hostility, Cartwright was successful because of his firmness and fairness with the Inuit. He joined in their games and provided for their needs. He said of them: "They are the best-tempered people I ever met with, and the most docile; nor is there a nation under the sun, with which I would sooner trust my person and property."

His relations with his fellow British were not so amiable. In the spring of 1772 a number of salmon fishermen employed by Noble and Pinson took possession of his salmon rivers, claiming that they had a right to do so under an act of Parliament. They claimed all salmon-fishing rights on the Charles River, forcing Cartwright to trade with the Inuit out of Fogo, Newfoundland. There were great losses when fire destroyed the Fogo post that year, and the firm of Perkins, Coghlan, Cartwright, and Lucas folded.

When Cartwright journeyed to England to defend his Labrador territory, the trip resulted in both triumph and tragedy. The Board of Trade granted him the right to hunt and trap in the Cape Charles area. But Cartwright, in an attempt to impress the Inuit, had taken his friends Attuiock and Tuglavina, together, with their wives, to England with him. The Inuit caused quite a stir in London. James Boswell's journal records: " Dr. Johnson did not give me half credit when I mentioned that I had carried on a short conversation by signs with some Eskimo who were then in London, particularly with one of them who was a priest." Unfortunately, during the visit one of the women, Caubvick, came down with smallpox, and eventually the others were stricken as well. All the Inuit died except Caubvick, who slowly recovered. But when she returned home, she spread the disease to other native people, many of whom succumbed. In 1779 William Phippard found Inuit skeletons on an island in Hamilton Inlet. Among the corpses was a medallion that had been presented to Caubvick by Cartwright's brother in England the year before. The skeletons were believed to be the bones of those who died from Caubvick's smallpox.

Although Cartwright experienced several failures during his sixteen years in Labrador, he always remained generous to a fault, even when dealing with those who had cheated him in some way. For him, Labrador was home rather than just a trading post, and in his journal he wrote more often of his natural environment and his hunts than of business. About 1775 he established a new post in Sandwich Bay at what was later known as Cartwright, and built himself a comfortable house there, Caribou Castle. He explored the Eagle River and named the White Bear River nearby. That year was a good one for him – his vessels went home loaded with fish, oil, salmon, and furs. During the summer he started a garden and set out peas, beans, radishes, onions, cress, cucumbers, corn, oats, and wheat.

But a few years later he suffered a loss of about £14,000 when several of his servants defected to join the crew of a Boston privateer, John Grimes, who before leaving Labrador plundered and destroyed Cartwright's posts. Yet Cartwright persisted, even during the American War of Independence, when fewer ships came to Labrador to fish and Cartwright was helped out with money from his brother John and from the Lesters of Poole. However, in 1784 he was forced into bankruptcy, and his Labrador possessions were sold to his old rivals, Noble and Pinson. Even on his trip to England in 1786 in the company of Benedict Arnold, he suffered loss when Arnold cheated him out of a stock of wine.

Whether or not Cartwright ever returned to Labrador is disputed. He did apply for another trade concession, noting in the petition the injustices suffered by small merchants at the hands of those with power. Foreshadowing the ambitions of later times, he advocated a separate government for Labrador under Quebec, with himself as justice of the peace. But he was denied the grant, and his notion of government for Labrador was rejected. Cartwright spent his remaining years in Nottingham, England, employed as a barrack master and known as "Old Labrador." He died in 1819. W.G. Gosling says, in his book on Labrador, that Cartwright's mind was occupied to the last with proposals to the Hudson's Bay Company to establish hunting and trading posts in Labrador, which the HBC eventually did in the 1830s.

Palliser and the Inuit

During Sir Hugh Palliser's years as governor (1764–68), a decision was made that profoundly affected the lives of the Inuit along the coast. As we have seen, relations between the seasonal British fish merchants and the Inuit were characterized by conflict and even bloodshed. Palliser believed that the fishermen were responsible for most of the trouble. Partly to protect them and partly to protect the Inuit from them, he took steps to confine the Inuit to northern Labrador. He made an agreement with the Moravian Church whereby, for his support in their conversion of the Inuit to Christianity, they would contain the aboriginal people north of Hamilton Inlet and keep them away from the English fishermen.[12] However, the agreement was not a complete success, and incidents of violence and treachery continued to occur. Since the various governors were "fishing admirals" who visited the waters of Newfoundland and Labrador for only two or three months of the year, they could do little to control the actions of the fishermen and traders, many of whom thought that the native people were their inferiors and ripe for exploitation.

The establishment of the Moravians' first station at Nain in 1771 started the process of displacing the market networks of the Inuit leaders and traders. This process was helped by the collapse of the market for baleen, the depletion of whale and walrus stocks in Labrador waters, and the effect of new weapons, such as the rifle, and the animal trap. In the first three hundred years of their occupation of Labrador, the Inuit had been an aggressive and opportunistic people, willing and able to exploit resources, initially for subsistence but later for trading. But with the increasing presence of Europeans, their settlements were moved, and their lives were changed forever.

CHAPTER THREE

Substitute Governors

Now, brothers, for the icebergs
Of frozen Labrador,
Floating spectral in the moonshine,
Along the low, black shore!
Where like snow the gannet's feathers
On Bradore's rocks are shed,
And the noisy murr are flying
Like black scuds, overhead;

Where in mist the rock is hiding,
And the sharp reef lurks below,
And the white squall smites in summer,
And the autumn tempests blow;
Where through grey and rolling vapour,
From evening until morn,
A thousand boats are hailing,
Horn answering unto horn.

"The Fishermen," John Greenleaf Whittier

While officially the British may have had jurisdiction over Labrador as of the early nineteenth century, they cannot be said to have governed in any real sense of the word. For the British, Labrador was a huge coast off which there were marine resources that could be harvested for businesses and markets elsewhere, and the people who settled on the coast, when they came to mind at all, were seen as obstructing those who came seasonally to prosecute that harvest. This was not a place where opposing interests were allowed. Certainly, the Labradorians were not people to be cared for in settled and growing communities. Such power as was exercised over them in the eighteenth and nineteenth centuries was by substitute patrons, non-governmental organizations, chiefly the Moravian Church, the

Hudson's Bay Company, and the Grenfell Mission. They filled the void left by a government that pursued and promoted the interests of others. The first of these to arrive on the coast of Labrador were the Moravians.

THE MORAVIANS

As a result of Palliser's agreement with the Moravian Church, a group led by Jens Haven received a charter to establish a mission among the Inuit of Labrador. Perhaps the oldest Protestant denomination, the Moravian Church had originated in what is now the Czech Republic in the middle of the fifteenth century. Before coming to Labrador, the Unitas Fratrum, as they were known, had established more missions around the world than all other Protestant denominations had during the two preceding centuries. By 1832 they had 209 missionaries at 41 mission stations in the West Indies, North, Central, and South America, Greenland, and Africa.

Fifteen years before Palliser, Johann Christian Erhardt, one of the brethren, had proposed to go to Labrador and establish a mission like the successful one in Greenland. His vessel, the *Hope*, arrived on the south coast of Labrador in July 1752. Later he sailed north to a place they called Nisbett's Harbour, a southern arm of Makkovik Bay. The Inuit were very pleased to see a white man who could speak their language, and Erhardt carried on a brisk trade with them and tried to erect a house for the winter. In September his ship left the harbour to seek other opportunities for trade. Ten days later it returned with the shocking news that Erhardt and five of his crew had left the ship with Inuit they had encountered and had not been seen again. Having no boats to seek the missing, the crew reluctantly abandoned the trip and returned to St John's. Later the remains were found, but never the circumstances of death.

In 1762 Jens Haven, a carpenter by trade who had served in the Moravian mission in Greenland, where he learned to speak Inuktitut, declared his intention to bring Christianity to the Labrador Inuit. In London he made the proposal to Palliser, the future governor of Newfoundland. Having received his full support, Haven and several others sailed north with three fishing shallops and arrived in Quirpon near the tip of Newfoundland's Great Northern Peninsula on 17 August 1764. Captain Cook, at the time surveying northern Newfoundland and Labrador, arranged for him to sail to Chateau Bay. But the Inuit had left, and it was not until a few days later that he met them back in Quirpon. The meeting is described in Haven's journal:

4 September 1764, was the joyful day I had so long wished for, when one Eskimaux came into the harbour to see if Captain Galliot was there. While I was preparing to go to him he had turned, and was departing to return to his countrymen, who lay in the mouth of the harbour, with the intelligence that the Captain had sailed. I called out to him in Greenlandish that he should come to me, that I had words to say to him, and that I was a good friend. He was astonished at my speech, and answered in broken French; but I begged him to speak in his own language, which I understood, and to bring his countrymen, as I wished to speak to them also; on which he went to them and cried with a loud voice "Our friend is come."[1]

The next year Haven, accompanied by three others, was sent in HMS *Niger* to Chateau, where they met hundreds of Inuit who had come south to trade. Speaking to them in their own language, Haven was encouraged and looked forward eagerly to the establishment of a mission. But the Moravians had trouble securing the 40,000 hectares of land that they thought necessary for the enterprise, and it was several years before they returned. They finally obtained their grant in 1769. On arriving near Nain on 24 June 1770, they found an old acquaintance, Segulliak, as well as Mikak and her husband Tuglavina. Mikak had gained considerable influence because of her trip to England with Lieutenant Francis Lucas, where she had met with the nobility, including King George III, who had presented her with a coronation medal. An attractive and intelligent woman, her charm was captured by John Russell, the eminent British portrait painter. Jens Haven, who had been in London at the same time preparing for the voyage to Labrador, realized what great assistance she could provide to his enterprise. After their return to Labrador, Mikak and her son Tutuak, did indeed use their notoriety to the advantage of the missionaries.

The Moravians acknowledged the Inuit right to their land and provided them with gifts in exchange for the areas they claimed. The Inuit made their marks on documents allowing the Moravians to use the land – the only treaties made with any Inuit in British North America. The Moravians chose Nain as the site of their first settlement and with their own sawmill cut the logs to build the original dwellings. When Lieutenant Roger Curtis of the Royal Navy visited the settlement the following year, his report was full of praise for the Moravians. They had built a substantial house and storehouse and had laid out a vegetable garden. Settled communities later became the pattern on the north coast as the Moravians tried to insulate the Christian Inuit from the heathens, whether the heathens were Britons or Americans or fellow Inuit. But it was clear to them that a people bound inextricably to the bounty of land and sea must continue to have access to it and that a total dependency on the mission was something it could never afford. Consequently, over time, although settled communities were built, the missionaries made a practice of visiting the Inuit at their harvesting places.

Most of the early missionaries were German, so the detailed records kept were in their own language, though they could speak Inuktitut. A great deal of correspondence flowed between the missions in Labrador, Herrnhut in Germany, and London. A monthly journal, *Periodical Accounts*, with contributions and statistics from all over the Moravian mission field, kept the missionaries in touch with one another. During its years of publication, it was one of the most widely read missionary journals in the English language. Some of the records the Moravians kept were not available until recently. However, following the fall of the Berlin wall and the reunification of Germany, Hans Rollman of Memorial University discovered at the Moravian headquarters in Herrnhut, near Dresden, pictures and records that will shed new light on the activities and experiences of the early Moravians.

The missionaries were chosen with care, for they were to serve in the mission field for life or until age dictated the discontinuation of their service. Wives were sent out to them, and the children of these marriages were sent away to school at an early age, often never to be seen again. The missionaries were supported from their headquarters in England and Germany, and every year a ship was dispatched to the mission field. Successive ships – from their first, the *Amity*, to their last, the *Harmony V* – hold honoured places in the history of transatlantic navigation. Not once in 150 years did they fail to deliver cargo.

As the missionaries' task was to bring Christianity to the Inuit, this meant replacing other gods and practices with those they believed to be the right ones. But the process was difficult. The concepts of sin, forgiveness, and redemption were alien to the Inuit, though they had had a satisfying spiritual and social life. Nevertheless, the Moravians supplanted the aspects of aboriginal culture that were contrary to Christian belief. They undermined the credibility of the Inuit *angakok*, or shaman, as well as the legendary figures of Inuit cosmology such as Nerchevirk, Torngarsoak, and Superguksoak. They also prohibited dancing, drumming, and singing. Now the rites of baptism, marriage, and burial entered the lives of the Inuit, as did the various festivals of the church. Polygamy and multifamily dwellings took longer to eradicate, for the Inuit culture persisted.

German words for numerals were applied in calculating time, so necessary for regulating attendance at church services and meetings, and for counting when exchanges were made at the mission store. As well, the Germans brought their stringed and brass instruments, along with their hymns and Bach chorales, which they taught the Inuit to play and sing. These were used to salute special occasions and were preserved over the years by the Inuit, who learned to perform them from memory. With their natural aptitude for music, the Inuit absorbed the tunes with alacrity, passing them on from generation to generation. On a still Sunday across the harbour in Nain you may still hear Bach in string and brass, a unique beauty of the northern Labrador coast.

The spiritual life of the Inuit had centred on the dance house, a combined church and community hall. The Moravians carefully persuaded their converts to replace the snow structures with wooden ones for both social and religious gatherings. Christian hymns replaced the dance songs, and the organ replaced the drum. But the Inuit had traditionally settled important matters in their dance houses, so the Moravians adapted this practice by organizing two councils to assist in the ministry and to maintain law and order. One council was appointed, the other elected. The appointed council consisted of three or four men and the same number of women, who were to help maintain order. Called Kivgat, they were village leaders and were expected to lead by example, the least lapse bringing instant deposal. In many cases the status was passed on to succeeding generations.[2]

The other council in each village was a committee of three or four men, elected by secret ballot every three years. Their responsibility was to look after the welfare of the village and to convey the wishes of the people to the missionaries. Called Atanik in Inuktitut, they were undoubtedly the first people to be elected in Labrador. And they had legitimacy, for the Moravians were sanctioned by the government of the day and were the virtual governors of northern Labrador. Not until 1946, when they voted in the election for the National Convention, did the Labrador people as a whole participate in any kind of democracy. Yet on the north coast the practice of public meetings with elected representatives persisted and flourished into the twentieth century. I can recall some that I attended, particularly in Nain and Makkovik, where speaker after speaker took the floor, as they knew to be their right and their custom, and made their points forcefully and directly.

The Moravians' settlement at Nain became their headquarters and remained so until the 1950s, when it was transferred to Happy Valley. In 1775 a mission at Okak, about 240 kilometres north of Nain, was established, and in 1781 another was begun at Hopedale. There the oldest Moravian structure, dating from 1817, still stands, having withstood fire and destruction. Nearby in the Mission House is a treasure trove of artifacts recording the Labrador Moravian heritage.

The missionaries were convinced that they must enter the trading business. As we have seen, by the time they arrived, trading for European goods had been underway for some time, either by Inuit middlemen or by French or English merchants. The desire – and, it could be argued, the need – for European goods had been firmly established. For the Moravians, the choice was to set up their own business, or to risk converts falling easily into the hands of southern traders, whose influence they knew would hardly be benign.

Meanwhile, unlike those on or near the Moravian stations, the Inuit south of Hamilton Inlet declined rapidly after 1765, when fishermen and trappers moving into the southern bays absorbed the aboriginal population. Without the protection of the Moravians they were vulnerable to outside influences, and on several occasions a number of Inuit were taken away for exhibit at various world fairs, usually with disastrous consequences. During the nineteenth century the remnants of the southern population, three hundred or so, were concentrated in Hamilton Inlet. Their assimilation took place so fast that Governor Sir William MacGregor, during his visit to the coast in 1905, declared that the Inuit had ceased to exist on the coast south of the Moravian establishments.

But they did still exist. Although the Inuktitut language disappeared south of Hamilton Inlet, aboriginal blood and customs were retained and are clearly evident today among members of those southern communities who make up the Labrador Metis Nation. John Kennedy of Memorial University maintains that Inuit enclaves in the south were not established until the end of the eighteenth century. In the Slade company's 1798 ledger for Battle Harbour, the unmistakably Inuit names of Shilmuck, Eteweeooke, Oglucock, and the Putlavamiut (Battle Harbour people) appear, and various Church of England clergy of the time refer to Inuit at Dumpling Island and Tub Harbour. The Moss diary[3] refers to Inuit at Francis Harbour, where the old graveyard gives testimony to the Inuit-Welsh ancestors of Todd Russell, president of the Labrador Metis Nation. The Anglican bishop of Newfoundland, Edward Feild, reported that many of the women between Forteau and Dumpling were aboriginal, mainly Inuit.

Because of the presence of the Moravians, the Inuit in the north took much longer to merge with white society. But after thirty years of Moravian presence, about half of those who lived in the northern communities professed Christianity. The majority had initially resisted conversion, but the prevalence of social conflicts, high mortality from

European diseases, and food shortages contributed to a religious awakening in 1804. Perhaps another cause was the teaching of Inuit children, which by this time had gone on for a generation. By 1801 many could read reasonably well. Schools had been established very early to teach reading, writing, arithmetic, geography, biblical subjects, and European history. Since instruction was in Inuktitut, the northern Inuit were provided with a level of education that was not matched at that time by any other Inuit population in North America.[4]

Whatever caused it, the "revival" spelled religious success for the Moravians. But after 1805 the mission became the establishment – indeed, the government of northern Labrador – and ceased to be an agent of social, religious, and economic change. Thereafter, the population at the mission stations increased rapidly as the Moravians expanded their presence, opening four more stations: in the north at Hebron in 1831; Zoar in 1865; Ramah, the most northern, in 1871; and Makkovik, the most southern, in 1896. Saglek and Nachvak also had been chosen for stations, but the Hudson's Bay Company got to them first. A final station opened at Killinek on the tip of the Labrador peninsula in 1905. The Moravians had contained the entire northern Inuit population in their Christian mission.

But a conflict was emerging for the Moravians. As mentioned above, although their basic purpose was religious, they believed they must be traders if only in self-defence. Yet this trading changed the way of life of the Inuit, for resources had to be harvested not just for subsistence but for the market. Whereas the Inuit had formerly hunted and fished for food, they now hunted and fished in order to buy trade goods. Since silver fox furs commanded high prices, the Inuit neglected the seal in order to hunt the fox with white man's traps. Although they never took to doing so with alacrity, they were taught to fish and to salt-cure their catch for the European market. This kept them on the stations and satisfied the Moravians' need for trade, but it was changing the life of the Inuit. Even though no cash changed hands and even though the missionaries discouraged the purchase of "luxury" items and tried to confine purchases to necessities, the Moravian version of the truck system created a dependency.

In the early part of the century, rival traders advanced on the Moravian precincts. Thomas Bird reopened the Kaipokok trading post in 1830, and A.B. Hunt started the first post at Davis Inlet in 1831. These independent traders paid the Inuit higher prices for seal, fur, and fish and offered liberal credit terms for products that the Moravians did not sell. Naturally, this appealed to many Inuit. Some of these traders and settlers took Inuit wives, and their children became known as Kablunangajuit (settlers). Among them were John Reed, Robert

Mitchell, and John Ford. Perhaps in the long run the most famous name among these early settlers will be that of Amos Voisey, who gave his name to a bay where the richest nickel mine in the world was later discovered. Voisey arrived around 1800 from England. He married twice, both times to Inuit women, and began a small trading operation in Voisey's Bay, which his son George carried on after his death. Today his descendants live in Happy Valley–Goose Bay.

John Lane arrived about 1830. Antoine Perrault from Quebec arrived in 1834 with the Hudson's Bay Company, though he soon established his own trading operation with the help of Captain William Bartlett, father of the famous Captain Bob who took part in Robert Peary's expedition to the North Pole. Perrault and his contemporary, Jean-Baptiste Jacque, had large families who still populate the coast. Thorwald Perrault was one of the leaders of the move to Goose Bay during the establishment of the base there and was one of the founders of Happy Valley, where his sons still live. The McNeils and the Lyalls came from Scotland, and both families have been prominent in Labrador. Thorsten Andersen of Norway set up as a trader at Makkovik. His family is still prominent along the coast, and Bill Andersen's sons Toby and Chesley are now the leading land claims negotiators for the Labrador Inuit Association (LIA). The settler families increased substantially during the twentieth century, and settlers with aboriginal ancestry are now recognized as Inuit by the LIA.

This steady influx from the south, including the transient Newfoundland fishing schooners, increased the anxieties of the Moravians. At the beginning of the nineteenth century the Newfoundlanders had advanced as far north as Hamilton Inlet. In 1866 there were twenty-five vessels in Hopedale, and in 1870 five hundred passed the northern harbours. In spite of their apprehension about the negative influence of the Newfoundlanders, the Moravians began to minister to this transient and floating population. In fact, an English-speaking brother was sent out for this purpose. The fleet continued to grow, its numbers swelling to between 15,000 and 20,000 people in a season. The sudden growth led to trouble and abuses. When boats, nets, and gear were stolen, there was no policeman on the coast to call and no government to intervene.

New perils were in store for the northern Inuit. In 1918 an influenza epidemic devastated the population of Okak and Hebron. The disease, which had swept Europe, was brought to the coast by a sailor on the Moravians' supply ship, *Harmony*, and quickly infected a majority of the inhabitants. Within five weeks, 207 of 266 people in Okak and 150 out of 220 in Hebron died, almost one-third of the total number of Inuit in northern Labrador. Whole families were wiped

out. Harry Paddon, a doctor with the Grenfell Mission, tells the tale
of a little girl who miraculously survived:

The whole community was stricken except one little girl of seven years of
age. There was here too a horde of wolf-like dogs, and with no one to feed
them they speedily reverted to wolf-like predatory life, tearing up and
devouring bodies, perhaps hastening death in some cases. The child ... was
limited to a diet of raw flour and berries, but ... could not barricade herself
against the dogs; she had no fuel left and on cold November nights the only
way to keep herself from freezing to death was by admitting these man-eating
beasts to sleep on the floor of her shack and to nestle up against their shaggy
bodies for warmth. For some reason they never touched her ... For three
weeks this ghastly existence went on. Then friends ashore ... came on a tour
of investigation. Horror stricken, they beheld the ravening dogs and the muti-
lated corpses. That there could be anyone alive never entered their heads,
and when the child appeared and ran towards them, they fled in terror.[5]

Paddon commented that it seemed "probable that the Labrador Eskimos
received their death blow in the great 'Spanish flu' epidemic of 1918
when forty per cent of the entire remaining Eskimos succumbed, and
whole villages were practically exterminated."[6]

Traders continued to move into northern Labrador in the early
twentieth century. All of them shared their knowledge and experience with the Inuit and learned from them the skills necessary for
survival in the near north. Perhaps the most prominent of these men
was Dick White. Certainly, he was one of the most erudite. In addition to maintaining a successful business and contributing substantially to anthropological efforts, he left astute observations of life on
the coast at that time. He was one of those "ancestors of the hardy
white men who today, on more than even terms, share with the Inuit
and wandering Innu the game resources of Labrador. Living in absolute freedom, depending on their own efforts to wrest a living from
nature, and knowing they can do it, asking no favours of governments
or anyone else."[7]

Born in St John's in 1878, White graduated in law from the University of London and was admitted to the Newfoundland bar in
1905. After practising law in St John's for several years, he joined the
team surveying the Quebec-Newfoundland border in 1909. In 1911
he and R.S. Elmsley of Ottawa went prospecting for base metals on
the northern tip of Baffin Island. White was hooked. Captured by the
North, he decided to give up his law practice and become a fur trader
in Labrador. But the Moravians opposed his application to trade in
Hebron in 1911. Consequently, White and his Inuit wife Ruth Townley

set up a trading operation at Voisey's Bay and later at Nain in 1913, hoping to intercept some of the Moravian trade with the Innu. The First World War interrupted White's fox farming and trading – he enlisted with the Canadian Expeditionary Force – but back in Labrador after the war he continued his trading and also his interest in the aboriginal cultures. He provided substantial assistance to the American scholar William Brooks Cabot in his studies of the Innu, and many of the artifacts collected by White are now in museums all over North America. Later he assisted E.P. Wheeler in the same way. He looked after the Innu too in times of difficulty and want, billing the provisions and ammunition he gave them to the Department of Indian Affairs in Ottawa.

White expanded beyond fox and mink, marketing local craftwork, cod liver oil, seal oil, pickled salmon and char, and the beautiful local stone, Labradorite, as well as advertising for tourists. He was a philanthropist as well, paying the expenses at schools on the outside for a number of promising local students as well as his own children. And after Father Edward O'Brien, the Catholic priest who served the Innu, had gone south for the winter, White helped by performing burials of the dead and reporting the deaths. Resourceful and successful, White was the source of the character Richardson in Harold Horwood's Labrador novel *White Eskimo*.

In addition to traders like Dick White, the Moravian's operations were plagued by financial difficulties, caused by the wartime disruption of overseas markets and by rising prices for consumer goods. In 1924 they changed from the credit system to a cash economy. This drove the Inuit back on their own resources, and they retired to the outer islands or to the river valleys of the interior, where game was more abundant for both food and trade. Finally, in 1926, the Moravians bowed to the inevitable pressure of outside competition and leased their buildings to the Hudson's Bay Company for twenty-one years.

Since the market for fur had been rising, the company encouraged trapping and provided the Inuit with the necessary food and ammunition. So the Inuit abandoned sealing to the detriment of their health, since a vitamin-deficient diet of bread, beans, and tea was no substitute for fresh meat. For a while the change seemed justified, as prices for fur continued to rise. But when the Depression of the 1930s hit, markets for fur virtually disappeared. The Hudson's Bay Company then suggested a return to sealing, but it was not so easy, for during the years of trapping the Inuit had neglected their rawhide sealing nets, many of which had rotted. Families were once more driven back on local game, even though they might have difficulty purchasing the necessary ammunition. With only the dole of six cents a day to support them, their existence became virtually hand to mouth.

Through all of this, as the Moravians had done from the beginning, they continued to work for the health of the population and the education of both children and adults – perhaps their greatest contribution to the coast. Although around 1900 the government in St John's classified the Moravian schools as church institutions, it did not appoint teachers, determine curricula, or supervise methods of instruction. Nor did it provide any funding until 1919, when it allocated $2000 for the boarding school in Nain. Yet government support for schools on the Island had been steadily increasing, and the act of 1916 had provided a grant of $367,000.

At Makkovik the mission had opened a boarding school in 1901, accepting pupils without discrimination from the age of six, using the English language and books sent from England. But again there was no organized curriculum, and since the teachers came from different European backgrounds, teaching methods varied from year to year. Yet there were outstanding teachers who made unique contributions to the coast and to the children who lived there. Kate Hettasch, the daughter of "Doctor" Paul, returned to Nain after her schooling in Europe and was put in charge of the Nain boarding school in 1930. Full of creativity and zeal, she taught on the coast for forty-five years and has left a rich legacy in text and pictures with the OKalaKatiget Society in Nain and the Moravian Archives in Bethlehem, Pennsylvania, not to mention the hundreds of lives she influenced. Beatrice (Ford) Watts of Nain, herself an outstanding Labrador educator, well remembers the influence of Kate in the classroom and beyond.

From the beginning, the missionaries had dealt as best they could with the health problems of northern Labrador. For most of the year they were the only source of medical help, and they performed with a surprising degree of competence – what Dr Harry Paddon probably would have described as "talented amateurism." They supplied medicine and even did operations in emergencies. "Doctor" Paul Hettasch once amputated an arm at the shoulder and another at the wrist, not only doing the surgery but also giving part of his attention to the amateur anaesthetist.

Dr Samuel King Hutton, a British Moravian, brought professional help to the coast in the early years of the century, but after 1911 when he closed his hospital at Okak, the coast received very little attention. The only medical professionals who visited the area were Dr Grenfell or Dr Paddon of the Grenfell Mission and a Newfoundland doctor who travelled as far as Nain once a year seeing patients on the mail boat. The health of the Inuit became so perilous that Bishop Albert Martin told his staff in 1908 that they were ministering to a dying race. Poor living conditions and malnutrition gave rise to tuberculosis, and sexually transmitted diseases increased as contact with outsiders became more common. Change for the better came only with Confederation in 1949 and Canadian funding for health care.

The coming of Confederation brought further changes to Inuit society, and inevitably brought about the end of the Moravians' role as the only government in northern Labrador. From 1949 control over services was assumed by government agencies. That same year Eastern Provincial Airways began its bush plane service to the coast, though occasional landings had taken place since the thirties. In the late nineteenth and early twentieth century the Inuit of northern Labrador experienced massive change, which wrenched them from the old ways but began to fit them somewhat for the decades that were to come. The era that Paulus Maggo witnessed in his lifetime, as recounted by Carol Brice-Bennett in the book on his life, ranged from kayaks and dog teams to satellite communications, high-powered snowmobiles, outboard motors, and aircraft.[8] It was a period of radical change.

The Moravians clearly made their own significant contribution to the history of Labrador and its governance. It is true that they suppressed precontact Inuit culture – the dances, the songs, the mythology. But these never really died, and the soapstone carvings of Gilbert Hay, John Terriak, and the other artists along the coast clearly reveal that the culture is very much alive in the minds and hearts of Labrador Inuit. The Moravians have also been accused of "well-meaning but misguided paternalism," a view that is reflected in the memoirs of the Rev. Bill Peacock, a superintendent of Moravian missions.[9] For many years the missionary was the ultimate authority, the person who controlled the flow of goods and laid down the guidelines for social life on the station. Tony Williamson of Memorial University has contended that having been treated as children for over 170 years, the Labrador Inuit were slow to develop initiative.[10] And it is interesting that while there are, for example, quite a number of qualified nurses and engineers from the communities on the north coast, it was only in 1980 that Renatus Hunter became the first Inuk from northern Labrador to be ordained to the Moravian ministry. He was not the first ordained Inuk. That honour goes to Simon Gibbons of Red Bay, an orphan brought up by Bishop Feild in his own household and ordained to the ministry of the Church of England in 1877. Yet in terms of what are usually regarded as Christian values, the Inuit before contact and after clearly cared for one another, shared food and equipment, cooperated in community affairs, and showed respect

for individuals. Acknowledging this, it is all the more lamentable that
in trying to cope with modern society, too many of them struggle
against alcoholism, abuse, and suicide. In a tragically ironic twist of
fate, the CBC tower in Nain – a device that helped open a window
on the world for people in that community – became for its young
the choice means of attempting suicide.

Although the Moravians supplanted Inuit governance, they did at
least introduce a measure of democracy into the communities long
before any other non-aboriginal government did so. Their records are
an extremely important contribution to Labrador history. They began
the first schools in northern Labrador, with the result that for some
time people in the north were better educated than many of their
counterparts farther south. They did their best to keep the Inuit
healthy, and indeed it is fair to ask how many Inuit there would be
north of Hamilton Inlet today if the Moravians had not been there.
But while they did the lion's share in preserving the race, there is no
doubt that they brought about permanent change.

THE HUDSON'S BAY COMPANY

After the Moravians, the next non-governmental organization to
exert control over Labrador society was the Hudson's Bay Company.
While it was by no means the first trading company at Lake Melville,
it became the most influential. By the time the Bay came to Hamilton
Inlet, the island of Newfoundland had representative government,
but little was known of such a system in Labrador, nor were there
any visible signs of it for decades. In the absence of government
representatives, elected or appointed, the company, with all its self-
interest, filled the role of patron.

After the amalgamation of the Hudson's Bay Company and the
North West Company in 1821, the country east of Hudson Bay was
explored and posts were established throughout the interior of the
Ungava Peninsula. In 1830 Nicol Finlayson established Fort Chimo
forty kilometres upstream of Ungava Bay on the Koksoak River. In
the spring of 1836 Governor Simpson, the HBC's "little Emperor,"
instructed Chief Trader Simon McGillivray to travel overland from
Mingan and set up a trading operation at the western end of Lake
Melville. Traders at Rigolet and North West River were subsequently
bought out. The intention was to establish a chain of trading posts in
the interior (which would be supplied from these coastal posts) to
control the trade with the Innu of the plateau. The trade route was to
be one that the native people had travelled from Hamilton Inlet and
the St Lawrence to Ungava Bay, passing through Petitsikapau Lake.

Fort Nascopie was erected in 1838 on the northwest arm of the lake near present-day Schefferville and close to the Churchill watershed. With a small staff and about three hundred Innu, it was operated on and off until the 1870s, but it was never profitable because of the expense and difficulty of transporting trade goods up the rivers.

The post at North West River was at the far end of Little Lake and Grand Lake, where Lake Michikamau is drained by the Naskaupi River, and where Louis Fornel established the first recorded fur-trading post in 1743. John McLean at Chimo was charged with the task of opening up an overland communications route with the post. In January 1838 he set off for Lake Melville (Esquimaux Bay), reached his destination without much trouble, and was back in Chimo by April. The following summer he attempted to reach it by a more westerly route, which led him to the "discovery" of the Grand Falls (later called Hamilton and later still, Churchill), the first non-aboriginal to see this extraordinary spectacle. In the middle of August 1839 he and his companion, Erland Erlandson, were paddling peacefully down Hamilton River "when, one evening, the roar of a mighty cataract burst upon our ears, warning us that danger was at hand. We soon reached the spot, which presented to us one of the grandest spectacles in the world, but put an end to all hopes of success in our enterprise."[11]

Although the first district headquarters was at Rigolet, it was soon transferred to North West River, and thereafter posts were established at Aillik, Tikkaratsuk, and Kaipokok, the latter providing stiff competition for Antoine Perrault. In 1859 the North West River post displaced A.B. Hunt for the Innu trade at Davis Inlet and in 1873 bought out the Hunt and Henley establishment in Sandwich Bay. Determined to break the Moravian stranglehold on the Inuit trade the Hudson's Bay Company established posts at Nachvak, Saglek, and Killinek in the 1860s and 1870s.

In the early 1840s the population of Lake Melville had included, in addition to the remaining aboriginals, people who had found their own way to Labrador and those who had worked off their five-year indenture to the Bay. Even after leaving the company's employ, it was difficult if not impossible to escape its influence. Most men had come over as Hudson's Bay Company servants, but even after they left, the system ensured that they would be dependent on the company for their existence; even if they were living off the land, they needed a grubstake, and it was likely that only by selling their furs to the Bay could they pay their debts. Thus, the Bay controlled much of their lives, and there was no appeal to any other authority.

It was the coming of Donald Smith that brought the Bay in Lake Melville its golden age. In 1848 he was assigned as assistant to Chief

Trader William Nourse. At that time North West River was a secure post, its chief rival being the company's own operation at the King's Posts and Mingan, as Smith knew from his experience there. Smith was steady, shrewd, and imaginative. His latest biographer, Donna McDonald, describes him as follows: "Dressed in a flaming flannel shirt and homespun trousers Smith spent most of his time bartering blankets and tobacco for furs. He also acted as judge and doctor. His treatment of wounds with a pulp made from the boiled inner bark of juniper trees was later studied by Lord Lister, who introduced the principles of antiseptics to surgery in 1865."[12] On three cleared hectares Smith grew turnips, cucumbers, potatoes, and peas. He built a three-kilometre track, Labrador's first road, for his ox-drawn sulky. When fur revenues declined, he began to trade in seal oil and he established a lively export business in cranberries and salmon packed in ice. He even built a small cannery, thereby introducing the canning of salmon to Labrador.

Smith asked the Bay to assign a geologist to North West River because there were, he said, "minerals here that will one day astonish the world." This showed remarkable foresight. In the 1950s Brinco, the international consortium created by the Smallwood government, had a number of geologists at North West River spread out over the Labrador wilderness searching for marketable ore. Later drilling confirmed that Smith's area of astonishing minerals contained commercial quantities of iron ore, titanium, lead, zinc, nickel, asbestos, and columbium, as well as a streak of uranium 137 kilometres long. (A uranium mine was almost begun in the 1980s, one deposit having been discovered by Walter Kitts and the other by Leslie Michelin, a Labrador prospector and former trapper from North West River. The bridge across North West River was partly justified on the grounds that it was the beginning of a new road to the mine site near the village of Makkovik. But distance from markets as well as environmental concerns placed the development in abeyance, where it still is today.)

Smith knew the value of having priests at a trading post and tried to get the Moravians to establish a mission in Hamilton Inlet. In 1857 Brother Elsner travelled to North West River, where Smith offered to build a house and church and pay the missionary in order to have a mission established. But Elsner reported that there were not enough people and they were too spread out. He noted that only fifteen people, including children, were resident at North West River at the time, while four families were within one day's travel. The total population of the area he estimated at about 170. No doubt he also concluded that when it came to competing with Smith and the Hudson's

Bay Company for hegemony in Lake Melville, discretion was the better part of valour.[13]

There were important changes within the Bay's area of influence between 1836 and 1900. The population increased, and with the subsequent competition for fur between the Innu and the settlers, the trapping grounds changed too. Hamilton Inlet was divided into two distinct activities: fur in North West River and fish in Rigolet. The changes included the establishment of a resident Methodist missionary, an itinerant teacher, and increased contact with the outside through tourists, adventurers, scientists, and mail boats.

During the era of the Hudson's Bay Company at Lake Melville, particularly around the turn of the century, a unique culture developed. Perhaps it was somewhat like that of similar areas of the North, where Europeans and aboriginals had met and mated. But in this place at this time it was unique. It is perhaps best described in its maturity by Elliot Merrick, an American writer who heard the call of the Grenfell Mission and stayed on to experience the life of the trapper on the line:

Our friends the scattered families that inhabit the bay are a unique race with oddly combined cultures: Scotch Presbyterian in religion, old English in speech and custom, Indian in their ways of hunting and their skill with canoes ascending the big rivers bound for the trapping grounds far in the country. Sometimes it seems as though they had taken for their own the best qualities of the three races, the Eskimo laughter-loving happiness, the Indian endurance and uncanny instinct for living off the country, the Scotchman's strength of character and will.[14]

During the late nineteenth century, when the Bay still ruled in Lake Melville, these people of mixed ancestry became the dominant population in central Labrador and the primary trappers for the fur trade. More and more men, mostly from the Orkney Islands but some from other parts of Britain and some from Quebec, settled in Lake Melville as "planters" and took wives and partners from among the Inuit women there. While initially the Bay's traders had hoped that the Innu would be their main source of fur, the Innu continued to be more interested in the caribou hunt. They were reluctant trappers, furs being for them a source of emergency food supplies. So it was that the settler Labradorians became the chief suppliers of the Bay. Through the late nineteenth and early twentieth century they built an extensive network of family traplines and tilts, often many days' distance from their homes. Their names are recorded in the Bay's journals of the period: "Having had a row with John Montague, John

Flett has now gone to inflict his company on Tom Blake Jr. who intends starting next Tuesday for Peter Michelin's path."[15] "Mayflower back this afternoon, with McLean family aboard. John Michelin and M. Best families in, in their boat from below, having landed Fred Blake at Lowlands from whence he was to come up in a small boat. Busy supplying planters."[16]

One of the most prominent was Malcolm McLean, a Scot who had come over to serve under Donald Smith. Later he launched out as an independent trapper and salmon fisherman. Married twice, he produced no less than twenty-two sons and daughters, nineteen of whom survived him. Supporting his family from the land and the sea, the only cash income he ever received was as caretaker of a defunct lumber company. He grew his own vegetables and kept his own livestock and chickens. Foreseeing the overcrowding of the traplines, he had started a sawmill, by the time he was seventy. With his white beard, black hat, and black coat that came to his knees, at the age of eighty-eight he was still tending his own salmon nets at his home in Kenemish so that his sons could work the little mill.

The Bay had no serious competition in the area until 1901, when Reveillon Freres of Paris decided to establish a number of trading posts, including one at North West River. But the Bay prevailed and bought out the French company in 1936. Raoul Thevenet, the Reveillon manager at the time, continued with the Bay for some years, later becoming an independent trader. His descendants live in the Lake Melville area to this day; one of them, Jackie Cooper, is the owner-operator of one of Labrador's premier sports fishing camps on Lake Minipi.

Between the coming of the Bay and the beginning of the twentieth century, the society of central Labrador was transformed. With the arrival of the Grenfell Mission at North West River and the beginning of the lumber operations, more and more people were attracted to the area. Most came to settle and to make a new life. But there were others, lured by the romance of Labrador, who came to explore. It held a mystique common to many parts of the North. It was the untracked wilderness – at least, for those who lived in crowded cities and towns. Many yearned for adventure or the freedom they had lost; others came to probe what for them was the last frontier. The early 1900s were a time of exploration both north and south. Fatal shipwrecks and lost expeditions were common. Arctic travel had not improved much over the centuries. But the explorers and adventurers who were successful in their travels to Labrador depended for assistance on local Labradormen.

Perhaps the best-known Labrador adventurer was an American, Leonidas Hubbard. In 1903 he attempted to be the first to cross Labrador from North West River to George River. He had the imagination and the desire – even the will – but he was ill prepared. Basing his scheme on an uncertain map, he led his small party up the wrong river at the head of Grand Lake, taking the Susan instead of the Naskaupi. Although Dillon Wallace, his companion, was sure they were on the wrong river, Hubbard deluded himself that they were on the right one. From the Susan they stumbled onto the Beaver, but it too petered out. Finally, although they could see Lake Michikamau in the distance, the cold was fast approaching and they knew they could not go on. Having exhausted their energy and their food supply, they began the retreat towards Grand Lake, where Donald Blake had a winter home. But soon Hubbard was near collapse. He decided that he could go no farther and sent Wallace and George Elson, their Scots-Cree guide from James Bay, on for help. After a courageous descent that braved the fall hazards of the Naskaupi, Elson finally made it to the tilt of Donald Blake. Donald and Gilbert, his seventeen-year-old brother, together with Alan Goudie and Duncan McLean, set out to rescue Hubbard. But they were too late. They found him dead in his tent along with his diary, which gave an arresting account not only of their travels but also of his final moments.

Partly because Hubbard's widow, Mina, felt that Wallace's subsequent books, *The Lure of the Labrador Wild* and *The Long Labrador Trail*, had capitalized on her husband's misfortune, she set out to defend his honour. Upset at the portrait Wallace had drawn of her husband, she grew to detest him and decided to complete her husband's dream herself. Recruiting Gilbert Blake as her guide and taking along the same George Elson, she began a race with Wallace, who had decided to make the same trip at the same time. It was a race unique in wilderness exploration: Dillon Wallace, determined to fulfill the dream of his closest friend; Mina Hubbard, venturing into the country that had killed her husband; and George Elson, returning to Labrador with a young woman who had placed her fate in his hands.

Obviously a strong and independent woman, Mina Hubbard succeeded where her husband had failed. In an event unusual for the day, a young woman not only beat the experienced Wallace to George River but also mapped the Naskaupi River between Grand Lake and the Ungava coast. Her book, *A Woman's Way through Trackless Labrador*, recorded her explorations and her appreciation of the area. Soon it may be made into a feature film based on the experience of young Gilbert Blake, the shrewd and resourceful young settler from North West River, whom she had recruited and who for her was undoubtedly the difference between success and failure.[17]

By the 1930s the trapping territory was spreading to more and more of the interior, and the traplines of the settlers began to overlap with land that had been historically occupied and used by the Innu.

Tanner, the Finnish geographer, estimates that in 1939 there were 15,000 traps on the Naskaupi and Hamilton river systems. There was a sense among Labradorians that things had been stretched to the limit. Conflict between the settlers and the Innu was inevitable. One story of an incident near Churchill Falls is told by Gilbert Blake in *The Labrador Settlers:*

William Montague, Henry Groves, Charlie Goudie, Arch Goudie and I were the first white men who went in there to trap among the Indians in the early 1900s; and they didn't like it. They tried to drive us out every way. But we were young men then and we didn't care, we stuck it out all winter.

Arch Goudie had just struck up his lines when six Indians came out one afternoon. They were so cross about us stealing their trapping. They had gone to Seven Islands and came back again after the winter. There were six men and they were so mad that one man took his gun and held it to Arch's head while the others robbed away all his grub and burned down his tilt. I didn't know this happened so there we were left without food, only a little bit I had.[18]

Giving another point of view, Raoul Thevenet reported that year that the settlers and Newfoundlanders had three to six hundred traps set during the hunting season and had overrun the native hunting grounds. He reported that the Innu were getting poorer every year and would surely have starved but for government relief. They were becoming very bitter against the white trappers, he said, and he feared conflict. But in reality, open conflict was the exception rather than the rule. Many settlers could speak the Innu language and had had friendly relations with Innu since childhood. Indeed, each had borrowed from the other and reliance on one another was common. Bella McLean Shouse, the daughter of Malcolm, describes her family's relationship with the Pasteen family, who regularly came to stay near her father's house at Kenemish:

My father always showed him [Pasteen] respect when he came out of the country in the winter, always invited them into the house, fed them, and let them sleep on the floor. My mother always had heavy quilts that was left by the Dickie Lumber Company and gave them to the Indians to lie on ... [The Pasteens] always brought us caribou which was exchanged for salt pork, flour and tea ... They had to make sure the Bay was frozen before going to North West River to sell their furs and get supplies for their families left in the country. The HBC or Reveillon trading company, whoever was the successful bidder for the furs, gave them supplies and sent their dog team and dog driver over to Kenemish with the big things like flour, pork, lard, etc. They didn't hang around if the weather was good, usually arrived at our place in the evening, next morning to North West River, spend the day trading, spend the night at the HBC kitchen, spend the next night back in Kenemish ... If the hunt was good, they would have some biscuits and a bag of loose candy for the children. I loved to watch them lash their sleds, everything wrapped in a tarpaulin ... From the time I can remember, my father and brothers never went deer hunting. When the Indians came out of the Mealies they brought us all the meat we needed. What with the partridges, rabbits, and our own beef, my father killed our beef animal each fall, this took care of our meat for the winter.[19]

Richard Budgell says the relationship between the Innu and the settlers was characterized neither by total harmony nor total strife. But it does seem as if the "distinctiveness of the Innu was well accepted by mixed-ancestry Labradorians, the fact that they played by different rules – 'Indians were free to go where they liked' – which may have related to the fact that they were acknowledged in some fashion to be unambiguously 'aboriginal' or pre-existing."[20]

Over the years the fall in fur prices and the drastic decline of the local caribou herd compounded the problems of the Innu. Many of them were reluctant to travel far inland for fear of starvation and of the deadly diseases that struck at this time. In order to survive, they increasingly had to seek assistance from the Government of Newfoundland. With the settlers becoming more dependent on wage labour, particularly after the coming of the air base at Goose Bay, the two groups gradually grew apart, and the river which they had shared became the dividing line after Sheshatshiu decided on municipal separation from the "settler" municipality of North West River. It would be a long road to regain the familiarity and respect they had had for each other in the past.

The decline of the fur market in the early decades of the twentieth century and the coming of the cash economy brought an end to the fur-trading enterprise of the Hudson's Bay Company, which turned its attention more and more to the retail trade. Later, the northern stores split from the company, and today in Goose Bay and North West River what were once outlets of the mightiest fur-trading operation of its time are now well-stocked convenience stores.

In its day, the Hudson's Bay Company had held sway over the lives of those who lived within its ambit. While the settlers were to the greatest possible degree self-sufficient, living off the land and sea, the company was a major factor in controlling their income and their sustenance. As game declined and settlers increased, the Innu came to depend more and more on the Bay. Its power lasted until the coming of the cash economy, with the advent of the lumber companies and, later, the air base.

THE GRENFELL MISSION

This was another powerful organization that filled the vacuum left by an absent government. Primarily a medical mission, it affected many facets of Labrador life: education, light industry (such as crafts), justice, welfare, and even political representation. Well into the early decades of the twentieth century, Labrador's best-known and respected spokespersons were those of the Grenfell Mission.

The mission had originally come to serve the needs of the fishery along the Labrador coast, especially the seasonal fishermen who sailed from Newfoundland each year in search of cod. In the heyday of the Hudson's Bay Company and the growth of the trappers' culture in Lake Melville, the Newfoundland fishery moved ever northward. There were the floaters (those who went to Labrador for the summer fishery and used their schooners as a base) and the stationers (those who moved to Labrador on schooner or steamer during the summer to fish from the land). Both groups encountered the livyers (permanent settlers of Labrador), who had increased steadily during the nineteenth century. The meeting was not always amicable, for there were only so many good berths or fishing places, and often there was competition for them. Although there was much intermingling and intermarriage, the relationship between those who came and those who stayed was often bittersweet, engendering attitudes that lasted for decades.

In 1825 the St John's Chamber of Commerce wrote to the colonial secretary in Britain pointing out how important the Labrador fishery was to Newfoundland. That year between sixty and seventy vessels from St John's and nearly two hundred from Conception Bay carried on the Labrador fishery, employing nearly five thousand men. Harold Innis in *The Cod Fisheries* reported that in 1840 a large number of ships carrying as many as four thousand people all told proceeded from Trinity and Conception bays to fish at Henley Harbour, Battle Harbour, Cape Charles, Deer Island, the Seal Islands, and Long Islands.

Soon Newfoundland schooners were routinely going as far north as Saglek, a few even venturing as far as Cape Chidley. They left lasting signs of their presence through numerous place names: Cutthroat, Ironbound Islands, Windy Tickle, Fish Island, and Newfoundland Harbour. The family of the famous arctic explorer Bob Bartlett operated rooms at Turnavik. Farther south, Captain William Jackman of Renews is remembered for his heroism in 1867 in saving the lives of twenty-seven shipwrecked people from the *Sea Clipper*, a schooner that had run aground and was breaking up on the rocks at Spotted Island during one of the most severe Atlantic storms. Jackman, shedding most of his clothes, dove into the rough seas, and while the brothers John and Samuel Holwell of Spotted Island assisted on shore with ropes, he swam out to the ship, returning with each of the twenty-seven in turn. These itinerant fishermen and their later relationship to Wilfred Grenfell were immortalized in the novels and absorbing adventure stories of the American writer Norman Duncan.

It was not just Newfoundlanders who sailed to Labrador for the season. The Slades signed on men in Poole, Dorset, to work in Labrador for two summers and a winter. Some never returned to England, settling in the coves and harbours along the coast. In the lists of the crews during the eighteenth and nineteenth centuries are the names Buckle, Rumbolt, Blake, Stone, Brown, Snook, Chubbs, Pye, Allen, Bird, Reid, Mangrove, Moores, Davis, Saunders, and Poole, as well as others who have been prominent on the coast for the past two centuries. Both Britons and Newfoundlanders made the choice to stay. And when they did, inevitably there was tension between those who stayed and those who simply came for the summer. Whose place was it, anyway?

As the fishery grew in importance and as more and more fishermen visited the coast, services were put in place. From 1811, at the instigation of the merchants who paid taxes but received no services, a magistrate was sent each summer. In 1824 an act was passed for a court of civil jurisdiction on the coast of Labrador. The court was first held in Rigolet in 1826 but was discontinued in 1833 on the grounds that there was not enough business. Yet there were grievances that needed to be settled. Newfoundland firms complained that they had to pay duty on cargoes for trade and barter on the Labrador while firms from Canada, Nova Scotia, and the United States paid none. The Newfoundland merchants' complaints paid off. On 10 June 1862 notice was given that all duties imposed would be collected, and in 1863 a court of limited civil and criminal jurisdiction was established.

By this time, steamers as well as sailing ships were plying Labrador waters. The steamships of large St John's firms took Newfoundland crews to their respective stations, those of Job Brothers going to Blanc Sablon, those of Baine Johnston to Battle Harbour, those of F.C. Jerrett to Smokey, and Captain William Bartlett's to Turnavik near Makkovik. But this led to conflict. The stationers and floaters complained that the crews brought in by steamship monopolized the fishing berths. Legislation was enacted in 1910 designed to limit the Labrador fishery to schooners, but it had little effect.

The large-scale Newfoundland fishery led to the first public steamship connection between Newfoundland and Labrador for the benefit of the transient fishermen. At first a boat ran between St John's and Mannock Island, near Hopedale. By 1883 the connection extended to Nain, calling in about twice a month. The service continued through the decades and still exists today, although many of its functions have been replaced by road and air service. Perhaps the best known and best loved of all the coastal boats was the *Kyle*, a ship that became guest and friend to those who waited for this lifeline to their small and isolated communities. Elliot Merrick, in his own inimitable prose, describes her arrival and departure at Indian Harbour in 1933:

We could make her out now, a low, slim ship, something like a destroyer, outlined in lights, pawing there impatient. Shouts came from the dark, the hiss of steam, the throbbing of her pumps. Fishermen's boats were clustered three deep alongside and astern, squeaking and crunching when they touched, a man in each with a boathook or a sculling oar, fending off; fishermen watching their chance to jump from one to the other as they rose and fell, fishermen swarming up the steamer's side and throwing a leg over the rail like attackers storming a citadel ...

Cascades of water were falling from the boat deck up above. Around the forward hatch searchlights shone warm and yellow. The winch chattered and stopped and chattered again. Barrels and boxes in slings came up through the hatch and disappeared over the side. The mate stood at the winch levers, and now and again he tightened or loosened a small wheel above the drum ... Jimmie, the bos'n, leaned over the side, signaling with his hand. It is easy to drop a puncheon through the bottom of a dancing trap boat, as it has often been done ...

"WHAW-W-W!" A jet of steam jumps from the funnel and the hideous blare smites the night again. On the fo'c'sle head the anchor winch starts to thump. Chain rattles in the hawse hole. Fishermen scramble to their boats, the ship already under way. Bells clang in the engine room, half astern, wheel hard over, full ahead. The sea thunders under her counter. Lines are flying, men are leaping. Fishermen's boats begin to pung. Last words shouted. She steams away into the inky night, masthead lights lurching, bound for another reef-guarded harbour of rock as though she steered by smell.[21]

Merrick captures, as no one else has, the sights and sounds of a ship that meant so much to those who occupied and used the Labrador coast in the early twentieth century. Long before the end of the fifty years she served the coast, the *Kyle* was a legend north and south, as the following song from Henry John Williams of Cartwright attests:

We're heading for our fortune folks, to youse we'll say goodbye.
We've got our welcome now wore out and the beer kegs all gone dry,
So I think we'll jump the *Kyle* now, where fishermen do flop,
Who fished out of their poor fathers' berths from the head to White Point Rock.

Services were put in place slowly over the decades. But there is no evidence that any formal attempt at colonization, sponsored by the government, ever occurred in Labrador along the lines of Cupids or Ferryland in Newfoundland or those of Courtemanche and Brouague along the north shore of the St Lawrence. The government saw the coast as a place to locate Newfoundland fishermen and as a place to cure fish. Just as the Island was an extension of Britain, Labrador was an extension of the Island. Ironically, those on the Island who might have effected change failed to see the similarities, even though they had themselves experienced the resentment that exploitation breeds. Even when laws were applied, such as the court of 1824 and the Customs Act, they were for the benefit of someone other than those who had chosen to live in Labrador. And even when services were provided, such as the mail service and the coastal shipping service, they were primarily for the benefit of the transient Newfoundland fishermen and their Newfoundland or West Country employers who came for the summer months. It is little wonder that Labradorians came to see themselves as second-class citizens, who more often than not were out of sight and out of mind.

The origins of the Grenfell Mission lay in a response to this burgeoning schooner and shore fishery. One of the services not provided by the government was health care. Ronald Rompkey, in his treatment of the life of Sir Wilfred Grenfell, describes the deplorable conditions on the Labrador coast that moved Britain's Mission to Deep Sea Fishermen to send relief:

About twenty-five thousand men, women and children sailed every year in July, mostly from Conception Bay, and lived in temporary huts on the shore. The annual migrants, as distinct from the permanent Labrador settlers ... survived there until October with no administration, no means of preserving law and order, no relief, and no medical care. They too were paid in provisions. For two or three years [according to Francis Hopwood, a visitor from the mission in England] a coastal steamer had been sent up with the mail, carrying on board one person, sometimes a student, with medical knowledge. "He is, however, beseiged by the wretched people and on one or two occasions when one of HM ships has visited the scene the people have begged the crews for the ordinary necessities of life," Hopwood added. The governor's secretary, for his part, told Hopwood that an acute shortage of clothing existed and that consequently women and children working ashore were being left "practically naked."[22]

The Mission to Deep Sea Fishermen decided to send a ship to assess the need and determine how best to meet it, and in August 1892 Wilfred

Grenfell – an adventurous young British doctor, whose religious zeal had been fired by the evangelist Dwight Moody – arrived on the Labrador coast. There he found the people he would serve for almost fifty years. During this first visit, Grenfell did what he could to meet their medical needs; but being a reformer, a religious zealot, and a social activist, he also handed out clothing and religious tracts, and held prayer meetings both on board his vessel and on shore. That first summer he sailed as far as Hopedale, where he stayed with the fishing fleet for ten days, tending to more than two hundred vessels before turning south again.

The following year Grenfell was back on the coast, this time with Dr Eliot Curwen and Sister Cecilia Williams. They found such unbelievable poverty and such squalid conditions that it was difficult to know where to begin. The Labrador fishermen suffered not only from poverty but also from economic exploitation, which they were helpless to change. This was the "truck" system. C.J. Poole in *Catucto* describes how it operated at Battle Harbour in the middle of the nineteenth century:

The company system was to give credit to the fishermen all Spring and Summer and when the fish was sold the accounts were squared or at least sometimes they were. During the Spring the fishermen would get such things as twine, pitch, oakum, nails, felt and tar to prepare their nets, boats and stages for the fishery. Then there would be the food items such as flour, butter, salt port and beef, dried peas and beans, black molasses and of course, English tea. Most all these items would go on the Summer account. Rarely would any money exchange hand for these items. The biggest item to go on the account during the fishing season would be the salt. This was the major expense and for almost every quintal of cod produced another half quintal of salt was used. Salt came loose and was handled by the wheelbarrow and bucket. All items were charged to the Summer account and it was hoped that enough salmon and cod could be caught to cover the expenses and then some.

Once all the cod and salmon were sold or shipped, as the fishermen referred to it, the skipper of the crew would go to Battle Harbour and settle up. The voyage was usually divided half to the skipper and the remaining half to the crew and skipper so the sharemen in large crews got only a small percentage of the catch.[23]

The system continued well into the twentieth century, though Grenfell did his best to change it. In this struggle he was largely alone; for as well as being up against the power of the merchants, Grenfell experienced the power and duplicity of the political system. For instance, a fisherman elected to the House of Assembly was appointed revenue officer, yet he cruised the coast with his own duty-free liquor; and the agent of Job Brothers thwarted the work at Indian Harbour, even though Job was a member of Grenfell's committee in St John's.

Once Grenfell realized that support from the Newfoundland government was not going to be overwhelming, he struck out on his own to raise funds for the medical work on the coast. This was a practice that he was to continue for the rest of his life, but not everyone applauded, for it showed how debilitated and needy the old colony could be. Among those whom Grenfell sought out was Sir Donald Smith, who was intimate with life on the coast after his twenty years in Labrador and who was now president of the Canadian Pacific Railway and the Bank of Montreal. Smith agreed to chair a committee pledged to raise $1000 annually for the mission. Moreover, he purchased and refitted the steam yacht *Dahinda* for Grenfell's use on the coast. The vessel, renamed the *Strathcona* to honour Smith (who became Lord Strathcona in 1897), plied the harbours and coves of Labrador for years, bringing facilities and medical assistance. Smith remained a strong and contributing supporter for some time.

Grenfell realized that to improve people's health he had to change their living conditions. His efforts to convince the Government of Newfoundland eventually bore fruit. In the November of his second season, Robert Bond, Newfoundland's colonial secretary, agreed to cooperate with the Hudson's Bay Company agents to relieve starvation along the stretch of coast between Battle Harbour and Sandwich Bay and to provide public works for the recipients of relief. Why the line was drawn at Sandwich Bay is not entirely clear. Perhaps the government wanted to leave governmental responsibility north of there to the Moravians.

In 1893 Grenfell opened a hospital at Battle Harbour with the assistance of a St John's merchant, Walter Baine Grieve, and he started another at Indian Harbour. A few years later a larger facility was built at St Anthony, which became the administrative headquarters and principal hospital for the coast for almost a century. It was clear that Grenfell was more than a doctor. He was a social activist, an agent of change, and a politician. Long before the people of Labrador were allowed to vote in Newfoundland politics, Grenfell acted as their unelected politician. Besides providing the first medical services to the coast, he put in place an educational system. He also built a number of nursing stations, staffed by nurses and doctors where possible. He instigated the first co-operative in Labrador (and perhaps in the province) at Red Bay to counteract the effects of the pernicious truck system.

Grenfell's charisma attracted funds and also workers for his cause, most of them volunteers. Many of them were scions of wealthy and prominent families in the United States and Britain, who having heard the call of Grenfell, came as WOPS (workers without pay). Nelson Rockefeller, the future governor of New York, worked at North West River under the sharp eye of Jack Watts, as did children of the B.F. Goodrich family. So did some of the Pilkington Glass family of England, who later contributed the beautiful stained-glass windows to the Anglican churches at Mary's Harbour and Cartwright. Other notables among the lists of Grenfell WOPS were the Americans Francis Sayre, Cyrus Vance, and Henry Cabot Lodge. Such was the ethic of the time, and such was the power of Grenfell to persuade, that prominent medical and surgical figures competed for work in the North for little more than the satisfaction of meeting human needs. This remained true well into the 1960s as the seeds of service and adventure that Grenfell sowed continued to bear fruit, particularly in New England and Britain. Dr Peter Steele, a British doctor who later participated in an Everest expedition, was in charge at North West River in the 1960s, before moving to the Yukon, while a former nanny of Robert Kennedy's children, Pat McCormick, served in the mission dormitory. Susan Sherk, who came from Massachusetts to work at North West River, still lives in the province, where she has held a number of senior positions. In the early years, the Newfoundland government, finding it difficult enough to run the few hospitals in St John's and one or two other communities, resented Grenfell's success. But by and large, his efforts were appreciated. And over time, relations with the government improved as more and more Newfoundlanders became involved.

Harry Paddon was one of those who heard the call of Grenfell and followed him to Labrador. Like Grenfell, he was a British doctor with a social conscience who filled the gap left by absent politicians in bringing about change to the Labrador society. Sailing for Canada in 1912, he was joined in Newfoundland by Mina Gilchrist, a Canadian nurse who later became his wife and partner, and became a strong and prominent Labrador figure in her own right. Discovering that there were many settlers in the Lake Melville area, Paddon sought Grenfell's approval to establish a hospital there. Travelling in a sail and motor ketch donated by Yale University, he set up first at Mud Lake and later at North West River. The *Yale*, with Harry Paddon the competent sailor and skipper, was a welcome sight along the coast for years to come. Paddon, on his trips around the bay and up the coast, brought the first consistent medical help that the people had ever had. He also brought his philosophy of self-help and independence, and his own common-sense methods of treating illness and disease.

Mud Lake had been the site of Lake Melville's first jobs in a cash economy – a lumbering enterprise that went bankrupt when its ship burned. During the first winter, Paddon and his partner, Arthur Wakefield, travelled the coast by dog team – up to five hundred kilometres north and south – stopping at every house to check on the health of those inside. Most of the men had gone trapping, but Paddon found the life of the villages fascinating, and over the years he came to admire the life the people led. He developed a great affection for them that was fully returned: "Father was greatly impressed" wrote his son Anthony, "by the women of Labrador, who managed their families, snared rabbits or shot partridge for daily food, made 'splits' or kindling, and split some of the hundreds of hunks of firewood which had been sawn up by the men before their departure. The women also baked bread, repaired clothing, or made new garments from cloth sold at the trading post. They served as midwives – often very skillfully – fished through the ice until it became too thick and fed the dogs."[24]

In 1915 Paddon moved to North West River and the green-frame Emily Chamberlain Hospital, which became the centre of that community as well as the centre for medical services along the north coast and for much of the south. Setting out from there by dog team in winter and on the *Yale* in summer, Paddon and those who assisted him tried to keep the people of the Labrador coast healthy. He built a house in North West River and with Mina began to raise a family. For Harry and Mina it was home – they considered themselves Labradorians. Indeed, Harry Paddon's "Ode to Labrador" is still sung, to the tune "Tannenbaum," and Labradorians consider it their unofficial anthem:

Dear land of mountains, woods and snow,
Labrador, our Labrador.
God's noble gift to us below,
Labrador our Labrador.
Thy proud resources waiting still,
Their splendid task will soon fulfill,
Obedient to the Maker's will.
Labrador, our Labrador.

North West River was the site of the Hudson's Bay Company post where Donald Smith had done his best to administer not only the Bay but the affairs of the area. It had been a trading post since Louis

Fornel established one there in 1743. Tucked away at the end of Lake Melville, about two hundred kilometres from the coast, it is really the mouth of the Naskaupi River after it courses through Grand Lake and Little Lake. Harry Paddon's son Harry Jr has called it "a veritable little paradise." So it appeared to me and my family when we lived there. Our older child, Hilary, was born there, while son Peter joined us in Happy Valley. A wooded shoreline ringed by gently sloping hills leads to long white beaches that glitter and sparkle on a sunny day, while across the thirty kilometres or so of Lake Melville the Mealy Mountains keep their snowy crown for most of the year.

On the south side in those early days stood Reveillon Frères' trading post and its outlying houses. In summer these buildings were surrounded by about seventy-five tents of the Innu, and the beaches were spread with canoes, dogs, and children. Harry Paddon Jr writes: "On the nights a Mokoshan or feast was held, the wavering light of a huge bonfire and the grumbling thunder of drums with the shuffle of a hundred dancing men and women and children would make our scalps prickle with the instinctive fear of something primitive, savage and unknown."[25] At the upper end of the north bank was the Montague family, and bordering the Hudson's Bay Company post were the Blakes. Below the trading post was the green-painted hospital, and below that the Goudies. Still farther down were the buildings of Porter's Trading Company. This was the village that was to become a medical and education centre for the coast – one might even say an administrative centre, for Harry Paddon took on not only the role of justice of the peace but also that of advocate and spokesperson for a coast that had no other.

The village had not changed much when my wife and I arrived in 1963 to work at Yale School,[26] where I was a teaching principal and she a principal teacher. The Innu were still living in tents, though houses would soon be built. A cable car spanned the river where before only canoes and speedboats had crossed. The school operated with a dormitory so that students from the north and south coast, who formed almost half the population of Yale School, could get a high school education. Established in the 1920s, the dormitory was still run by the Grenfell Mission. The mission was still a driving force in the community in the 1960s. It had its own electric generator, its own gardens, its own stores, and its own maintenance force, led by the energetic and redoubtable Jack Watts. Originally from Brigus, Newfoundland, Watts had come to Labrador as a wireless operator with the Marconi Company, and at Indian Harbour he heard the call of Paddon. With his wife Annie Baikie, Watts joined the mission, becoming its formidable maintenance and construction superintendent.

Tanned and lithe and topped by a thatch of white hair, he could be seen striding briskly through the village, checking on the garden, the garage, the laundry, or the dorm – when he was not high above in the mission's Beaver bush plane, heading for Makkovik or Nain. He was succeeded by his son Ronald. As well, the mission had its own ground transport. It was, of necessity, a self-contained unit.

In the early days of Harry Paddon's practice, conditions had been much more primitive. There was no communication with the outside world between the sailing of the last coastal steamer in October and its first sailing in June. Of course, telegrams could be sent from Battle Harbour, where there was a Marconi station, but to get there involved a 500-kilometre trip by dog team.

The trip from Battle Harbour was a factor in one of Paddon's early efforts at social justice. There had been no shortage of local recruits for the First World War; even incomplete records turn up about fifty. Among those who volunteered from the Lake Melville area were Percy Smith, a Hudson's Bay Company clerk, Fred Goudie, Murdoch McLean, the son of Malcolm, Robert Michelin, and "Johnnie" Blake who fell on the field of battle. Perhaps the premier recruit was John Shiwak, whose outstanding skill with the rifle made him particularly valuable as a sniper. His commanding officer described him as "an excellent scout and observer and a great favourite with all ranks." Lance Corporal Shiwak lost his life rushing a narrow bridge near Masnières in the Cambrai tank drive in France. Others missing in action included Dan Groves, Charlie Mesher, and Billy Mackenzie. After the war, the Labrador veterans were left at Battle Harbour to find their own way home. Indeed, the people of North West River did not know the war was over until the veterans walked into the community in January 1919.

Harry Paddon was furious: " It did seem a bit hard when these unrepresented citizens had given all they had to give, and when a party of timber cruisers could be sent to Rigolet in December, if required, that our volunteers should be dumped ashore in Battle Harbour over 300 miles from home, and left to pay their own board till ice travel began and then their transport back home. It took me five years to get them a just refund, but the colonel of the Newfoundland Regiment backed me up, and eventually it was paid."[27] By then, Newfoundland had had representative government for almost a century, yet there was still no one except this Grenfell doctor to speak for the Labradorians and to ensure fair treatment for those who had gone to such lengths to serve their country.

Paddon had a friend who assisted him with his social action as well as with political action from time to time. Henry Gordon is still remembered for his heroism in the coastal diocese, particularly during the Spanish flu epidemic. He was the Anglican priest at Cartwright, a community he described as far superior to any of the others in the district. This, he thought, was because many of the residents were descendants of carpenters, coopers, tinsmiths, and other craftsmen brought out by the early trading companies. Like Paddon, he had been educated at a British public school, with its values of courage and service. Like Paddon, too, he was a capable sailor and outdoorsman – if not a muscular Christian, something very close to it. Henry Gordon Academy in Cartwright bears testimony to the high regard in which this exceptional man is held today by the people of Sandwich Bay.

In 1918 the Spanish flu wreaked havoc in southern Labrador, as it did in the north. In Sandwich Bay, Gordon travelled day and night to help those in need, caught the flu himself, but recovered to work on. Despite his efforts, many of his parishioners died. He wrote in his journal: "I had to live amid the dead and dying for over a month, digging graves, tying up bodies, and looking after little orphans. The doctor tells me bluntly I have to clear out for six months or he won't be answerable for the consequences, and I know that I am only a bag of badly-shaken nerves myself."[28] Gordon was angered by the meagre response of the Government of Newfoundland, which amounted to a gang of men and several thousand boards of lumber for the burial of the dead. He wrote:

I came across some copies of a Newfoundland paper in which I was absolutely staggered to read for the first time the abominable behavior of the Newfoundland Government towards Labrador in her terrible plight last fall. The SEAL (our last steamer in the fall) had returned to St. John's with a report of the awful state of the distress on this coast due to the Spanish Influenza. A deputation waited on the Government to ask for the dispatch of as Relief ship, with medical aid and food. The Government had not only refused to send a ship, but one of its leading ministers deliberately remarked, "Let them starve, the Government will be saved the trouble of feeding them." At present I am so mad about it that I can hardly give my mind to anything else. The attitude of the Newfoundland Government towards Labrador was always a scandal, but this is adding insult to an already long list of injuries. Labrador pays at the very least $10,000 a year in taxes to the Newfoundland Government; she has not one single representative in the House of Assembly, she has no resident Magistrates, Police, Relieving Officers, no roads, no winter wire or wireless communications, no railway, nothing that any people need for the advantages of life. And to think that this Governing Body, which takes all and gives nothing, should condemn a magnificent race to starvation and death. One's heart has almost broken with the sufferings of those poor people.[29]

If the government would do nothing, Gordon and Paddon would. Their establishment of dormitory schools were an important turning point in the history of education in Labrador. These institutions housed and taught not only those who had been orphaned by the flu but many more who came from the coast, providing a home for orphans and giving a generation of Labradorians improved educational facilities.

While Gordon appealed to the British, Paddon went on a fund-raising trip to the United States. A local committee in Cartwright began raising funds, and a committee in St John's under the secretary treasurer Hugh LeMessurier was very supportive, as was the vestry of St Thomas's Church. All in all, $25,000 was raised, and although there is no evidence of any government money, the foundation stone for the Sandwich Bay dormitory school was laid in Muddy Bay by Governor Charles Harris in 1920. As well as serving the children from the Sandwich Bay area, it also served from time to time those from other parts of the coast, including the north.

The school later burned and was replaced by Lockwood School in Cartwright. But the venture took hold, and together with the school and dormitory in North West River, as well as others, the practice of dormitory schools became a reality and a very successful one. It survived in Labrador until the 1970s, and the graduates can be seen throughout Labrador today in positions of authority and influence. Of course, residential schools were fairly common throughout the North for a period, many of them run by religious orders, and most were funded by one government or another. But the tragic circumstances out of which these Labrador institutions grew, and the fact that the plan and execution were put together by two dedicated leaders – neither of whom was an educator by trade – show the vacuum the government left on the Labrador and how magnificently it was filled. Unlike many other residential schools, those in Labrador have remained entirely free of charges of abuse. Indeed, Chesley Lethbridge, who came to Lockwood School from his home in Paradise River in the 1940s at the age of eleven, was able to say of Dr and Mrs Forsyth, who lived at the school: "They taught you how to look after yourself. The Forsyths were very fine people. They were a mother and father to me and all the children there."

Over time, Paddon emerged as a Labrador presence. He was an experienced Labrador doctor covering many kilometres both in winter and summer. He knew the Moravians in the north and worked well with them, facing the situations he met with common sense. In addition to his medical work and his contribution to education, he promoted industrial and agricultural work, taking a particular interest in the mission gardens at North West River. He also believed in Labrador's great hydro potential, its mineral wealth, and its valuable timber stands. He despaired of the poverty that still existed, especially among the native populations. But he was optimistic that this could be overcome and that, with the right policies, Labrador could be an extremely prosperous place.

However, Dr Charles Curtis in St Anthony, who succeeded Grenfell as head of the medical mission, did not share either Paddon's vision for Labrador or his vision for the mission presence there. Paddon was unable to gain from him much interest in the Innu or Inuit, nor did Curtis seem to realize the importance of the work of the Moravian missionaries or the necessity of the Grenfell Mission to work closely with them. Differences began to separate the two men, with the result that Paddon's position with the mission became unclear. St Anthony, feeling the pinch of the Depression in the 1930s, thought that North West River was an expensive location for a small hospital, and Curtis went there to assess the situation for himself.

After Curtis's visit, the Grenfell board considered leasing the Emily Chamberlain Hospital property to the Bowater Lloyd Company after the Commission of Government (which by then was governing Newfoundland) expressed an interest in starting a sulphite mill in Lake Melville, with an attendant community at North West River. Paddon, who had made his home there, was devastated, not knowing what medical facilities the company would provide for the town, though of course he was pleased that someone else had shared his vision of the development of the forest resources of Labrador and was doing something about it. But the Second World War shattered the mill proposal and Paddon was left to wonder what plans for North West River the International Grenfell Association would have now. He was heartened that the mission had decided to keep his boarding school open for another year, but remained uncertain about the future. Sadly, he did not live to find out what would happen. In the autumn of 1939 he travelled to the United States on furlough and to spend time with his sons, who were at school there, and while in the United States he fell ill and died, at the age of fifty-eight.

Mina Paddon's dedication to their work and her devotion to the Labrador people enabled her to overcome her grief and loss, and she returned to the work at North West River. Her son Tony, fully expecting to succeed his father, completed his two remaining years of medical training before joining the Royal Canadian Navy, in which he had a distinguished wartime career on ships of the line. In his memoirs he comments on the situation that Mina Paddon faced in North West River and the courage she showed in keeping it running. She became a legend in her own right among the Labradorians:

After my father's death, things had become very difficult for my mother. During the war years, she carried on as best she could, with very little money or staff, or support from Mission Superintendent Dr. Charles Curtis at St. Anthony headquarters. She was responsible for everything: the medical supplies; the yearly food supplies; the school, teachers and housemothers; the requisitions; the planning; and, above all, the hospital and patients. In addition, there were the displaced settlers and Inuit who had uprooted themselves to work at nearby Goose Bay airport. She could hardly have managed her multitude of duties without the daily backup of her redoubtable assistant and foreman of outdoor work, Jack Watts. My mother was infinitely grateful to Jack, and together they made an amazing team, weathering many a desperate crisis together.[30]

For her contribution to Labrador, Mina Paddon, known with deep affection in North West River as "Gran," was made an officer of the Order of the British Empire.

Following the war, Tony Paddon, born in Indian Harbour and having grown up as a son of the Grenfell Mission, with all the challenge and excitement and opportunity for service that it provided, returned to take over the medical and social work of his father. The time he spent in St Anthony before going on to Labrador gave him an insight into the attitudes of the Labrador people towards the St Anthony hospital. It was clear that many of them, particularly the Inuit and Innu, were not comfortable going there. He was convinced that the Labrador operation should be separate. But his views, like those of his father, ran contrary to those of Dr Curtis, who considered that the Inuit were a Moravian problem and that the people of Lake Melville could be left to the mercies of the air base at Goose Bay, a purely military operation.

Nevertheless, young Paddon returned to North West River determined to develop a special zone of care for the Labrador people. He also immersed himself in social and educational work, as his father and mother had done. New schools and dormitories were built for students from the coast and for those who were without homes. He saw the mission enter the age of radio and airplanes, the age of modern nursing stations and medical facilities. And he followed in his father's footsteps as an intercessor for Labrador, even after it had political representatives. Tony Paddon could always get the ear of Premier Joey Smallwood, and when he did, Smallwood paid attention.

Eventually, his contribution to Labrador life was recognized by his appointment as Lieutenant-governor of Newfoundland and Labrador in the 1980s. Meanwhile, the centre of gravity for the Labrador operation shifted to Goose Bay, and North West River became merely a nursing station. Eventually the mission gave up control altogether, and the administration of medicine was taken over by a public board, as educational facilities had been in the late 1960s.

In its time the Grenfell Mission brought innovation and change to Labrador, particularly in health and education. As well, outstanding instructors such as Jessie Luther in St Anthony and Kitty Keddy in Cartwright worked with local women to produce excellent crafts, especially hooked mats, for markets in Britain and the United States. From designs by Grenfell himself or by visiting artists such as the American Stephen Hamilton, these mats today fetch thousands of dollars from collectors. And although, like the Moravian Mission, it has been accused of paternalism, there is no doubt about the benefits that the Grenfell Mission brought to Labrador. In its heyday it too was a political force, an agent of change, its leaders filling the vacuum left by absent politicians.

THE CHURCHES

Other non-governmental organizations that served the needs of Labrador were the churches. It is useful here to trace their contribution to the welfare of the people, for they too had an important effect on life and society. We have already seen the kind of fundamental change that the Moravians brought to the life of the Inuit on the north coast of Labrador.

Roman Catholic

It is clear that the families of those Innu now in Sheshashiu had contact with a Catholic priest, Father Pierre-Clement Parent, who became a missionary at the Mingan seigneury in 1769. But the priests stayed for only part of the year and limited themselves to baptisms, marriages, and distributing material printed in Innu Aimun by their Jesuit forerunners. The arrival in Canada of the Oblates of Mary Immaculate in 1844 marked the beginning of the second phase of conversion for the Innu. Like the Jesuits, the Oblates learned the Innu language and moved among the people from Lake St John to the Strait of Belle Isle. Early on, their intention was to convert the Innu from the interior who had been coming down to the Gulf of St Lawrence sporadically since the beginning of the century. Over time, more and more of them came. Between 1850 and 1866 entire families of those now in

Sheshatshiu were baptized, married, and instructed in the faith by Catholic missionaries. Indeed, the Hudson's Bay Company complained that this travel was taking away their trappers and hunters. So when a Catholic priest came to Lake Melville in the 1860s, the Bay gave him every possible aid. The priests wanted to convert the Innu, and the Bay wanted to keep them near the posts for trading purposes, so the two sides saw some mutual advantage in working together.

Father Louis Babel, the discoverer of iron ore in Labrador, was the first to hold a mission in Lake Melville in 1867. Arriving on the Bay steamer he baptized in Sheshatshiu, Fort Winokapau, and Fort Nascopie. For more than twenty-five years after that, the Oblates held regular missions at Sheshatshiu in the chapel built in 1872. But the long trips were expensive, and the Oblates abandoned Sheshatshiu before the turn of the century, urging the Innu to visit the missionaries along the St Lawrence.

In 1920 missions to the Labrador Innu were undertaken by the diocese of Harbour Grace, Newfoundland. Already caring for the religious needs of the migrant Labrador fishery, it became the Catholic overseer of the Innu until 1945, when jurisdiction passed to the vicariate apostolic (later, the diocese) of Schefferville. With the decline of Schefferville, the see was moved to Labrador City in 1979. From Harbour Grace, Father Edward O'Brien visited Sheshatshiu every year and held a mission for a few weeks as the Oblates had done before. In the summer of 1927 he extended the mission to Davis Inlet, marrying, baptizing, and generally looking after the welfare of the Innu as he went. In his boat the *St Christopher*, at one time crewed by the young Sid and Philip Blake of North West River, "Father Whitehead" became a familiar sight along the coast.

Father O'Brien became a strong champion of the Innu. In anticipation of his visit to Davis Inlet, the Hudson's Bay Company traders would issue new clothing and canvas tents, because they knew that the priest would not countenance the people living in inferior conditions. His affection and respect was returned; one Innu, Manteskueu, recalled: "The women used to braid their hair and tie it up. Father Whitehead really admired the women with braids in their hair. The people began to realize he was a good priest and they respected him very much. Whenever we heard he was coming to the village, we would gather and give him a welcoming party, and receive him with respect. Then he would announce the time when mass would be held. Innu men and women had great respect for their religion and spirituality."[31]

O'Brien kept in touch while away and was informed of deaths by the trader Dick White, with whom he corresponded. It is undoubtedly O'Brien who ordered the first headstones for the Labrador Innu that stand today in North West River. He kept valuable records and took numerous photographs, which later formed the basis of a series of excellent paintings of the Innu by the Wabush artist Sheilagh Harvey. As well, he produced the first censuses and repeatedly sought the help of the Government of Newfoundland on behalf of the Innu. Under his influence the Lake Melville Innu became firmly attached to the post and mission at Sheshatshiu.

In 1945, when the jurisdiction of the Catholic Church shifted to Quebec, the missions among the Labrador Innu once again became the responsibility of the Oblates. In 1949 a permanent priest, Father Cyr, came to stay at Davis Inlet. He built a residence and produced electricity from a nearby brook. He also started a school, confining the children to the village while their fathers continued their hunting in the interior. He was followed by Father Pirson and then by Father Peters when Pirson moved to Sheshatshiu in 1952. For twenty years Catholic priests served these communities, speaking the Innu language and interceding on their behalf to obtain houses, schools, and government services.

Yet of late a darker side of the Catholic presence has emerged with allegations of mistreatment and abuse of the Innu by Catholic priests and brothers. In *Gathering Voices*, their own "People's Inquiry" of 1992, the Innu charge that the priests who abused were "sick" and not saints or holy people. In testimony that is obviously extremely difficult to recall, the Innu reveal that abuse did indeed take place. Yet their judgment is that perhaps a white court is not the most appropriate venue for judging such crimes and that a traditional Innu healing circle might be more helpful.

Elsewhere in Labrador the Catholic Church has served and serves today the Catholic communities at West St Modeste and Pinware in the Labrador Straits and farther north at Black Tickle.

Methodist

The Methodist settlers who came to Labrador brought their faith with them and kept it alive by passing it on to their children. Armenius Young, who served the church in Hamilton Inlet in the early years of the twentieth century, describes the continuance of the faith in his book *A Methodist Missionary in Labrador*:

Ambrose Brooks, a young Englishman who had recently come to Labrador, and who afterwards became the father of Mrs. Daniel Campbell ... called to see Phippard, then an old man. He found him sitting in the sun by the doorway of his hut, with the Bible in his hand, with tears in his eyes, in a very lonely and despondent mood. He too soon passed away; but not before he had spread an unconscious influence for good, and inculcated, though perhaps in a crude form, some principles of the Christian religion in the heathen Eskimos.

I learned from Mrs. Campbell that her father was a good singer and was interested in the education of his children. He spared no pains in teaching them to sing and read. This might have been the extent of their education, for Brooks thought that his half-breed children could get along very well on the Labrador without the knowledge of writing. The children, however, were ambitious and by perusing their father's letters, and with what little help they received from him, they learned to read and write. In this way practically all the children of middle Labrador learned to read and write. Brooks' wife became a Christian and when she died the grand testimony left behind was that she was going to be with Christ.[32]

Although the Rev. Hickson had come to preach in Labrador as early as 1824, there was not a full-time minister in the area until the latter part of the nineteenth century. In fact it was a Methodist minister, Arthur C. Waghorne, who encouraged Lydia Campbell to write her memoirs, the first account by a settler and the only account by a woman of life in Hamilton Inlet in the nineteenth century.[33]

The Methodists stationed ministers in Hamilton Inlet and Lake Melville throughout the twentieth century, and their successor, the United Church of Canada, still does so. Armenius Young gives an account of the life of a minister in the early part of the twentieth century: the long and arduous boat rides and dog team trips, the treks through the woods to visit isolated trappers on their territory, the fight against alcohol brought by the loggers to the far end of Lake Melville, and above all the joy of companionship and charity and generosity of spirit. The people he served were, and still are, among the most hospitable to be found anywhere. For although want was present far too much of the time, those he visited never failed to share what they had and to give of their best, as they do to this day.

The Rev. Lester Burry of the United Church had a unique career in Labrador. Using a series of boats, all of which he called *Glad Tidings*, he ranged up and down Lake Melville and Sandwich Bay, preaching, marrying, burying, and helping in many other ways. Later he introduced the first snowmobile to the work of the missionary in Labrador. Most importantly, he devised a system of communication for the trappers on the line far up the Naskaupi River: by means of homemade receivers they could hear what was broadcast from the transmitter at Burry's church. He sent them messages from home and gave them the news of the day. Burry was a man of imagination and creativity, remembered fondly long after his twenty-seven years of service to

Labrador were over. In fact, he was the first to represent Labrador in any democratic forum or assembly in what would become the Province of Newfoundland and Labrador. He was elected for Labrador to the National Convention in 1946, the first time the Labrador people ever voted and the first time they had an elected representative.

Anglican

While the Anglicans who settled in Labrador brought their faith with them, there is not the same evidence to show how it was maintained. In the south, there is no equivalent of Lydia Brooks Campbell's memoirs in Lake Melville. The recorded history of the church begins in 1848 with the arrival of the church ship, *Hawk*, in Forteau Bay carrying the bishop of Newfoundland, Edward Feild, and two of his clergy, the Rev. Hoyles and Rev. Harvey. Feild was the first bishop to visit Labrador and the first to attempt to answer its needs. From Forteau he sailed as far as Sandwich Bay, stopping at most of the fishing stations. He estimated that the settler population at that time was about a thousand.

Following his visit, Feild requested the Society for the Propagation of the Gospel (a British organization whose aim was to send Church of England ministers to parts of the Empire that could not afford their own) to send three clergy for Labrador to be stationed at Forteau, Battle Harbour, and Sandwich Bay. Although the request was granted, the service was not regular; it was difficult to staff the Labrador parishes, and the clergy who did come stayed only a few years. As well as preaching the gospel and administering the sacraments, the Anglican clergy, in the absence of elected officials on the south coast, brought the squalid conditions in which the people lived to the attention of the government from time to time. The Rev. Colley in his report in 1889 noted: "The Government collects taxes, but gives very little in return. I brought before them the destitution of the settlers, and also wrote an account of their state to one of the local papers."[34]

Canon J.T. Richards spent nearly all of the first half of the twentieth century at the Flowers Cove mission, which for some time included the Straits area of Labrador. Early in his ministry he petitioned the government to bridge the rivers in the area, but his petitions, he says, were "relegated to the waste basket without a moment's thought." There is anger and frustration in a lengthy article he wrote for the Newfoundland diocesan magazine in April 1911: "We don't mind stomping through several miles of bog, ankle deep ... on these coasts, though we often proved this to be hard work. It is the impossible that makes us groan; and a bridgeless river with current running waist high is certainly impassable. Let the Government place bridges over the three rivers of Forteau, L'Anse au Loup, and the L'Anse au Diable, and establish a ferry to cross Pinware River twice a day, and it will have conferred a favour on the inhabitants of the Labrador side of the Strait of Belle Isle for which they might be thankful."[35]

After what must have seemed a long time the bridges did come, along with other amenities of life. But the geography continued to challenge the clergy who served on the Labrador. To meet the challenge, the Rev. Carl Major, the parish priest at Mary's Harbour from 1959 to 1964, conceived the idea of a parish airplane. In his appeal to the church, he noted that other denominations on the coast – the Pentecostals and the Plymouth Brethren – had planes and were thus better able to serve the needs of the people.[36] In 1960 the Diocese purchased a new Piper Super Cub, and Major got his licence in record time. In the absence of a scheduled air service, the plane served much more than the religious needs of the area for the duration of Major's ministry there.

Even after Labrador people got the vote and representatives were elected to serve their needs, the geography was such that political visits were infrequent and communication sporadic. Consequently, the clergy along the coast continued to provide activist intervention not simply in community affairs but in running school boards and other public services.

Pentecostal

The Pentecostal Church arrived on the Labrador coast during the establishment of the timber-cutting operation in Port Hope Simpson. Burton Janes, archivist for the Pentecostal Assemblies, records that leaders such as Eugene Vaters were concerned in the 1920s about the lack of a mission in Labrador. In 1930 Thomas Mitchell, Eli Burton, and William Gillett travelled along the coast of Labrador in a vessel they had built, the *Gospel Messenger*. The first Pentecostal Assembly in Labrador was founded in Port Hope Simpson in 1936. Thereafter other congregations were established, notably by William Gillett at Postville in Kaipokok Bay, where he built a school, a mill, and a business, in addition to pastoring the assembly. In 1959 he and his wife travelled to Charlottetown to start a congregation there, which still thrives, as do those at Port Hope Simpson and Postville. Meanwhile, in 1953 Thomas Mitchell and Thomas Evans had sailed to L'Anse-au-Loup and Fox Harbour, where they established congregations, and that same year the Rev. MacKinney arrived in Happy Valley, where Lincoln Shiwak hired several Innu men, at his own expense, to cut logs for the church. Pentecostal congregations have sprung up as far north as Hopedale.

Like the clergy of other denominations, the Pentecostal pastors were more than preachers; they were builders who took a leading role in community activities. With the growth of Labrador West, the Salvation Army, as well as the Pentecostals, became established there, contributing to the educational as well as religious life of the communities.

Without any real help from government, the foundations had been laid for schools, medical services, and churches, and traders both big and small had established some businesses and maintained others. Challenging though it was, the Innu who ranged through the woods of the Ungava Peninsula, like the Inuit and part-Inuit settled around the Moravian compounds in the North, and like the trappers in Lake Melville and Groswater Bay (who learned the art of survival from both the Inuit and the Innu and in turn passed on their own European heritage), and the French, British, and mixed bloods of the south coast all the way to the Strait of Belle Isle – whoever they were, they held to their communities, cared for each other as best they could, and relied on their own locally recognized leaders. They had little choice but to rely on the benefactors near at hand, for the government that was nominally theirs was far away and inaccessible.

CHAPTER FOUR

The Government

The Canadian attitude to Newfoundland is very like the American attitude
to Canada, an amiable indifference coupled with a complete ignorance of
local susceptibilities. No doubt the reaction of Newfoundlanders to Canada
is in many ways similar to our reaction to Americans.

J.W. Pickersgill, May 1943

I asked a high Canadian official, "Do you want Newfoundland?" He said,
"No." "Do you want Labrador?" He said, "Yes."

A.P. Herbert, author and MP for Oxford University, 1950

WHO IS THE REAL GOVERNOR?

For a long time, as we have seen, the situation on the coast of Labrador
was virtual anarchy. Any government interference was on behalf of the
French and British merchants who sought its resources of fish or whale
or seal. In the eighteenth century, while Britain and France fought for
control of the North American continent, the control of Labrador, in
theory as well as practice, was mainly with British Newfoundland.
Eventually, in 1809, formal jurisdiction over the littoral was vested in
Newfoundland. At this time, although as many as six hundred vessels
a year prosecuted the Labrador fishery, there was not a large number
of permanent settlers and there was no local government.

In the 1820s Newfoundland began to take some interest in Labrador. A civil court judge, William Patterson, was sent to the coast in
the summer of 1826, and he proceeded to hold court there each
summer until 1834. But the paucity of cases and the high cost of court
expenses caused the government to cancel the appointment. Besides,
Lambert de Boilieu's description of one judge portrays not only the
absence of sober second thought but indeed the absence of sobriety.[1]
Although the government was unwilling to make expenditures in the
area, it continued to exact customs duties and other revenues
throughout the nineteenth century. After 1832, when Newfoundland

gained representative government, this constituted taxation without representation for the people of Labrador.

In 1863 the Colonial Office recommended representation for Labrador in Newfoundland's House of Assembly. But Newfoundland's prime minister, Hugh Hoyles, rejected the suggestion. He saw Labrador as merely a venue for Newfoundland fishermen and meant to keep it that way. As a result, Labrador did not have representation or political recognition for at least eighty years. No attempt was ever made to defend or explain this act of discrimination. No excuse was possible: the population was as large as several of the Newfoundland districts when they were first created, and the distances involved were not much more formidable that those of the Great Northern Peninsula, which for many years was only one district.

The government did not provide funding for education; the churches or the missions did that. And the government did not provide money for health care; Grenfell did that.It was only in the early decades of the twentieth century that any government became seized with the presence of Labrador, and this was because of the resources that either had been discovered there or were being exploited. As a result, both Quebec and Newfoundland, each of which had been a tacit if absentee governor at one time or another, began to vie for possession once more. Quebec fired the first shot.

In 1902 Alfred Dickie, a Nova Scotia mill owner who was cutting wood at Mud Lake, received a letter from the Quebec minister of lands and forests informing him that he was operating a business without a Quebec licence. Dickie responded that he was operating with the permission of the Newfoundland government. Unimpressed, Quebec lodged a formal complaint in Ottawa that Newfoundland had extended its jurisdiction into the interior of Labrador, and Ottawa duly carried the protest to London. As both Quebec and Newfoundland claimed Labrador, Joseph Chamberlain, the British colonial secretary, suggested that Canada obtain a legal decision. Quebec and Newfoundland both set out to establish their claim to Labrador.

The jurisdictional situation was murky. Care had not been taken to define exactly who owned what. Following the economic hegemony of France, the Treaty of Paris in 1763 had placed Labrador "under the care and inspection" of the Governor of Newfoundland. Of course, in reality, the best it got was inspection from time to time. At that time the Labrador coast was described simply as the area "from the River St. John to Hudson's Straits." The assumption was that Newfoundland's jurisdiction included all the territory not included in Quebec or in the Hudson's Bay Company charter.

Quebec officially regained control of the region in the Quebec Act of 1774. Nevertheless, the governor of Newfoundland, who was commander in chief of the naval squadron based in St John's, was authorized to supervise and protect the fishery operations in the region. But merchants who were seeing their investments destroyed by American privateers during the War of Independence protested this dual responsibility and demanded effective government. As we have seen, George Cartwright proposed a separate local government for Labrador, including its own resident governor. No doubt he would have filled the slot gladly, and if he had, the course of Labrador history might have been different. But this did not happen, and the British government simply transferred jurisdiction back to Newfoundland in 1809.

Quebec was so strongly opposed to this that in 1825 a new British North America Act established a southern boundary between Labrador and Quebec. The boundary was a line leading due north from Blanc Sablon and connecting with a line running due west along the fifty-second parallel as far as the St John River. The boundary point at Blanc Sablon was chosen because it represented the eastern limit of French Canadian settlement. This was the first time that occupancy by groups of people living on the Labrador peninsula was used to determine a boundary, and it was the first attempt to define an explicit boundary in the interior of the peninsula. Then in 1898 the Canadian government extended the boundaries of Quebec northward. An act proposed a boundary line running from the coast of James Bay along the Eastmain River, then following the line of latitude at 52 degrees 55 minutes, through lakes in Labrador to the Hamilton River, along the Hamilton River to Hamilton Inlet "until it strikes the westerly boundary of the territory under the jurisdiction of Newfoundland." But this ignored the 1825 British North America Act, which had set 52 degrees latitude as the southern boundary of Labrador and therefore the northern boundary of Quebec.

Obviously, Quebec wanted an extended boundary because it believed it had a claim to Labrador but also because A.P. Low's surveys had alerted it to the potential there for minerals, water power, and timber. But legal possession would not be easy. The dispute over the licence to the Dickie Lumber Company brought the issue to a head.

Patrick McGrath, a journalist and politician who was Newfoundland's primary investigator for the case, obtained important information from J.A.J. de Villiers of the British Museum, one of the most prominent cartographers of his day. He assembled maps of Labrador, as well as maps showing how "coast" was defined in other places, and wrote an accompanying commentary. But these efforts were almost nullified in 1924 when Newfoundland suddenly considered selling Labrador to Quebec. At the time, the Newfoundland government was in extremely poor financial shape and very unimaginative, both politically and economically. Newfoundland had overextended itself in its expenditures on the First World War and on the railway. Moreover, markets for fish were near collapse.

Wilfred Grenfell condemned the proposed sale as short-sighted. Labrador, he pointed out, was a land rich in natural wealth, and Newfoundland would be blind to its own interests if it parted with the territory for temporary cash.[2] Nevertheless, negotiations between Newfoundland and Quebec were carried on through 1925, with letters exchanged between Walter Monroe, the prime minister of Newfoundland, and Louis-Alexandre Taschereau, the premier of Quebec. The correspondence reveals that Newfoundland was prepared to sell Labrador for $30 million. However, access to the coast was important, particularly for the Newfoundland fleet that went there every summer. So later that year Monroe offered Labrador to Quebec for $15 million, provided Newfoundland retained rights to a three-mile strip along the shoreline for the use of its fishermen. But Taschereau decided not to deal and to leave the matter of Labrador jurisdiction to the Judicial Committee of the Privy Council in England.

There is no evidence that the people of Labrador were ever consulted on the sale of the land on which they were living. Although there were only a few thousand permanent residents at the time, they presumably did have some rights. But the Newfoundland government was short of cash, and it could not afford to worry about what the people of Labrador thought. However, other Newfoundlanders cared what they thought. Signed statements of residency were collected from many Labradorians. The evidence on the boundary dispute filled five thousand pages and eight volumes, with oral presentations accounting for another sixteen hundred pages. This in itself was of immense value as a historical record for Labrador, and it has provided scholars with a treasure trove of research material. With this abundant testimony in hand, Sir John Simon, representing Newfoundland, argued that the shoreline constituted a territory "with defined sea frontage which stretched to the height of land," or from the coast to the central Labrador plateau.

On 1 March 1927 the Privy Council came to the conclusion that the case of Newfoundland had been "made out." The only exception to the height of land as the Labrador boundary was the fifty-second parallel, established in 1825 as the southern Labrador boundary. The

Romaine River, rather than the St John, was set as the western limit, thus benefiting Quebec. The boundary was declared to be "a line drawn due north from the eastern boundary of the bay or harbour of Anse au Sablon as far as the fifty-second degree of north latitude, and from thence westward along that parallel until it reaches the Romaine River, and then northward along the left or east bank of that river and its head waters to the source and from thence due northward to the crest of the watershed or height of land there, and from thence westward and northward along the crest of the water-shed of the rivers flowing into the Atlantic Ocean until it reaches Cape Chidley."

McGrath was exultant as he spoke of the effects of the decision two weeks later: "The decision absolutely closes off Canada from access to the North Atlantic ... The drawback to Canada's physical complete-ness which the possession by us of this vast region on her eastern frontier represents, and the interference with the development of her own areas lying west of it which must almost inevitably follow."[3] He had no doubt that development in timber, minerals, and water power would come, and he urged the "wise and far-seeing" exploitation of its resources for "the abiding advantage of this country."

But those in authority did not hear McGrath, nor did they care to hear him. After the boundary question was settled, Newfoundland was still experiencing financial difficulties, and the government of Richard Squires was prompted to again offer Labrador for sale. In 1929 it was asking $110 million for the sale of Labrador to the Dominion of Canada – a deal that very nearly went through. (By 1930 the price had risen to $130 million.) Malcolm MacLeod of Memorial University speculates that if the deal had gone through it would have changed the course of Newfoundland history. Totally relieved of a debt that had been thirty years in the making, he says, Newfound-land would have weathered the hard times of the 1930s without bankruptcy. No bankruptcy, no Commission of Government. Perhaps no Confederation. Of course, without Labrador, Newfoundland would have been without important bargaining levers with Canada. What MacLeod does not speculate on is the fate of Labrador had it been sold to Canada. What would have been its future if, like the Northwest Territories and Yukon, it had dealt directly with Canada and not through Newfoundland? Or would it have been swallowed up by Quebec?

In any case, Quebec did not acquire jurisdiction over Labrador. When in 1949 Newfoundland joined Canada, it did so with Labrador as delimited by the Privy Council. It is true that Joseph Smallwood, the leader of the Newfoundland delegation negotiating the terms of union, had proposed to the British high commissioner that the Canadian government should lease Labrador from Newfoundland for fifty years at a rate of $6 or $7 million, an amount that would have covered the estimated budgetary deficit of the province. But the other members of the delegation rejected this scheme lest it encourage Newfoundlanders to think that Canada's willingness to bring Newfoundland into Confederation sprang solely from a desire to get its hands on Labrador's resources.

In the skirmishes between Newfoundland and Quebec over Labrador the first round clearly went to Newfoundland. But what about the following rounds? After 1949 the two provinces struggled for economic supremacy in Labrador. Historian Peter Neary has said, "Two metropolitan interests – those of Montreal and those of St. John's – backed by two powerful regional identities, however analogous, have clashed head on in Labrador."[4] The first development came during the 1950s with the iron ore deposits straddling the very boundary that the Privy Council had determined. While the mining boom gave Newfoundland two new towns, Labrador City and Wabush, the ore is carried to the steel mills of North America and the world via the Quebec North Shore and Labrador Railway. Consequently, its terminus, the port of Sept-Îles, has benefited enormously from shipments of Labrador ore. Peter Neary's judgment is that "in a sense P.T. McGrath's claim in 1927 that the Judicial Committee's decision 'absolutely closes off Canada from access to the North Atlantic' has been turned on its head."[5]

Because the market for Labrador resources is in the heart of North America, Quebec blocks Newfoundland's access. Newfoundland's resources, whether iron ore or water power, have had to pass through Quebec, and the toll has contributed substantially to the growth of the Quebec treasury. Indeed, when in the 1960s the representatives of Brinco put their case for the development of hydropower to Premier Lesage, they pointed out how the development would negate the 1927 boundary decision. Philip Smith, in *Brinco: The Story of Churchill Falls*, describes the argument they made:

Among the other advantages of the Hamilton Falls scheme put forward over the lunch table were that, since it would be financed by private capital, Quebec would not have to borrow hundreds of millions of dollars for power development at a time when the government urgently needed money to improve the province's education, health and other social services; it would provide jobs for Quebec workers and opportunities for Quebec suppliers and manufacturers; and it would enable the province to hold other potential sites for economic hydro-electric development in reserve. Furthermore, an abundant supply of cheap power at tidewater around Sept Iles could attract new industries to the growing North Shore area of the Province. And (perhaps the most compelling argument in the circumstances) the development of Hamilton Falls power for use in Quebec would recognize the geographical facts and override the political boundary that Quebec had traditionally opposed, making the whole area one economic entity.[6]

It is interesting that in the above discussion the interests of Quebec were stressed, as in other discussions the interests of Newfoundland were stressed. There were no negotiators who had in mind the interests of Labrador and the effect that cheap power would have on its development. It was as if the interests of Labrador and the people who lived there were forgotten by all. The underlying assumption was that Labrador's resources must be developed for someone else, whether that someone was the island of Newfoundland, the province of Quebec, or the market of Wall Street.

While Quebec did not officially recognize the 1927 decision, it did so tacitly. For instance, in the early 1950s, Premier Maurice Duplessis of Quebec and Premier Joseph Smallwood of Newfoundland instructed the Iron Ore Company of Canada to calculate royalties from the Knob Lake mine according to the amount of ore mined on either side of the border it straddled. And, of course, when the power from Churchill Falls flowed west, it had to pass over an acknowledged border, for it was at that point that Quebec exacted its charge. Later the two provinces had to share information, at least on the professional level, concerning the George River caribou herd, which roamed both Quebec and Labrador. Clearly, there was a boundary. When the boundary came up during the Quiet Revolution, René Lévesque was more realistic about it: "They won and we lost," was his terse comment. Nevertheless, not everyone in Quebec was as sanguine about it, and Quebec maps well into the 1980s showed Quebec as running east all the way to the Atlantic Ocean. In fact, in 2001, when a proposal came forward to change the province's name in the Constitution of Canada, making it officially "Newfoundland and Labrador," Quebec's treasury board minister, Joseph Facal, warned that if changing the name meant changing the border, they would oppose it. This, in spite of the fact that officially Quebec had never acknowledged a border in the first place.

THE COMMISSION OF GOVERNMENT

In 1932 the Government of Newfoundland faced bankruptcy and appealed to Great Britain for help. The mother country appointed a royal commission, headed by Lord Amulree, to investigate the financial and social structure of Newfoundland and to recommend changes in government aimed at putting the dominion in a stable financial position. In an unprecedented move, Amulree recommended the suspension of responsible government and a temporary period of government by a commission responsible to Great Britain. This "Commission of Government," consisting of six commissioners appointed by the British government, took office in February 1934.

Wilfred Grenfell made a number of recommendations to the commission. He suggested the building of more roads to assist rural development and the abandonment of the railway and the coastal steamers in favour of motor traffic. This, he claimed, would improve the transportation of goods, bring in tourists, and give access to the bogs, berry marshes, and game. In these recommendations he was ahead of his time, for the same ideas came to fruition later in the century when the railway and ferries were traded by the province for roads, including one across Labrador.

Ironically, by giving up responsible government, Newfoundland gave Labrador the first government it ever had – at least, the first government to pay appreciable attention to the permanent settlers or to serious resource development. Sir John Hope Simpson was the most impressive of the British commissioners. He was a severe critic of the small elite that ruled the country, and his policies were aimed at breaking the control of the powerful merchants and bringing more opportunities to the many who were the primary producers. Discounting itinerant governors, he was likely the first senior politician to visit Labrador. His visit in 1934 took him to St Anthony where he met Grenfell, whom he came to admire greatly, and on to North West River, where he stayed with Harry Paddon. Again, the admiration and respect were mutual.

In 1936 a survey was begun of the forest resources at the western end of Lake Melville and the lower reaches of the Hamilton River for a large British newsprint firm. These activities put North West River on the map as never before. There was new employment for trappers in the summer months, a number of them acting as guides and canoeists or as compass men for timber surveyors. The owner of a motorboat stood a good chance of having a lucrative season. Four airplanes were based at North West River, which now had a population of about three hundred. "They know they stand on the edge of a precipice, perhaps," Harry Paddon said, "or at best a parting of the ways."

Another of Hope Simpson's ports of call was the mouth of the Alexis River. Some of the families there, like the Notleys, who had been in the area since the mid-1800s, used Alexis Bay as a winter home. But the thirties brought a population explosion. In 1934 J.O. Williams, a Welsh entrepreneur described by the British Foreign Office as "one-third visionary, one-third businessman, and one-third speculator," obtained a loan from the commission to establish the Labrador Development Company for the purpose of cutting pit props at Alexis Bay, St Michaels Bay, and St Lewis Bay. At the company's request, the new community in Alexis Bay was called Port Hope Simpson. For the people of the area, this was their introduction to jobs for cash. Several hundred loggers were hired from nearby coastal communities, and so were unemployed men from the Island. Most Newfoundlanders came from the northeast coast and the northern peninsula, particularly the community of Griquet, while the Labrador settlers came from as far south as Forteau and as far north as Sandwich Bay.

In his report on the affairs of the Labrador Development Company, Judge Brian Dunfield said that by 1936 the community had a population of five hundred and that some of Williams's promises had been kept: fourteen houses had been erected, along with a staff house and hospital, a community hall, and several other facilities, including wharves. But problems plagued the operation, not the least of which was Williams's erratic behaviour, and the outbreak of the Second World War which impacted negatively on the export of pip props to Britain. In 1939 Williams sent his son Eric to oversee the operation, but conflict developed with Keith Yonge, the manager. Tragically, Eric lost his life trying to save his daughter during a mysterious fire in 1940. An elaborate grave marks his final resting place in Port Hope Simpson.

In 1947 the Labrador Development Company went into liquidation, and by 1951 the population had fallen to 252, many of the residents having gone to work at Goose Bay. However, the next year the Bowater paper company gave the community new life when it began cutting pulpwood for export to its mill in Corner Brook. When Bowater also closed down in 1968, many of the residents tried to survive on seasonal fishing from their original communities – Georges Cove, St Francis Harbour Bight, Sandy Hook, Fishing Ships Harbour, and Occasional Harbour – using Port Hope Simpson during the winter. Some of the original names still remain in the community today: Burden, Kippenhuck, Notley, Parr, Penney, Rumbolt, Russell, Sampson, Strugnell, and Ward. Until recently, only Andrew Strugnell kept the local woods industry alive with his cutting and sawmilling operation. Now the completion of the Trans-Labrador Highway from the Straits has given Port Hope Simpson not only options for purchasing elsewhere and options for shipping its goods, but optimism that the timber stands which the Commission of Government so ably identified will once again become viable. Recently the community was identified by the provincial government as the regional airport for that area of southern Labrador, giving it a new lease on life.

Sir John Hope Simpson took on the fish merchants and brought new ideas and energy to the fishing industry. The year of his Labrador visit, about 2500 tonnes of fish were caught by parties who would not have been able to fish without assistance organized and financed by the government. The government collected the fish and sold it, paying the fishermen the balance, if any, between the price received and the advance made, a method that was to be duplicated almost exactly in the middle years of the century by the Canadian Saltfish Corporation.

It was also the commission, most notably Hope Simpson, that initiated the development of the iron ore potential in western Labrador. It gave permission for the Weaver Coal Company of Toronto and Montreal to survey about 50,000 square kilometres of interior Labrador. Weaver was to have exclusive mineral rights to the area, on which it agreed to spend a million dollars and to have some access to water power as well. The government would collect a rent of $64,000 per year and royalties on all minerals produced. Weaver became the Labrador Mining and Exploration Company, which still collects royalties on the iron ore produced.

From a social and political point of view, perhaps the most useful initiative of the Commission of Government was the creation of the Newfoundland Rangers. A force like the RCMP but with a much more comprehensive mandate, the Rangers were the first permanent government officials to be posted to Labrador. Previously, in 1880, during a special emergency, the government of the day had conferred the powers of justice of the peace on the Moravian Bishop Borquin and later had invested the same authority in Wilfred Grenfell and Harry Paddon. As well, from the early years of the twentieth century, a magistrate and a police officer had travelled as far north as Nain every summer. The magistrate had selected game wardens from among the local people, the most famous being Sam Broomfield. Nevertheless, prior to the creation of the Rangers, very few of the Inuit, Innu, or even the whites of Labrador had ever seen a policeman.

The Rangers were generally well received: "On the whole [they] were treated with guarded respect, useful to have around, though you mustn't make too free with them or let drop any information that might lead to an embarrassing appearance before a magistrate on charges of breach of the liquor laws that everyone regarded as laws made to be broken."[7] As well as performing as the first rural police force in Newfoundland and Labrador and as protectors of forests, game, and fisheries, they acted as liaison between the people and the government. Some such liaison had become necessary with the suspension of responsible government at the end of 1933. Until then, members of the House of Assembly had been the liaison, at least for the Island. In fact, at that time the members had had a great deal of power, far more than we would now consider appropriate. They distributed public works monies, appointed postal carriers and postmasters, and often made arrangements between St John's merchants and outport agents. Consequently, their sudden disappearance from the political scene left many outports on the Island without this St John's contact, so the Rangers took on this role along with all the others.

For Labrador, the coming of the Rangers was a huge step forward. Having never been represented in the Newfoundland parliament, it had never had that same kind of access at the centre of power. One of the few services, even though it may have been infrequent, was the mail service. But who appointed Newell and Murphy, the mail carriers who delivered by boat in the summer and by dog team in the winter? Dr Paddon? Rev. Gordon? "Doctor" Hettasch?

The commission was more cognizant of the existence of the people of Labrador and their rights and more even-handed in its treatment of them than previous governments had been. For example, although the Moravian Mission remained the arm of government, the Rangers were instructed to enforce the concessions that St John's had made to Labrador people. The concessions included the Rangers' authority to permit the taking of rabbits, birds, small game, and caribou in the area covered by the Moravian Mission, provided that the mission confirmed the need. This was a positive change of attitude on the part of St. John's. Before Commission St John's, as a 1920 letter from an official of the Newfoundland government, Gower Rabbitts, to Warden Sam Broomfield shows:

Your recommendation of changes in the seasons for Foxes and Otters will be considered but I am afraid nothing will be altered this season. Yours of 2 February has your statement about the publishing by you of laws different from those published by this Board. I have to inform you again that the seasons set out in the Game Laws are the only legal seasons and any persons breaking these Game Laws should be prosecuted in a court at the earliest opportunity. Of course, if they really needed the Meat as food for themselves or their families, they would be able to prove to the satisfaction of the Magistrate trying the cases and he would not convict them.[8]

But who were the magistrates and how often were they around? Fish swim, and birds migrate. Later in the century a staggered season was enforced for migrating birds, but before 1933 it did not seem to matter to St John's that there might be different needs, not to mention different seasons, in Labrador. In 1921 a petition had been sent from northern Labrador pointing out that "neither deer nor hare nor partridge are we permitted to kill ... Our boot-skins are only lying up and spoiling for the lack of deer sinew."[9] Again in 1924 a petition was sent to the governor, signed by William Barbour, Martin Martin, Isaac Rich, and Ereald Dinn, protesting that "they are not satisfied with the law for killing deer. They want plenty of fresh deer meat to eat and want the sinew for making skin boots. Three deer is not enough for food and only sinew enough to make boots for their own use, to say nothing of boots to sell, which they need to help make a living ... They would like the deer season to be March/April instead of January, as they cannot get any other fresh meat these days, or birds or seals, only frozen seal meat thawed, which is not healthy."[10] The trader Dick White added his voice to the protests. In a letter to Prime Minister Alderdice in 1934, he suggested:

Let this flour be given in charge of the Moravian Missionaries at each place or nearest thereto to distribute as needed. As for the other articles usually given on relief such as molasses and tea, even the poorest hunter's earnings can cover these in a bad year and so long as there is flour available in an emergency no one would starve with the free hunting privileges at present enjoyed. But if the Game Laws were enforced here as in Newfoundland and people had to observe close seasons, then, indeed they would be short of food, and it would take a few cargoes of provisions to support them. The point I make is that while they can kill game, etc., all the year round they need little else.[11]

There is no record that any of these requests for more realistic policies with respect to seasons and quotas in Labrador were ever acted upon. But with the coming of the commission and the Rangers, game laws were cognizant of local conditions and circumstances.

The Rangers opened six detachments in Labrador in 1935–36. The chief ranger tried to choose those who had some previous connection with Labrador. Of the eight he chose, at least five had had previous experience on the coast, although only one, Frank Mercer, had actually been a policeman in Labrador before. He had gone north early in 1934 as one of "Puddester's cops" – eight members of the Newfoundland Constabulary sent to Labrador by Sir John Puddester, commissioner for public health and welfare. Their task was to look after the welfare of the local people, some of whom had been left destitute by the collapse of the fish trade and the failure of the inshore fishery. The only other evidence of a police presence in Labrador was when the Newfoundland Constabulary had been stationed briefly at Stag Bay south of Makkovik in 1923 in response to a short-lived gold rush.

Mercer was one of those who, through his association with the land and the people, became very attached to Labrador. He later joined the RCMP and was eventually transferred back to Labrador as staff sergeant in charge of the area. Retiring after a distinguished career with the RCMP, he joined the Department of Labrador Affairs. Over the years he had many adventures in the North. He was the basis of the character Finnan the policeman in Harold Horwood's novel *White Eskimo*. The story is based roughly on Mercer's pursuit and arrest of Esau Gillingham in northern Labrador on the charge of murder. Mercer was at Hebron in 1936 with two other Rangers when Inuit travelling south from Nutak reported that a man had been killed at Gillingham's cabin near the mouth of the Okak River. Mercer, the senior of the three, with corporal's rank, decided to go and investigate, taking with him an Inuk named Zacharias Ikkusik as dog team driver and guide. Horwood took the story of bringing the body to Nain and the subsequent indictment of Gillingham and wove it into a captivating tale, with characters based on such people as Dick White and a caricature of a Moravian missionary, together with his own recollections of Labrador. In the novel Gillingham became a hero and Mercer's character somewhat less than that.

Some of the territory was very difficult to patrol in those days. Labrador was totally isolated in winter, with no regular flights and only one mail delivery by dog team between Christmas and the opening of navigation in June. North of Hamilton Inlet there was just one winter medical visit by Harry Paddon from North West River. The Commission of Government realized that it knew very little about the needs and aspirations of the country. To remedy this, monthly, quarterly, and half-yearly reports describing every aspect of local conditions were required of the Rangers. Sent to the commissioner of natural resources, they were often copied and distributed to the other five departments of government. Within a short time the commission was the best-informed government that Newfoundland had ever had and the only one thus far to be informed to any great extent about Labrador.

The government later became even more involved in the affairs of Labrador. When in 1942 the Hudson's Bay Company announced the closure of its trading posts on the north coast, the commission stepped in to take over the company's operations, including its leases from the Moravians. Thus, for the first time, the government was taking a direct role in the economic welfare of the region. At last it had taken over responsibility from a non-governmental body. Hebron, Nutak (which had replaced the older settlement of Okak after the flu epidemic of 1918), Davis Inlet (with the Innu and a few settler families such as the Saunders), Hopedale, and Makkovik all came under the aegis of the government. These communities contained almost the entire aboriginal population, Innu and Inuit, north of Hamilton Inlet.

Although the coast had been serviced by the Hudson's Bay Company's ships, *Fort Garry* and *Nascopi*, the mail steamer from St John's had never proceeded beyond Nain and sometimes not beyond Hopedale. Now the government laid the responsibility for northern transport on the Newfoundland Railway, and regular supply ships steamed to the north coast. This system of vessels subsidized by the government essentially continued as the main supply system for the coast, though with many changes, including the transfer of the service to the federal government at Confederation. It still carries on today, although responsibility has been transferred back to the province. Airstrips, of course, have radically changed the pattern of transportation, and tourists now mix with local travellers on the coastal boats. But the boats still run and may do so for some time to come, at least north of Cartwright. So the torch was passed, as the company ceded to the government the monopoly on trade and transport along the north coast.

The responsibility for trade was delegated to the Department of Natural Resources. Its instructions were to use the necessary working capital not for financial profit but for the rehabilitation of the people and for raising their low standard of living. Now the government took the lead on all matters except education and health, which remained in the hands of the Moravians and the Grenfell Mission. There was no question from this time on about who was the administrator, not only de jure but also de facto.

The policy of the stores was rehabilitation, and the store managers were welfare officers as well as traders. They were instructed to make every effort to improve housing, to aid sealing and fishing ventures, and to stimulate local industries such as sawmills. To achieve its aim of rehabilitation, the Northern Labrador Trading Operation (NLTO) discouraged trapping and encouraged sealing and cod fishing. Its officials reasoned that fresh meat and fish would provide a cheaper and healthier diet than the store food consumed by trappers. They believed that the market for animal fats and fish would continue at least through the war. The gamble paid off. Higher returns for fish stimulated the Inuit to double their efforts so that by 1946 they were marketing twice as much cod as in 1942. In those years, earnings tripled, relief slipped to almost nothing, and the people appeared to be well on their way to recovery.

Although NLTO advocated hiring local Labrador people for its operations, most of the staff were actually former Bay employees or former Rangers. Thirty-year-old Sergeant Walter Rockwood, who was appointed government agent in northern Labrador, had served at Nain as a member of the Newfoundland Constabulary and was later a commissioned officer in the Rangers. Following four years teaching at schools for the deaf in the United States, he had spent two years as a welfare officer on the Burin Peninsula of the Island. Now, as agent, his powers were similar to those of the governor of a territory, with the judicial powers of a magistrate. He was to be judge, governor, and trader – a highly unusual combination. Perhaps for this reason his appointment was referred for confirmation to the Dominions Office in London. Rockwood became the most powerful administrator in the history of northern Labrador, and when in 1952 the successor of NLTO, the Division of Labrador Services, was organized as a branch of the Department of Welfare, he was invited to become its first director.

Government had finally arrived in Labrador. Although the Innu still travelled the rivers and lakes of the interior relying on their own leaders for guidance while depending on the traders for relief from want and on the church for religious support, in most of Labrador the Government of Newfoundland had been established as governor. Not only had it taken initiatives that affected the lives of the people, but it had taken steps to develop resources that would transform the interior of Labrador. It had also put in place services that were at least somewhat responsive to the needs of the people. Great demographic shifts were to come that would move many of the people out of their old communities and into the new ones that arose as a result of the coming of war and capital. While the old parts of Labrador would remain, new parts would be created, and intercourse between them would be attempted. A Labrador identity that they shared would grow, though solidarity between north, south, centre, and west would be difficult to bring about.

CHAPTER FIVE

Coming Together

Growth, for the past 15–20 years, has literally been forced upon them. For many it has been both painful and confusing. They have come from microscopic communities of two or three families – from a life of independence – into, what appears to them, monstrous size communities of 200–15,000 people. There they were suddenly expected to have all the skills required to live in such communities harmoniously and, consequently have become dependent on many outside forces.

Beatrice Watts, Labrador in the Eighties

THE SECOND WORLD WAR

A transforming event for the north coast, and indeed for the whole coast, was the Second World War. The course of the war depended on the supply of materials from North America to Europe, and the Canadians and Americans searched for a place that would be a jumping-off point for air ferries. They found Goose Bay. Although Labradorians had been exposed to wage labour at Port Hope Simpson and with the lumber companies that operated previously in Lake Melville, this was the first time that cash for work was available so readily and for a sustained period. People all along the coast, especially from the north, were attracted to the jobs at Goose. The populations of Makkovik and Hopedale were particularly reduced as families migrated to Lake Melville. Alfred Winters and several others walked more than 150 kilometres across Labrador from Makkovik to Goose Bay for work on the base there.

The war changed the lives, dramatically and permanently, not only of the people in the north but of those in the Lake Melville area and indeed all along the coast. Until then, Labrador had been a land of three separate parts. In the north there were the Inuit and part Inuit, along with the Innu and some settler families at Davis Inlet, Voisey's Bay, and Sheshatshiu; then there were the people of the southeast coast and the Straits, some from Newfoundland and some not; and in the Lake Melville area were the Orkney Islanders and the part British. The inhabitants of the different regions had lived more or less separate lives as the original people and those who came after them settled into their own territories. True, their lives had been affected by technology and the changing worldmarket place, and they had learned from one another and learned how to live with one another, but each group had remained more or less on its own ground.

The Second World War and the building of Goose Bay changed this. Drawn away from the shrinking markets for fur and fish, people from north and south came to Goose to seek employment at the base – and, as it turned out, found new lives for themselves. John Montague reported to Gordie Rendell on the CBC Goose Bay "Labrador History" series: "A year before the Base started I talked to the Hudson's Bay manager and he told me they had about ninety trappers. The year the Base started they had five or six. The fur was down and most all went working for McNamara. I've been trapping ever since 1921 myself, never missed a year."[1] While many of those who went to work at the base were later drawn back to their place of birth, to the land they loved and the old homes they knew so well, most of the workers settled in Goose Bay or Happy Valley and made it their new home. Soon Inuit, Innu, and settler were living in close proximity in a modern setting, all of them trying to come to grips with fundamental change in their lives.

The Goose Bay air base, built to ferry aircraft to Europe and for antisubmarine patrols over the North Atlantic, made a significant contribution to the war effort: "It more than doubled ferrying facilities; it supplemented air coverage of convoys taking the far northern route; it was a convenient staging field for United States air communication with Greenland and Iceland; and it provided a shorter route to Great Britain from Montreal and the interior of the continent where the larger aircraft industries were located."[2] Its story begins in 1941 when Newfoundland, acting on the recommendation of the Permanent Joint Board on Defence, agreed to lease the land to Canada for ninety-nine years for military purposes only, with no transfer of Newfoundland's sovereignty. Canada was to bear the cost of the enterprise, while the question of how the base would be used for civil aviation would be resolved only after the war.

In June 1941 a plane carrying Eric Fry and a Canadian scouting party landed in North West River to look for a suitable spot for the airfield. Met by R.G. Gillard, the Hudson's Bay Company manager, and Mina Paddon, they engaged Sid Blake's boat, with the skipper Dan Michelin and Sid's son Edward, and headed for Goose Bay. John Groves, a local settler, pointed out several sites, including Robert

Michelin's berry patch on the plateau overlooking the bay. Fry liked what he saw: the site had easy access to the Hamilton River, was suitable for construction, had adequate drainage, and lots of room for runways. Robert Michelin, a pre-eminent trapper and guide, who had been prepared to give his life for his country in the First World War, now gave it his berry patch for an air base. Three days later Colonel Elliott Roosevelt of the U.S. Army Air Force (and son of the president) arrived on exactly the same mission. He, too, found the site entirely suitable and agreed with Fry that it should be called Goose Airport. The spot commanded a spectacular view, in the words of Labrador songwriter Byron Chaulk, "overlooking the waters of Lake Melville so grand, one of the greatest in all this great land." To the south it was framed by the snow-capped Mealy Mountains and to the north by dark hills dominated by Mount Mokami. Pilots coming and going were treated to a vast expanse of blue waters ringed by green hills and a lavender sky that seemed to go on forever.

The awarding of the contract brought McNamara Construction for a long stay. Its boss, Bill Durrell, would not only oversee the building of Goose Airport but later, on the recommendation of C.D. Howe, the Canadian government's "Minister of Everything," he would head the construction of the Quebec North Shore and Labrador Railway, one of the most significant projects of its day. The contract called for the building of an air base with concrete runways and accommodation for five thousand officers and men of the Canadian Army, Royal Canadian Air Force, and U.S. Army Air Force, as well as three thousand civilians. There were to be two modern hospitals, one for the Americans and one for the Canadians, seven gigantic hangars, modern bakeries, steam laundries, central heating, a pumping station, water supply, sanitation, docks to accommodate four ocean-going cargo ships at one time, administration and recreation facilities, and fifty kilometres of roads. Later there would be movie theatres, bowling alleys, and canteens. In short, in the Labrador wilderness, which had been the preserve of the settlers and the Innu, where the nearest tilt might be a day's march, a town large enough to accommodate up to eight thousand people was to be erected. Later, in the 1960s, the population, still served by many of the same support services as they are to this day, rose to about twelve thousand. The industrial machine had arrived in Labrador, and life there would never be the same.

Both settlers and Inuit who had had previous experience with work for wages in Port Hope Simpson, Lake Melville, and the Northern Labrador Services Division (NLSD), were drawn to the workforce in Goose out of what many of them now knew was necessity. The channels in Goose Bay had to be charted, and Russell Chaulk and Robert Michelin were invaluable in that endeavour because of their intimate knowledge of the waters. In September 1941 the Canadian icebreaker *N.B. MacLean* arrived at North West River and hired Chaulk to pilot it into Goose Bay. Chaulk did his soundings from his canoe with a cod jigger and safely piloted this first ship, and many others that followed, past Groves Point and into Terrington Basin. He later became the first harbourmaster for Goose Bay.

Many more worked on land. John Michelin, who had been a trapper and later became a guide to travellers across the Labrador Peninsula, headed a crew that felled the trees and made the saw logs. Durrell described these new workers' arrival:

It wasn't long after the advance party of McNamara workmen had established their camp before natives from Mud Lake, North West River, Traverspine, Otter Creek and Carter Inlet began to arrive. I gave them all work at standard rates of pay. The only fly in the ointment was that according to custom all brought their wives and families, and their dogs along with them. I can honestly say that before a year had gone by, most of the natives of Labrador, from Cape Chidley in the north down to St. Michael's River in the south, had worked for the McNamara Construction Co. This was a good thing for the natives because it gave them more money to spend than they had ever enjoyed in their lives before.[3]

The Innu at this time were still nomadic, still not settled in communities, and still living in tents, without modern education or even an adequate knowledge of the English language. While the settlers and Inuit felt the need to work, particularly in view of the downturn in both fish and fur, their hearts were still on the sea and land. Isaac Rich recounts the change that took place in his life and that of his family as a result of the building of the base:

We knew that they were goin' to build the Base here and they did want a few men for surveyin' in the beginning so I was one of them that got the job. It was the beginning to be a dark outlook for the future if this war was goin' to carry on like it was, and the price of fur was goin' down, so we grabbed the chance and took the job.

When I knew the construction company was comin' here I decided I'd come right here to the Base and have my family come with me so I could go home every night. Before I went to work with the construction company I put up a small log cabin at Otter Creek. My wife definitely did not want to come up here but I just made the decision. Come to look back on it, it was quite a thing to ask the wife to come right directly up here with only a small thin canvas tent, but it looked as though there was chance of making a livelihood, better than we had before.

We would say, "Can I stand being told what to do for six months?" The idea of being your own boss and then to go under another boss, no odds how good he is, and being told to do something instead of doing it your own way, well it's hard to explain. You didn't feel as though it was possible to do that or to be in one building about 40 feet by 50 feet to walk around when you could be roamin' back in the country somewhere. It's surprising you had that feeling, it was more than you could stand almost, when the trees begin to turn yellow and the different winds you feel in the fall of the year. Those were the hard days. But that's beginnin', it's worn off now.[4]

The establishment of the base at Goose Bay caused a major demographic shift in Labrador. With the exception of the Innu, who still travelled the woods and rivers of the Labrador interior, men and women came from all along the coast to work and settle in Goose Bay. Previously, most of them had been captives of the truck system that Grenfell and, in his own way, Hope Simpson, had tried to eradicate. Now the construction companies and the air force paid them cash, giving them an economic freedom they had never known.

But the freedom to settle was restricted. Private homes were forbidden within an eight-kilometre radius of the large stretch of land that Canada had received. Max Winters, originally of Makkovik, remembers the small community of twenty-five families at Otter Creek when he was a boy. But even these families were forced to move because they were too near the fuel storage tanks. But the people were determined that they would have homes for their families and a community of their own. Gilbert Saunders, John Broomfield, and Thorwald Perrault, all from north of Cape Harrison, chose spots for themselves on the bank of the Hamilton River. Arriving by boat from Otter Creek, the men and women pulled themselves up over the bank with the help of the willows and pitched their tents at what grew to become the town of Happy Valley. Alice Perrault, in her history of Happy Valley, tells of these early times:

The sound of hammers could be heard quite late at night. The work was done by kerosene lamps, or lanterns, but after three weeks, the houses were ready for the families. True, they were not large (10 × 18). A good deal of material was provided by the Americans, and it was quite common to see large packing cases being towed across the creek. Stoves were from oil drums and our little homes were warm, though not completely finished.

Our provisions, oil and gas, had to be bought at North West River, our nearest shopping place. As the men were only able to get off for a short while, we had to think ahead and purchase enough for a few months. Sometimes in the winter they often went in one of the trucks which was hauling gravel from North West River. It was an all day job, and sometimes meant staying overnight and then walking the 25 miles from North West River to our home.[5]

The RCAF had helped provide a building for church services, and it was here that Alice Perrault was soon able to begin the first school. From these beginnings was to rise the largest community in Labrador, bringing together those from the Labrador coast and those from the Island. It was not until 1946 that a road to the community was built and the base agreed to send a truck to transport the workers. Until then, the men had to walk the eight kilometres to the base or go by boat. Although the base did donate some materials for building and provided some medical help in emergencies, by and large it turned a blind eye on the Happy Valley community.

By 1950 the residents still had no rights whatsoever except the right to leave. They had no title to land and could be ordered to move at any time. They were not permitted to own or operate private vehicles, and no commercial establishments of any kind were allowed. Water and sewer services were not available, and building standards were minimal. When Fred Rowe, the provincial member for Labrador at the time, approached the base command about the amelioration of conditions in Happy Valley, the response was negative. Happy Valley, he was told, was an illegitimate community; North West River was not connected by road and was twenty-five miles away by water; evacuating hundreds of civilians from Happy Valley in the event of another war would be a logistical problem for the base authorities. In any case, they thought there were undesirable elements in the community that would pose a security risk, though these phantoms were never identified.

Yet on the Island there were three large bases: Pepperell, surrounded by 100,000 residents; Argentia, with at least five communities in close proximity; and Harmon, ringed by the town of Stephenville and other communities. No one had thought seriously of removing them. The fact was that one thousand Canadian citizens were being denied their rights. Rowe argued that there was no justification for the denial of basic amenities such as food, clothing, taxis, automobiles, and movies. There was no evident problem with alcohol or with other problems that could not be controlled in the usual way.

When the base authorities refused to budge, Rowe took the issue to Brooke Claxton, the minister of national defence. Rowe suggested that the land be passed back to the Government of Newfoundland, which would make it available to the people. The recommendation was accepted by both governments. A nursing station began service in 1950, operated by the Grenfell Mission, and a Hudson's Bay store was opened at Goose in 1950 and in Happy Valley in 1953. The year 1952 brought the first post office, operated by Una Saunders in the home of Gilbert Saunders. By the time a movie theatre opened in 1956, the population was about a thousand. In 1958 telephones were installed and a town council was formed. The following year diesel generators were shipped in, and in 1964 a fire hall was built and a new hospital opened to replace the old American jail, which Tony Paddon had obtained for medical services in 1950.

Meanwhile, a local radio station had been started by the employees of Terminal Construction Company. When the RCAF took over the base, they inherited the radio station and operated it with volunteers. But it was not until 1957 that the CBC was ordered to absorb it, which it did reluctantly. Joe Smith, who had been in the RCAF and was to play a key role in the extension of technical services in Labrador, arrived in 1959 to make Goose his home and Labrador broadcasting his lifelong commitment. Smith installed equipment both for the CBC and for many other Labradorians who needed it, and kept it in good repair for decades. Managers would come and go, but Joe Smith went on forever. Even then, radio was run in abstentia from St John's while local personnel manned the equipment and played the tapes that were sent in.

It was the Americans, specifically the Nineteen Thirty-Second Communications Unit, who started the television station (with films only), albeit overseen by a CBC manager sent from the Island. Hockey games might be six weeks old. Not until 1971 was a permanent link established with the Island. So for the first thirty years after Confederation, one part of the province did not hear from the other on a regular basis. Even after 1971 the feed was all one way; Labrador began to get the Newfoundland news, but the Island still knew nothing about what was going on in central Labrador. With the exception of those who read the Newfoundland papers and those who had short-wave radio, the two parts of the province existed in splendid isolation from each other. The two solitudes, which had so much catching up to do, led separate lives.

After the war, Happy Valley continued to grow and develop, with the base as its main economic support, as it is to this day. The Cold War spawned the U.S. Strategic Air Command, a strike force against potential invasion from over the pole. It was this activity that gave Goose its postwar raison d'être until the arrival of several NATO countries for training in low-level flying. As well, additional bases were built on the coast at Cartwright, Hopedale, Saglek, and Fox

Harbour, doing for the populations of these communities what Goose had done for Happy Valley. Fishermen performing skilled and unskilled work were paid astronomical wages, with which they provided their families with amenities previously unknown to them. In the meantime, dog teams gave way to snowmobiles, and smoked salmon, char, and caribou were replaced to some degree by the less nutritious offerings of the mini-supermarket.

Men and women who had spent a great deal of time in the woods and on the sea were still able to do so in their leisure hours. Once the coveralls came off and the grease was removed, a man could head for his tilt or his favourite fishing spot. So while the bases provided the stability of a cash income, families could still enjoy their caribou and trout and bakeapples. In a way, the bases became part of the community, providing on the one hand dances, movies, and other entertainment, but on the other hand the threat of unwanted pregnancies, marital breakdown, and venereal disease. The old challenges of poor seasons for fish and fur in a place removed from fluctuating markets gave way to the new challenges of the consumer society and life in the faster lane. Labrador communities had changed fundamentally.

CONFEDERATION

In 1945 the British government, having neither the wish nor ability to keep its far-flung empire, began to divest itself of its overseas territories, including Newfoundland. Clearly, responsible government could now be returned to the old colony, as had been understood would happen when in 1934 it was suspended. After all, Newfoundland had not only been self-supporting throughout the war but had contributed financial assistance to Britain. Even so, the war had not brought any structural change to the Newfoundland economy, which might very well collapse in the event of a postwar depression. If this were to happen, Britain might find itself called on once more to provide financial assistance. The ideal solution, from Britain's point of view, was for Newfoundland to join Canada. But would this be acceptable to the people of the Island and Labrador? All previous attempts at union had failed. To find the answers to this question, Prime Minister Clement Atlee called for the election of a National Convention in 1946.

Lester Burry, the United Church minister at North West River, became a candidate and was elected as the representative for Labrador, gaining 787 of the 984 votes cast. At last, Labrador had representation! Burry had served the United Church from his base at North West River for twenty-seven years, his first house being an old log structure originally built in the 1800s for the Hudson's Bay Company's Donald Smith. Travelling in his boat the *Glad Tidings* and by dog team in winter, Burry had served the interior and the coast faithfully and well and had come to be loved throughout the parish. He continued his dedicated representation at the National Convention. Don Jamieson has said of him:

Burry's effectiveness lay in his gentleness, sincerity and depth of experience. He was one of the few speakers who could command respectful silence in the usually rowdy assembly, as, without rancour, he told of the alienation of the Labrador people and their belief in Confederation as a way out of decades of neglect.

They had no special love for Quebec, but their links with the people of the island of Newfoundland were tenuous, often hostile. Their Convention spokesman, Lester Burry, was most effective in ridiculing the newly discovered concern of so many Newfoundlanders for Labrador. The best way to retain the territory, he argued, was to give the northern residents the better living standards offered by Confederation.[6]

While Burry clearly represented his people well, it was perhaps Bill Keough, the representative from St Georges (and later a central figure in the Smallwood cabinet), who most effectively reflected on the state of mind of the Labrador people: "It seems to me that until now the people of Labrador have fared none too well at our hand. We haven't gone out of our way to provide them with even minimum public and social services. In the days when we did have responsible government we never even thought it worth our while to extend to the people of Labrador a ballot. Indeed, we didn't get around to giving a second thought to Labrador until it seemed as if we might get something out of it. It would be interesting to know the thoughts of Labradorians when they hear some of our political pundits raising the roof over the raw deal Newfoundland's gotten from somebody or other."[7]

Keough expressed the thinking of the Labrador people perhaps better than he knew. He even called them Labradorians, a term that many on the Island would still have had trouble with in the late twentieth century, although more and more of them would come to use the inclusive name "Newfoundland and Labrador." When Newfoundland was chastising Ottawa for lack of understanding and lack of adequate response to local identity and local needs, it still did not acknowledge that it stood in a similar relationship to Labrador. Viewed in the context of later attitudes, the remarks of Keough were all the more prescient.

The presence of the Innu and the Inuit were barely mentioned in the National Convention debates. Although Smallwood did refer to their presence, it is unclear how he anticipated their affairs being handled after Confederation – though it seems he believed that the Government of Canada would assume the responsibility. When the terms of union were struck, there was no mention of aboriginal people. It was as if they did not exist. The argument that they were equal citizens of the province clearly is not valid in light of subsequent legislation and court judgments or in view of the conditions in which they lived at the time. In terms of their ability to function in a modern environment, they were not equal citizens and would not have become so without affirmative action which, in the final analysis, only the federal government was able to supply.

For whatever reason, – whether it was their knowledge of Canada through their experiences at Goose Bay or their faith in Burry – 1858 Labrador residents (more than 80 per cent of those who voted) supported Confederation in the first referendum. In the subsequent provincial elections after Newfoundland joined Canada, they supported the Liberal Party, as most of them would do in the years ahead.

Fate was reluctant to grant representation to Labrador – the first election there was delayed because of the weather. Nevertheless, Harold Horwood eventually became the first member of the House of Assembly ever elected for Labrador. At last, there was a permanent government in place, duly elected by all, to deal with the needs and aspirations of the people. And there is no question that the union brought immediate financial benefits in the form of family allowances and pensions of one kind or another; and later, in 1957, unemployment insurance to all but the Innu. These measures, together with the arrangements for education and health, meant the further erosion of Moravian influence and authority in the north, and to some degree that of the Grenfell Mission too, though both organizations continued to be consulted closely on policy well into the middle of the twentieth century.

The Aboriginal People

The Newfoundland government acknowledged its responsibilities for the provision of social and economic services to the population of Labrador, and – as we have seen in the case of Goose Bay – tried to provide them as quickly as possible. However, with regard to the aboriginal people, the policy continued to be fraught with ambiguity. Who had the responsibility and was in charge of their affairs? After Confederation, exchanges of correspondence attempted to clarify things. Smallwood clearly preferred that the federal government take and keep the responsibility. But just as clearly, Ottawa did not want to accept it. In 1953, a letter to Herbert L. Pottle, the provincial minister of public welfare, set out the federal position: "There is no legal requirement for the Federal Government to assume any responsibility whatsoever, either financial or administrative, in regard to the residents of Northern Labrador ... Even if the Federal Government agree to assume continuing responsibility in some form for the residents of Northern Labrador, it could not in practice do so with propriety as it appears virtually impossible to determine who is an Eskimo and who is not."[8]

Official documents of the period clearly shows that the federal government consistently and wrongfully interpreted the silence of the terms of union on the subject of aboriginals as allowing it to avoid direct responsibility for them. Consequently, Ottawa encouraged the assumption of responsibility by the Government of Newfoundland. The basis for denying federal constitutional responsibility was that the aboriginal people of Labrador were enfranchised. So they were damned if they did and damned if they didn't. Until the National Convention, no one in Labrador had had the vote. After they got it, the aboriginals were abandoned by the federal government on the basis that since they now had the vote, they should not be put under the Indian Act and therefore did not come under section 91(24) of the British North America Act. The federal government erroneously chose to determine its constitutional responsibility based on whether Indians could be included under the Indian Act. In his 1993 *Report on the Complaint of the Innu of Labrador to the Canadian Human Rights Commission*, Dean Donald McRae of the Common Law Section, University of Ottawa Faculty of Law, concluded that this same situation still existed.

In a letter to Prime Minister Lester B. Pearson in 1964, Premier Smallwood set out his understanding of how events had transpired and what the position of the two governments was. But rather than insisting on federal acceptance of fiduciary responsibility, he allowed his federal counterparts options:

At the time we were negotiating the terms of union, the government of Canada, as I understand it, did not accept the view that Eskimos were Indians under the constitution; nor was the government of the day anxious to have the Indians of Labrador accepted as Indians under the British North America Act and brought under the administration of the Superintendent General of Indian Affairs ... Subsequently, however, the Government of Canada did recognize a certain moral responsibility towards the Indians and Eskimos ... We would be prepared to have the Government of Canada take over full

responsibility for the Indians and Eskimos of Labrador, as you would presumably have a right to do under the Constitution ... If the Government of
Canada would still prefer ... to have the Indians and Eskimos of Newfoundland treated in precisely the same way as other inhabitants of the Province,
we are quite prepared to continue on that basis provided the Government of
Canada will give us the same degree of financial support as is given directly
by the Government of Canada in respect to Indians and Eskimos living in
other provinces.[9]

The latter option has in fact been the course of action followed, with
some modifications, up to the present time.

In 1951 the responsibility for trade and social welfare in northern
Labrador was transferred to the provincial Department of Welfare,
and a new agency, the Division of Northern Labrador Affairs (DNLA),
was created to succeed the Northern Labrador Trading Operation.
This new division was to administer the federal funds that began to
flow into the province after Ottawa acknowledged its moral, if not
legal, responsibility for native people. In fact, from the beginning, all
people in the northern Labrador communities and those in
Sheshatshiu benefited from the funding. On the other hand, this was
not the case for those south of Cape Harrison, though many of them
had aboriginal blood, as the founding of the Labrador Metis Association would later attest. From the time of Confederation, the north
laid claim to funds that the south did not have, and this led to a clear
imbalance in the provision of community services, which was not
rectified until the coming of regional development programs such as
DREE (the federal Department of Regional Economic Expansion).

Federal funding for aboriginal people increased in 1954 with the
signing of a ten-year agreement that assumed most of the responsibility for Indian and Inuit health services. In 1965 this agreement was
expanded to include funding for the construction, maintenance, and
development of Inuit and Indian communities. In 1970 and again in
1975 the agreement was renewed, and under the later agreement the
leadership of the Inuit and the Innu had a voice for the first time in
the disbursement of funds. In effect, the agreements made the provincial government, through DNLA, the most pervasive force the
communities had ever seen, affecting all aspects of life. At last, the
government was governing, though how effectively and responsively
we shall have to judge.

The agreement between Ottawa and St John's in 1954 committed
the health of northern Labrador to the International Grenfell Association (IGA), which was to operate under the authority of the Newfoundland government but charge all its expenses to Ottawa. In

Hamilton Inlet and south of it, the IGA (at the cost of $92,000 annually) maintained four nursing stations and two twenty-five-bed hospitals, besides operating a small hospital ship, which in summer cruised the coast as far north as Hebron. At least once every summer a government doctor still travelled on the mail boat as far as Nain, seeing patients on the ship. The Marconi wireless station at Hopedale and the two-way radios with which the government equipped its trading posts made it possible in emergencies to seek medical help from Newfoundland. But as yet there was no resident doctor on the coast to make full use of that device.

Shipping supplies in summer and air freighting them in winter caused difficulties and great expense. Even today, Labrador has the highest prices in the province, with gasoline in recent years being up to a dollar per litre in some places. Until about 1959, many of the planes carrying administrators or supplies to the coast flew from Gander, and these long and expensive flights were further complicated by uncertain weather conditions. While Goose Bay soon became the transportation and communications hub for eastern Labrador, in fact airstrips in the coastal communities, with the attendant communications and landing devices, did not appear until the 1980s, when they were established as a result of federal funding. Until then, Beavers and Otters, including the air ambulance from North West River and St Anthony, landed on skis or floats. Even in the early seventies there was no scheduled air service to the Labrador coast. It was the airstrips provided by the federal government in the 1980s that completely transformed transportation on the coast.

As in other parts of the North, one of the early health initiatives was a major campaign to eradicate the scourge of tuberculosis, which was endemic as a result of housing and sanitation conditions. In 1955, at the request of Tony Paddon, Dr Charles Curtis, the superintendent of IGA, travelled the coast as far as Nain. After entering every Inuit dwelling in the community, he found only one that he considered fit for human habitation. At Nutak and Hebron, he was told, conditions were even worse. His organization was treating the coast's tubercular cases at the hospital in St Anthony, but he contended that it was useless to restore the people's health only to send them back to squalor. Accordingly, he recommended the following measures: to bring the Hebron and Nutak people south, where there was wood to heat their homes; to use a percentage of the federal grant of $200,000 for a housing project; and to attempt to find some solution for the deplorable economic and living conditions of the Inuit.

Evidently, the Moravian Mission agreed with this course of action. Similarly, government officials argued that in the south better housing, education, and health services could be provided. Moreover, they claimed, the market for fur had declined and there was little market for foxes; the char fishery was in the summer only, and it was believed that there was potential employment as a result of a uranium find near Makkovik. So in May 1955 the provincial Executive Council voted to close the Nutak depot and transfer all its families to Nain or farther south. The Nutak people were scattered to Nain, Makkovik, Hopedale, North West River, and Happy Valley.

Now the Hebron people were alarmed and wrote to their MHA, Fred Rowe, telling him that they did not want to move, at least not until they could be assured of good jobs and good housing. A reply came back from the deputy minister of welfare that there was no plan to evict the residents and that if there ever was, they would be given a year's notice. But in the summer of 1958 the Moravians, suffering financial hardship and a lack of ministers, decided to abandon Hebron. The government felt it had no choice but to close its store, and it took that decision later in the year. But the move was badly planned and executed, evidently because of protracted financial negotiations between the provincial and federal governments.

Not all officials were supportive of the move. Tony Paddon, while he supported the move from Hebron, proposed that it should be to a new community to be built at Napartok Bay, not far from Hebron. Walter Rockwood, who was now director of DNLA's Department of Welfare, sent a memo to the deputy minister of welfare acknowledging the poor housing and lack of fuel in Hebron, as well as the inaccessibility of the area for medical purposes, but pointing out that the availability of food at Hebron was better than elsewhere. Rockwood seemed to think that more thought should be given to the move and more preparations made. He also thought that there should be more consultation with the people. His memo argued against the move: "We have the views of the people concerned, as expressed in their letter to Dr. Rowe, dated 9 August. They do not wish to leave their homes, hunting and fishing grounds at this time for fear of suffering hardship. They say that when they can be assured of having steady work with good wages they will be prepared to move."[10]

The province had decided to build twenty new houses at Makkovik in 1959 and turn them over to twenty families from Hebron, and to bring south the settlement's remaining thirty families in 1960. However, Rockwood said the relocation would have to take place in one move. If the store remained open during the winter, he believed the people would stay. And if the missionary was withdrawn, this would place the whole burden of care on DNLA. Eventually the order came to close the store, in spite of the earlier assurances that the people would get one year's notice of a move. Now the government had not twenty but all fifty families to relocate.

Most of the Hebron families spent the first winter crowded into temporary shelters at Hopedale, and a year or two later many of them were moved south to hastily built and inadequate cottages in Makkovik. Only a few families settled in Nain. For them, it would be possible to return to their original home, at least from time to time. But those farther south would find it virtually impossible to go back. Moreover, they were clustered in houses in a special section of the community away from the rest. In addition, they did not speak English, nor did they use the same Inuktitut dialect as the Inuit of Makkovik.

For the first time in their lives, adult Inuit were made to feel different and inadequate compared with others in the community, even other Inuit. They had no knowledge of the nearby countryside and therefore were not immediately successful in hunting. They suffered a loss of respect from their peers and a loss of self-esteem. Reliance on welfare only made matters worse. Poverty, demoralization, and frustration led people to consume alcohol in excess, which contributed to family violence, accidental deaths, criminal offences, and the further breakdown of family relations. The desire to reunite families caused many of the Inuit to leave Makkovik over the next decade. In fact, a large number of Hebron exiles eventually settled in Nain, where they added to the growing population. Social and economic strains arising from this increase upset the ecological balance and contributed to community pressures that have never been resolved.

There was a great deal of resettlement in the province in the first two decades after Confederation. But in most cases, particularly in the latter years, there was consultation with the people, as Gordon Pinsent's novel *John and the Missus* dramatically records. In the case of Hebron, the will of the people was clearly subordinate to the will of those responsible for their welfare, no matter how well meaning the latter may have been. Rockwood, who was opposed to the move, pointed out forcefully that the people had not been consulted. They had been promised a year's notice before any move, he said; that promise had not been kept. They had requested houses and jobs before moving, but housing provisions in the receiving communities were grossly mismanaged, evidently through federal-provincial wrangling. Language was clearly not a barrier; that barrier had been overcome decades before. What was a barrier was the ethic of the day – that aboriginal people were not capable of managing their own affairs and were dependent on the state and associated patrons. Years later, at its 1998 annual meeting, the Labrador Inuit Association was instructed to seek redress for the move. It is seeking an apology, compensation, and healing. There is also talk of a new community north of Nain, for which the proposed Torngat Mountains National Park could provide some economic benefits.

At Confederation, Labrador north of Cape Harrison was being serviced by the four Moravian schools, a Roman Catholic school in Davis Inlet, and by one that the Pentecostals had opened at Postville in the 1940s. However, in 1952 the Department of Education reclassified the Moravian schools in northern Labrador as "community" schools, to be administered by a district school board chaired by the head of the Moravian Mission, the Rev. William Peacock. Thereafter, they used the same texts and exams as all other parts of the province. Attendance was compulsory for children of school age. The board appointed the teachers and paid them regular provincial salaries, plus a $200-a-year cost-of-living bonus.

In these schools English was now the sole language of instruction, even though about half the students came from homes that habitually used Inuktitut. Only in Nain were some of the beginners taught in their native tongue. Not until the seventies and eighties, when more jurisdiction was restored to the communities and regional school boards were created, did Inuktitut return to the classrooms and a program of cultural studies was initiated.

While medical, educational, and social welfare services improved in the north, non-native administrators now exercised control over the communities, displacing the elected aboriginal bodies that had managed affairs under the Moravians. The first town council formed in Nain in 1956 had five members: the Moravian minister as chair, the store manager, the community nurse from IGA, the chief elder representing the Inuit, and a delegate from the settlers – an oligarchy largely of non-aboriginals. Since 1951 the jurisdiction of DNLA had gradually expanded until it was managing funds from other provincial departments, including education, municipal affairs, and health. Through its arm, the government was taking firm hold of the northern communities. Much of the leadership fell to the chief administrator, Walter Rockwood. Knowledgeable about Labrador and obviously committed to its welfare, he tried to advise those on the Island of its identity and needs. In an early memo he called for sympathetic understanding:

Labrador is a young giant, potentially greater than its foster parent, and fast approaching maturity. Unless Newfoundland awakens to this fact it will be bypassed. Newfoundland cannot provide the capital for the development of Labrador's resources, but of all the neighbouring provinces it ought to be the best suited to offer sympathetic understanding and to provide efficient administration. This, perhaps, is all that Labrador expects. However, the

problems cannot and will not be understood without real effort, and super-
ficial knowledge is dangerous. But under existing circumstances there is
scarcely any reason to believe that the problems will be better understood in
the immediate future than in the past.[11]

The attitude that drove policy appears to have been one in which the
dependent aboriginals were led by the government agencies. Native
people were not expected to think or do for themselves; it was the
white leadership, either on the coast or in St John's, that knew what
was best for them. Local people were not so much consulted as
informed and directed. Indeed, apart from the Moravians, few officials spoke Inuktitut. Of course, paternalism was the ethic of the day,
and Rockwood was a product of his time. But he was genuinely
interested in trying to improve the life of the people, even though
his policies may not always have been right or accepted. He believed
in "economic rehabilitation," and it is difficult to see how either the
Inuit or the Innu could have continued to survive as hunters and
gatherers indefinitely and not come to participate in the modern
economy. In time, like other aboriginal groups on the North, they
chose to participate through co-operatives rather than developing
individual businesses. But once they had organized themselves, they
did participate.

In the meantime, Rockwood did his best to express the reality of
Labrador and its relationship with the Island:

Too often in everyday conversation the term "Province" is used as if it
includes only the island of Newfoundland, and not the much larger area of
Labrador. Only when the vast iron ore deposits, waterpower and timber
resources of the latter are mentioned is it remembered that it too is a part of
the Province. Compared to the Island itself, Labrador is a young giant, potentially greater and fast coming to maturity. The highest mountains in the
"Province" are not on the Island; the Mealy Mountains near Goose Airport
are higher than the Long Range Mountains, the rugged Torngats farther north
are higher still. Lake Michikamau is larger than Grand Lake, and there is
certainly nothing in the Island of Newfoundland to compare with the Grand
Falls of the Hamilton River. In the field of man-made developments, Labrador
already has the only standard gauge railway in the "Province."[12]

Rockwood certainly believed in self-help, and he also believed that
the resources and expertise he had available to him were inadequate
for the job and that the federal government should take over the
responsibility. His thoughts and actions were not unlike those of Max
Budgell, a Labradorian who worked under him. Budgell is best

remembered for his trek across Labrador to join the Canadian Army during the Second World War. When the Hudson's Bay Company closed the post he operated at Davis Inlet, he decided to enlist, and in what was surely one of the most unusual enlistment marches in the annals of the Canadian Army, he trekked to Sept-Îles, a distance of some two thousand kilometres. For three months he travelled with a party of twenty-five Innu who were returning home. "This was just a normal trip for them," said Budgell, " they were walking home after hunting and trapping in the north, the way we would walk home from a pub." Every night the party slept on spruce boughs on the snow, a roaring fire warming feet that were wet and cold from the abundant spring water. The final straw came when after walking two thousand kilometres through some of the most challenging terrain in the country, Budgell was thrown in "the clink" because he was an alien. Labrador and Newfoundland were not yet part of Canada, and since he was without proper papers the authorities, perhaps fearing foreign espionage, initially resisted Budgell's heroic attempt to serve his king – which he went on to do with great distinction.

Budgell spoke the Innu language and had a great insight into Innu thinking and culture. In a letter to Rockwood in 1958 he outlined a plan for taking the Innu to the interior by aircraft to fish. It is clear that he had consulted with them:

First, and perhaps most important, the Indians are enthusiastic ... our problem won't be to persuade men to go ... I discussed the possibility of a supply cache inland with Joseph Ashini and several other influential members of the band; they agreed together a supply cache would be best suited at Michikamau ... The Indians told me on Grand River there is, or has been, these past three years a supply cache operated by a Seven Islands Indian (Matthew Antoni). Supplies are flown in from Seven Islands and production of beaver and mink is high ...

Fish was selling in Montreal in 1951 at 90 cents a pound ... We could combine commercial fishing and fur trapping ... The market I have in mind for Indian production would be Goose Airport where fish flown from Halifax is retailing at 80 and 90 cents a pound.[13]

Already the Innu were well along their tragic slide into dependency. In 1930 those in the south had been persuaded by Father O'Brien to leave their summer camping ground at North West River and move to the south side of the river, where the community of Sheshatshiu is today. After the Hudson's Bay Company closed most of its posts in the 1940s, the Innu became more and more dependent on the post at North West River, more dependent on the company's credit, and more dependent on the church, on the IGA hospital, and on government charity. Until then, they had been spending about ten months in the woods of central Labrador. In the mid-1950s Father Joseph Pirson began to teach a mainstream curriculum, and in 1960 a school was built. There was no attempt to accommodate the hunting cycle, and the withdrawal of family allowances was threatened if parents did not send their children to school. Brighter young people such as Bart Jack and Ben Michel were sent away to J.R. Smallwood Collegiate in Wabush, while others attended Catholic schools in St John's. In 1962, 68 per cent of Innu families were still leaving for traditional hunting grounds, but by 1967 the effects of government and church policies were obvious: that year, only two families and four men left the village to hunt. The longer time the Innu spent in the community meant more frequent contact with diseases, especially tuberculosis, which took their lives and weakened their social fabric.

It was the growth of this social deterioration that Rockwood and Budgell had sought to arrest in the fifties. Budgell had believed that with an initial capital expenditure of $2000, the plan could work and the Innu would eventually become self-supporting in their traditional habitat doing what they did best. Indeed, Quebec Innu were already in the area, as his letter indicates, no doubt occupied in the same way. But the government cancelled Budgell's plan when there was a cost overrun. Budgell resigned in disgust. It is not clear who was responsible for cancelling the plan. Apparently, the decision came from someone higher than Rockwood. The loss of the Labrador Innu was the gain of the Quebec Inuit. Budgell moved to George River, north of Labrador's Lake Michikamau, where he had proposed to begin the Innu venture, and there he helped start the first Inuit co-operative in Canada. In 1959 the co-op bought equipment with $12,000 borrowed from the federal Eskimo Loan Fund and began to put in place a plan roughly similar to the one Budgell had proposed to the Government of Newfoundland.

What might have been different if Budgell's plan had been adopted and he had stayed to implement it? The catching and shipping of whitefish from Lobstick Lake and other places was tried again in the 1970s and is being considered once more at the present time. The shipping of arctic fish to world markets works elsewhere in the North and could work in Labrador with sound planning and management. In the seventies Budgell resurfaced in the province as executive secretary of the Royal Commission on Labrador. Perhaps if Rockwood had had more men like Budgell, or if the government had listened more closely to their policy suggestions, the trauma that gripped both Innu and Inuit communities at the end of the century might have been avoided to some extent.

In 1954 a federal-provincial health agreement allocated more funds for the Innu and the Inuit. At the insistence of Father Pirson and Dr Paddon, houses were constructed at Sheshatshiu for the elderly and disabled. By 1963 fourteen permanent homes had been built in the hope that they would foster a greater attachment to the community. Attempts to employ the Innu for wages as firefighters, in uranium exploration, and at the hospital were only marginally successful. Only a handful of Innu, such as those with the provincial forestry department at Otter Creek, held regular jobs, and only one, Edward Rich, worked at Goose Bay airport for any length of time.

Until the beginning of the twentieth century, the hunting grounds of the Naskapi had centred around Indian House Lake on the George River, where the people gathered every fall to await the caribou on their migration route. There, the Innu who used the trading post at Davis Inlet had contact with Naskapi from the Fort Chimo area (Waska neken Innu). After the caribou herds changed their migration route about 1916, near starvation drove the Innu to depend even more heavily on the trading posts. But their situation continued to deteriorate. Those who had gravitated to Fort Chimo were moved to Schefferville in 1956, where they settled near the Montagnais village that had been established there six years earlier by Father Cyr. These two bands continued to live together until 1981, when the federal government resettled the Naskapi on a reserve near Peter Lake, nineteen kilometres away, where they are today. Thus, the barren ground Innu had been permanently split into two camps.

At Davis Inlet a Catholic priest had made annual summer visits since 1927, and one was posted there permanently after 1952. At the instigation of Father Peters, the new village of Davis Inlet (Utshimassit) was built between 1966 and 1969. After the fur trade collapsed, although there was improved health care for the people of Davis Inlet, there was a greater dependence on food from the government store. Despite good intentions, settlement brought a tragic decline in the Innu lifestyle. Houses lacked running water or electricity, and, incredibly, there was no adequate water supply at the site chosen – a major factor in the later decision of the community to move to Natuashish (Sango Bay). On this site, which is closer to traditional Innu hunting grounds, (the old Davis Inlet village was on an island), a completely new and modern community is arising on which the Government of Canada has already spent about $150 million. Health problems had occurred among the young as a result of drug and alcohol abuse. Later, young Innu switched to glue and gas sniffing, as the dramatic TV footage of the tragic fire of 1992 recorded, when Davis Inlet children were trapped in a burning house. Whether the move to a new home will change the lives of the Davis Inlet Innu for the better remains to be seen.

Their society had long been fragmenting. The Innu had lost their economic and social decision making in return for welfare. Men, traditionally the hunters and providers, no longer had a role within society and turned to alcohol to compensate for their loss of dignity. As government aid increased, so did alcoholism, family violence, and suicide. There was also bitterness towards the Euro-Canadians who dominated the village.

In *Struggling with My Soul*, George Rich describes the challenges faced by the new community: "We had to get used to new neighbours. There were teachers, nurses, store managers, and other new people to work with the Innu. These people were all white. The only jobs available to Innu were as janitors in the school and as relief workers for the hydro generating station. The lucky ones who had been obedient to the missionary got the first chance at these jobs ... The restless Innu could not easily turn away from their way of life and move to a more permanent settlement. Almost immediately they began to turn to alcohol."[14] In his moving personal testimony Rich describes his struggle against the effects of sexual abuse and the drinking that led to his marriage breakup. Only after somehow finding the strength to break the hold that alcohol had on him did Rich find the way ahead. Many of his fellow Innu, both young and old, still struggle against the trauma that post-nomadic life imposed on them. Only lately have there been signs that some healing may be about to begin.

The bitterness of the Innu was fuelled by the construction of the Churchill Falls project, which caused hundreds of waterways to be diverted and more than 1300 square kilometres of forest to be flooded. Prime hunting areas at Michikamau and Ossokmanuan lakes vanished beneath Smallwood Reservoir. The Lac Joseph caribou herd, once numbering about 5000, lost key parts of its range, including a major calving ground west of Michikamau Lake. As well, burial sites, holding perhaps thousands of years of Innu history, were wiped out. Campsites and bones over one thousand years old – valuable evidence in a later Innu land claim – disappeared.

During the 1950s and 1960s Brinco, the international consortium that Smallwood had created for the development of provincial resources, explored large sections of Labrador. Using North West River as its base of operations, its subsidiary Brinex hired Labrador men to work as labourers, cooks, and prospectors. In 1956 uranium deposits were discovered at Kitts Pond and Michelin Lake in Kaipokok Bay. Expectations were high that mining would begin, and by 1975 plans were being considered to open mines at both places. But there was a great deal of opposition all along the coast on environmental grounds, and the project, being far from the fluctuating markets, did not go ahead. As we have seen, Confederation had brought with it the Canadian social safety net. Meanwhile, in the Lake Melville area and elsewhere on the coast north of the Straits, defence installations provided employment for local Labradorians. In the north the government provided a support base for the communities and tried to stimulate employment.

The South Coast

On the south coast life after Confederation continued much as it had been, dependent almost exclusively on the fishery. As we have seen, in the nineteenth century more and more Newfoundland ships sailed to the Labrador coast, and some of the fishermen stayed. These settlers developed a system that Prince Dyke has called "seasonal transhumance." In effect, this involved having two homes: one on the coast or the outer islands for the summer when the fish were running, and one in a bay for the winter, where there was a supply of wood and game and some shelter from the wind and cold of the North Atlantic. Fishermen and their families lived at Cape Charles, for example, for the summer months, moving into Lodge Bay, Cartwright's old home, for the winter.

Dependent as they were on the fortunes of the fishery, life was a struggle, made all the more difficult by what John Kennedy of Memorial University has noted as isolation from important institutions. In the nineteenth century, people living along the coastline from St Lewis to Spotted Island were far from merchants, churches, and schools. This portion of Labrador had received few services from the Newfoundland government except for those that were provided for the transient fishermen. By the summer of 1864 there was a day school at Battle Harbour, and the following summer schools appeared at Cape Charles and Venison Tickle. The state paid the itinerant teachers and supplied books for a curriculum of arithmetic, writing, and reading the Scriptures. This system continued into the early twentieth century, when it was replaced by boarding schools. Other services were provided mainly for the Newfoundland fleet. In 1867 Judge Pinsent had recommended a postal service and that year the *Ariel* was dispatched to the south coast with mail. The first lighthouses north of the Straits were erected at Double Island and Indian Harbour. About 1907 the government took over the Marconi wireless stations on the coast.

While the prime object of the fishermen's attention was cod, a herring fishery flourished on the south coast from the 1930s to the 1950s, creating a source of employment for many local people. Francis Banikhin from St John's started a fish plant at Cape Charles and later at Banikhin's Island about 1937, his wages attracting workers from as far away as L'Anse-au-Loup. But the plant burned down in 1957 and Banikhin retreated to Newfoundland. He was a Ukrainian Jew who had come to St John's in 1917. Seized with the economic potential of Labrador, he proposed to Hope Simpson that the Grand Falls of Labrador be developed by Jewish immigrants. Once a connection had been established to the coast, he foresaw the development of millions of dollars' worth of hidden resources, financed and operated by German Jews. Although Hope Simpson supported the proposal and transmitted it to London, Thomas Lodge, another commissioner, called Banikhin's proposal impractical and P.A. Clutterbuck, the Newfoundland expert in the Dominions Office, was far more scathing in his denunciation. Power development in Labrador would have to wait for money that was politically correct.

The depletion of the Norwegian whale stocks led to an expansion of whaling along the coast. A station at Antle's Cove, near Cape Charles, opened in 1904, followed by Hawke Harbour in 1905 and Gready in 1927. Norwegians owned and controlled most of the southeastern Labrador whaling stations, and Norwegians took most of the higher-paying and more desirable jobs. Nevertheless, they were generally well received and brought some of the first wage labour to the south coast. But the fifty years of whaling had little long-term impact on the communities of the region.

Some trapping was carried on in the area, and in fact a fur trader emerged who became a rival of the Hudson's Bay Company. Samuel Butler Russell Fequet, a native of Old Fort on the Quebec North Shore, opened a post at Paradise River in 1900. Later, he bought the premises of Hunt and Henley at Pack's Harbour and in 1918 relocated his business to Cartwright. In the 1930s he opened a store in North West River, which was still operating in 1941. Today, Howard Fequet, also a successful entrepreneur, operates out of the old store of S. Fecquet and Sons at Cartwright, part of which he has turned into a local museum.

In 1915 Grenfell persuaded Clarence Birdseye from New York to set up fox farming at the abandoned post of Reveillon Frères at

Muddy Bay. (It was while he was in Labrador that Birdseye developed his method of "quick freeze" from watching local fishermen, such as Garland Lethbridge of Paradise River, fishing through the ice in winter and spring.) Birdseye's fox-farming operation and similar ones by other companies provided competition for the fur of wild animals, and pressure from transient fur buyers led to conflict among the local trappers. As a result, both Sam Fequet and his sister's son, Steve Macdonald, travelled the coast to try and drum up business. For a while the competition improved the market greatly, but the First World War ended Birdseye's operation. In any case, fur trapping on the south coast never became central to the economy as it did in the Lake Melville area.

As in the north, resettlement occurred in southeastern Labrador. As we have seen, some people moved to Port Hope Simpson when the woods industry started up, though in most cases the move was not permanent. Then, with the construction of Goose Bay, some were lured there by the offer of wage labour and many stayed to make it their home. Some voluntary moving had always taken place, and this continued after Confederation. People from West Bay moved to North River in Sandwich Bay, and those in Otter Bay moved to Norman Bay in order to be nearer better wood and water. Prior to any government resettlement incentives, people moved to Cartwright from Sandy Hill, Goose Cove, Dove Brook, and Spotted Island. The places most people went to were Cartwright, Mary's Harbour, Charlottetown, and Port Hope Simpson.

With the development of the government resettlement policy, many more moved. In fact, between 1967 and 1970 one-quarter of all the people in southeastern Labrador were resettled. This produced new social divisions in the host communities, putting space and educational pressures on schools and reducing traditional harvesting areas. All did not move within the region. For instance, some of the Stone family from Henley Harbour moved to Corner Brook, returning seasonally to their fishing rooms. On the other hand, the families at Black Tickle, which owed its origins to the Irish immigration to Newfoundland and was predominantly Roman Catholic, were dissuaded from moving on the grounds that this would result in religious conflict. Consequently, Black Tickle remains today on the edge of the Atlantic, struggling for survival against the fluctuations in marine resources.

As in the north, resettlement in the south had a significant social impact. Just as there was a Hebron section in Makkovik, so was there a Batteau and a Spotted Island section in Cartwright. At Mary's

Harbour the river divides the older north side from the newer neigh-bourhood, where some people from Battle Harbour and Indian Cove resettled. All this movement increased dependency on government programs of one kind or another.

Farther south, in the Straits, the descendants of settlers from the Channel Islands and Newfoundland harvested the resources of the sea, with all its vicissitudes. Cod fishing and sealing brought cash, as did trapping. The people's diet was supplemented by preserved wild berries such as partridgeberries (known as red berries in other parts of Labrador), bakeapples, and wild birds in season. There was also some subsistence farming and animal husbandry. In the 1930s Sam Jones purchased the first cow from Canon Richards in Flowers Cove, and others bought hens for a supply of chickens and eggs. Although there were reports of poverty, the culture of sharing ensured that people lived reasonably well in spite of the ups and downs of the cod fishery. In the early part of the twentieth century the main exporter of fish in the western part of the Straits was Job Brothers at Blanc Sablon, while farther east the Red Bay co-op was the major outfitter and provider. The latter had been formed at a meeting chaired by Levi Pike in 1896. From time to time, other fish buyers appeared: the Penneys, the Reids, and Matt Organ from Bonne Bay.

As in the north, the Grenfell Mission filled gaps left by an absent government. Nurses and doctors attended to medical needs, but the IGA was also deeply involved in education, a jurisdiction that was dominated by the churches on the Island. The teachers recruited by IGA were volunteers who paid their own travel expenses and were expected to collect school supplies.

The 1927 boundary decision created problems both for the settlers in the Straits and for the Government of Newfoundland. Historically, the communities of Blanc Sablon in Quebec and L'Anse-au-Clair in Labrador had been neighbours who considered themselves all part of one shore. L'Anse-au-Clair and Forteau people had travelled reg-ularly to Blanc Sablon for supplies. But the borderline drawn between the two brought a customs post and duties on goods and materials that previously had slipped back and forth easily. After the boundary decision, life became a game of trying to outwit the Ranger, the enforcer of customs duties on behalf of the Newfoundland govern-ment. Bessie Flynn, OC, an outstanding woman who made her own contribution to Labrador in a number of ways, recalled that in order to avoid the sharp eyes of the law, people from Forteau would often return from Blanc Sablon after midnight, stopping their engines at a point of land to the west of Forteau and rowing into the harbour.

Sergeant Ed Delaney, a Ranger sent to the Straits in 1945, took it upon himself to do his own survey of conditions. Not only did he see the difficulties that the border created for local residents but he accused the Straits merchants of exploiting local people with inflated prices, and he recommended that the government ensure that there was no difference between prices in Newfoundland and Labrador. CBC writer and broadcaster Doug Letto stated that Delaney's report was a "stinging indictment both of the role played by the merchants and the complicity of government officials such as the Ranger and the Customs Inspector, to whom these revelations could not have been news."[15]

Delaney also found an absence of education, health, and mail services in the Straits. He was particularly critical of the education system: "Education in the Straits is not making any progress. The Government is pouring in money for nothing ... Graded teachers are loath to come here and every fall most of the schools do not get Teachers until there is absolutely no chance of their getting a school on the island of Newfoundland. There are 12 or more settlements in the section from Red Bay to L'Anse au Clair, in most of the settlements there are several bright pupils who cannot go beyond Grade X because that is the limit of the teacher's education."[16]

It is clear that Delaney was one Ranger who more than adequately filled the vacuum left by the absence of political representation. He understood the reality that Labrador was still a territory to be exploited by the government in St John's and said so in no uncertain terms. His solution to the teacher supply problem – a system of bonuses – was ahead of its time; it became policy many years later. The same difficulty in acquiring qualified teachers on the Labrador coast continued. As superintendent of education, I found myself in Boston in 1970, just after the Bruins had won the Stanley Cup. Because provincial bonuses had not been enough to attract Newfoundland teachers to the region of Labrador north of the Straits, I was there, with the help of the Rev. Bob Bryan of the Quebec-Labrador Mission Foundation, hiring zealous, philanthropic graduates of New England prep schools, who otherwise might have served with the Peace Corps or become WOPS with the Grenfell Mission.

Like other areas of Labrador, the Straits had voted overwhelmingly for Confederation. For those who had lived next to Blanc Sablon and the Quebec North Shore, Canada was nothing new and had always been a neighbour. But Confederation immediately made life easier. Not only did the customs duties disappear, but the Canadian social safety net made life more secure.

After Confederation, government attention was focused on the fishery, still the economic mainstay of the area. A committee of bureaucrats found the existence of an old problem: the high cost of salt, with which the fish were preserved. The committe reported that ways and means should be found of easing this burden on fishermen of the Labrador coast. Of course, the cost of doing business on the coast is higher than elsewhere, a problem experienced throughout the North. Yet with the possible exception of Guy Earle, who purchased the Battle Harbour property from Baine Johnston, most merchants were either unwilling or unable to make a supply of salt available to Labrador fishermen at a reasonable price. In the late 1970s the federal government created the Canadian Saltfish Corporation, a crown corporation serving the fishermen of eastern Quebec, northern Newfoundland, and Labrador. Through agents, this body supplied salt to the fishermen, bought all salt fish they had for sale, and held it until the marketplace offered a fair price, thereafter returning any gains to the fishermen. Operated by a series of considerate and experienced managers, the corporation served the coast well until the 1980s, when it overextended itself by ventures into the fresh fish trade.

This kind of co-operative effort appears to be the model that works on the Labrador coast, as the experience of the Labrador Shrimp Company and Torngat Fisheries will attest. More recently, the long-time Labrador fisherman and fisheries adviser Max Short recommended the Northern Coalition, a consortium of co-ops in northern and southern Labrador, northern Quebec, and Baffin Island. Created in 1997, this body has taken advantage of increased shrimp allocations to return even greater profits to its members for reinvestment in other ventures.

LABRADOR WEST: THE MINERS

The second major demographic shift in Labrador came with the development of the iron mines in the west, a development, as we have seen, that had its roots in the days of the Commission of Government. But now the major population influences came from the island of Newfoundland and from Quebec rather than from Labrador itself.

At about the time of Donald Smith, Louis Babel had noted the iron ore potential of Labrador. Babel was a Swiss Oblate ministering to the Innu. For several years after 1866 he reported that an area near Lake Winokapau was *abondant en minéraux* and an area between Nativity Lake and Menihek River was *abondant en fer*. Albert Peter Low, who travelled and mapped extensively the Labrador area on behalf of the Geological Survey of Canada and who left us detailed records of his travels between 1892 and 1895, used Babel's notes as the basis for more thorough and fruitful research. Low travelled some 11,000 kilometres by canoe, dog team, boat, and foot over the Labrador Trough, a half-moon reaching from the northern tip of Ungava south to Schefferville and Labrador West, and thence to Lake Mistassini. He noted iron formations in the Dyke Lake area, about 160 kilometres northeast of Wabush Lake and along the Koksoak River in the Ungava Bay area. The base maps he prepared remained the only ones available for the next forty years, and they have never been entirely supplanted. While Low's main concern was describing the huge deposits of iron-bearing sediment, he predicted the partnership of iron ore and hydropower long before it actually came about.

In 1936 Claude Howse, then assistant government geologist – who was to play an important role not only in the development of iron ore but in the Churchill Falls project – received a request from the Weaver Coal Company of Montreal for a prospecting concession of some 50,000 square kilometres in western Labrador. Howse recommended it, and the concession was granted. Weaver, soon to become Labrador Mining and Exploration, retained J.A. Retty and Julius M. Cohen to look for precious metals. But it was Mathieu André, an Innu guide from Sept-Îles, who in 1937 alerted Retty to a mineral showing in the area of Sawyer Lake, eighty kilometres northwest of Churchill Falls. Retty at once recognized a remarkable iron ore deposit – hematite mixed with a little magnetite or sulphur, premium quality for making steel. The samples contained 69.7 per cent iron ore. While Quebec claimed the extensive deposit for its own, in fact it was spread across the boundary of 1927. Mathieu André, who later became chief of the Sept-Îles Innu band, was eventually given a $7000 finder's fee, a far cry from what aboriginals will undoubtedly receive today from the discovery of nickel in northern Labrador or the development of the Lower Churchill.

In 1942 Jules Timmins acquired Labrador Mining and Exploration, formed the Hollinger North Shore Exploration Co. Ltd., and interested the American businessman George Humphrey, of the Hanna Company, in the deposits. That same year a base camp was set up at Havre-St-Pierre and further exploration was carried out. The initial party included Dr A.E. Moss, a geologist who was to have a long and successful career with the Iron Ore Company of Canada.[17]

It was C.D. Howe who pointed out to Jules Timmins the necessity of a railroad for bringing the ore to tidewater. Howe suggested as well that Timmins consider hiring Bill Durrell, who at the time was supervising construction of Goose Airport. Timmins did, and in 1948 Durrell began planning and overseeing the construction of the

Quebec North Shore and Labrador Railway, linking the port and Innu village of Sept-Îles with the iron ore deposits at Knob Lake.

It was a huge and imaginative project for its time, and the challenge of building such a railway seemed to attract some unusual men. The workers included Dave Nichols, later president of Loblaws and President's Choice; Andrew Sarlos, in time a prominent investment banker; and Peter Gzowski, the future writer and broadcaster, whose father Harold was a superintendent on the project. The railway was completed with no government subsidies at a cost of $350 million. Tremendous difficulties had been overcome. Mountains, rivers, and lakes were crossed, and blackflies, bitter cold, snow, rain, and vicious storms were endured. New construction methods had been devised, including the use of aircraft. The project served as the setting for Hammond Innes's novel *The Land God Gave Cain*.

The line crossed the Moisie River, a prime waterway of the Innu in their nomadic journeys across the peninsula. There is no evidence that they were ever informed, let alone consulted, nor was there any consideration of the effect the railroad would have on wildlife, particularly the caribou. These were the days before native rights and environmental assessment panels. Later, when the time came to dam the Lower Churchill, the Innu remembered, and they ensured that their rights and environmental protection were fully considered.

After the railway was completed, the mining areas straddling the Quebec-Labrador boundary were developed. In 1949 the Iron Ore Company of Canada (IOC) was formed after 362 million tonnes were outlined, and in 1954 production began at Knob Lake. Terminal facilities were built at Sept-Îles, from where the ore could be shipped up the St Lawrence to the Lower Great Lakes ports, south to the American ports, or overseas. Market conditions were good, and the IOC shareholders were intent on getting the maximum return on their investment. In 1957 a record 10.8 million tonnes was shipped from Sept-Îles.

Labrador City

In 1958 the Iron Ore Company announced that it would develop the Carol Project under manager Ab Moss. Carol was the name of the wife of IOC's geologist, Buzz Neil, and IOC preferred to keep the name. But it lost the debate. Joe Smallwood had his way and Labrador City was born. Work was begun on the Smallwood mine and the pilot pellet plant. Initially, the company decided to build the pellet plant in Sept-Îles. However, when Smallwood was informed, he threatened to tell the whole world why this was such an extremely poor choice.

As a result, the pellet plant was built in Labrador City. It was Small-wood two; company no score.

When Charlie Jubber flew down from Schefferville with a gang of men early in 1959 to set up the company stores, there were only about fifteen people in a camp of mud and dust. The Hudson's Bay Company, which would soon be replaced by Bowring Brothers of St John's, had a store in a caboose near the railway terminal. But facilities were primitive. Water was pumped from Wabush Lake, and there was a community toilet (heated), with six seats on either side. Accommodation was in bunkhouses.

Gradually others arrived to work on the project. Evelyn Watts (who later became Mrs Charlie Jubber) had been with the Grenfell Mission in Happy Valley. Having answered an ad in the *Evening Telegram*, she arrived in 1960, the first nurse, indeed the first woman, at the camp-site. Later, at the urging of Ab Moss, she recruited her sister June and her cousin Rhyna McLean. Both were from North West River. Evelyn was the daughter of Jack Watts, the highly respected and effective general superintendent of the Grenfell Mission and the right-hand man of Mina Paddon and her son Tony. Rhyna McLean was the granddaughter of Malcolm McLean of Kenemish, a pre-eminent Labradorian of his day. They were the first indigenous Labradorians, and they immediately ran into a strong prejudicial attitude. Having a drink with the Mountie, Guy D'Avignon, at the hotel in Wabush, Watts and McLean were taken for natives – "Eskimos" – by the bartender and asked to leave. Watts fired off an angry letter to the *Evening Telegram*, which had the desired effect: in future alcohol would be served to "natives."

From the beginning, Quebec and Newfoundland companies vied for business. Quebec companies such as Bechtel and Richard and B.A. Ryan had a previous history with the company. On the other hand, it may have been difficult to get Island contractors to bid. The Island was far away, and the only practical way to reach it was by air. Quebec goods and materials were closer and could be transported easily on the Quebec North Shore and Labrador Railway. The Newfoundland Tractor Company was invited by IOC to furnish their Caterpillar equipment for the site, but the Pippy family decided not to accept. Subsequently, the Hewitt Company from Sept-Îles was given the contract, and it has thrived in the area to this day. On the other hand, Bowrings was there from the beginning, as was Ashley Electric with its hard-working and capable foreman, Grayson Crawley. In Wabush the Crosbie family was heavily involved almost from the beginning. Ches Crosbie, who earlier had an interest in the Ashuanipi Fish Camp, later bought the Wabush Hotel as well as the shopping centre in Wabush, which included an Ayre's outlet, a drug store, and other businesses.

In 1960 sixteen houses went up on Marconi Street in Labrador City, just down the street from the Catholic parish hall, the first church structure in town. There Father Roussel, known locally as Father Pinball, an Oblate from Quebec, set up his pinball machines, pool tables, and slot machines to raise money for the church. When the time came for mass, the curtains were pulled over the pinball machines in what one local wag described as an obvious "undercover operation." Marie Greene House remembers her confession ending abruptly when the strains of "Kitty Wells" drifted from beyond the curtains. "Really, Father," she protested, "it isn't my kind of music." Eventually, Our Lady of Perpetual Help was built out of local fieldstone, the $600,000 needed having been raised from the proceeds of the gaming devices, as well as from the first taxi service and a snack bar that attracted hungry miners. At one point, Father Pinball's payroll was second only to that of IOC. Soon the Anglicans and United Church set up a combined operation with more conservative funding methods but with a racy name – The Joint. Francis Buckle, originally from Forteau, was one of the early ministers. (He recently retired in Labrador West as archdeacon of Labrador.) The Salvation Army and Pentecostals came later.

Labrador City was no ordinary Labrador or Newfoundland town. People came from all over Canada and all over the world. And it was full of young people, who soon realized that they had to be their own grandparents and quickly bonded to build a unified and vibrant community. From the beginning, although Smallwood kept a tight rein on development in both Labrador City and Wabush, the government was a marginal player. The company was all things to all people.

Labrador City grew rapidly. More and more houses were built as more and more families poured in, mostly from the Island. For some, it was a far cry from what they had left behind. Two young brothers who had never seen a flush toilet before kept pushing the plunger and running to the basement to find out where the water went. Aircraft, both large and small, were landing on the dirt strip from Montreal and St John's. A liquor store was authorized. So was the steelworkers' union. IOC paid its teachers $5000 more per year than school systems on the Island, so highly qualified teachers set to work immediately to initiate an enhanced version of the Newfoundland curriculum. Vernon Snelgrove was brought in from the Island to set up the school system. Dorice Marcil, who had had experience in the North, including at Schefferville, was the first Catholic teacher. A communications tower was put in place for radio and telephones, and the railway was completed to the Wabush Narrows in 1960, with the acting mayor, Art Rendell, driving in the last spike. By March of that year there were four hundred people; by June there were eight hundred.

IOC constructed a completely modern, environmentally attractive town out of the wilderness, where houses were rented and sold to employees at extremely favourable terms. As well, the company built a hockey rink, curling rink, golf course, and ski hill, in addition to such necessities as water and sewer systems. The influx from other parts of the province was from the Island rather than from Labrador. Not a single Innu was ever employed in the area, and few Inuit were. In the early years the Innu were not prepared for such employment. The first Innu school was completed at North West River in 1959. The previous year an office of DNLA had been established there, although Indian agents had been among the Innu of the North Shore for some time. But transport from east to west was a problem as well. Labrador was the hinterland not of St John's but of Montreal. Walter Rockwood pointed out to the government that it was easy for the Innu in Seven Islands to access the iron ore development at Schefferville either by train or air, but it was virtually impossible for the Innu of Labrador, who had also used this area traditionally. Of course, the establishment of Eastern Provincial Airways ameliorated to a great degree air transport from Goose Bay to Labrador West. But the problems of transport for those who lived on the north and south coasts persisted. There were no scheduled flights on the coast at this time, and it is a mystery how people from the coast found their way to Labrador West and Churchill Falls. The fact is that few did, except for those from the Labrador Straits.

The official opening of the IOC mine was planned for July 1962. Smallwood insisted that no high-ranking Quebec or federal officials be invited – a difficult situation for the company because it had received considerable federal assistance. Smallwood was to set off the first blast to open the mine named in his honour. Ken Kidder (whose daughter Margo was later to play Lois Lane to Christopher Reeves's Superman) was the explosives engineer. He had the electricians set up a system whereby when Smallwood pushed the plunger at his location, a light would go on in an underground tunnel where the blaster and his assistant would detonate the blast. But the official party was late, and the blaster and his helper had become bored and inattentive. As a result, for about three or four seconds after Smallwood pushed the plunger nothing happened. After what must have seemed an eternity, the blast went off. A relieved Smallwood commented that he had always wanted to move mountains.

Wabush

Wabush Mines came about in a very different way. John C. Doyle flew to Newfoundland in 1952 in search of business for his company, Canadian Javelin, and his newly acquired Boon-Strachan Coal Company. His timing was impeccable. By coincidence, he happened to sit next to Claude Howse, who in the course of conversation revealed how IOC had inadvertently transferred back to the province a 6200 km² strip, rich in iron ore, to the south of Wabush Lake. Doyle suddenly lost all interest in coal.

Following Doyle's approach, Smallwood, on the advice of Howse, handed the land over to Nalco, a company he had created for the development of the province's resource potential. Doyle offered $250,000 in cash – as someone said, the first time the province had got money instead of giving it. But Doyle was an outsider trying to break into the closed mining club. When he failed to interest North Americans in the project, he tried Europeans. In the meantime, Smallwood helped by opening the provincial treasury and allowing Doyle to build a spur line connecting the Quebec North Shore and Labrador Railway to the mine.

Eventually the North Americans came to the table. In return for the Wabush Ore property, the consortium of American, German, and Italian companies, as well as Stelco and Dofasco, agreed to give Doyle a $2.5 million down payment and annual royalties of $1.8 million per year, rising to a maximum of $3.2 million after five years. It was one of the greatest coups in postwar mining. Like IOC, the Wabush company insisted on a pellet plant in Quebec at tidewater. This time Smallwood could not stop it, even with the help of Jack Pickersgill, the federal cabinet minister. The company threatened to move the whole operation to Erie, Pennsylvania, if it could not build the pellet plant on the St Lawrence. Smallwood had lost a round.

Like Labrador City, Wabush started off as a muddy campsite. Previously, several Innu, including Charlie Vollant, had lived there, and they were asked to move to Indian Point; later they moved to Sept-Îles. Nearby, a pilot plant began operation in 1960, and construction started on a stockpiling and shipping facility at Pointe-Noire, Quebec. Soon more trailers appeared around the log cabin of resident manager Jim Robb (its fireplace still stands). Gerry Barriault and other original residents arrived by train or by Eastern Provincial Airways from Newfoundland or by Northern Wings from Sept-Îles.

Trailers housed the bank and the Bell telephone exchange. The hospital was a bunkhouse where John MacGregor, the son of Lolly and Pat, became the first baby born in the new community.

The town grew quickly. By 1963 there was already a housing shortage. The Sir Wilfred Grenfell Hotel was always full, and Tom Gillespie ran a boarding house to take the overflow. Until 1964 many of the workers were transient, and Andy Spracklin remembers many a rowdy night at the local tavern, the Snake Pit, followed by many a tearful morning. The older airstrips were replaced in 1961 by an airport that served the two Labrador towns and the nearby Quebec town of Fermont. But the area was growing so fast that $11 million was required in 1978 to build the present completely modern airport. A shopping plaza was opened in 1965 by Crosbie Enterprises. It contained a liquor store, a pharmacy run by Joe Dicks, a supermarket, a post office, and an outlet of the Newfoundland company, Ayre and Sons.

The Carol Players, who later dominated provincial theatre festivals, were formed in 1964, and that same year Ewart Young began *Dateline Labrador*, a magazine that covered the whole of the territory.[18] The year 1964 also saw the opening of J.R. Smallwood Collegiate, a school that housed separately both the Catholic and Protestant denominations as the Newfoundland law required. In 1967 it captured national attention when *Maclean's* magazine reported that the $2 million school built by Wabush Mines had 36 teachers for the 240 pupils – a teacher for every seven children at a cost of more than $8000 of building per child.

In November 1978 work began on a $4 million industrial park, providing the infrastructure for local businesses and attracting new ones. The fall of 1981 saw the first municipal elections when Derm Flynn became the first elected mayor, followed by Bill Kelly in 1985.

Growth of the Two Towns

The two companies had built two towns six kilometres apart. Both had grown and prospered, becoming one of the major employment centres in the province. Together they contributed substantially more to the per capita portion of the gross provincial product and to tax revenues than any other industrial complex. Labrador City was mining 27 million tonnes per year, from which 9.9 million tonnes of concentrate were produced, and of this 9 million further were processed into pellets. At Wabush 13.6 million tonnes of ore were mined annually, of which 6 million tonnes were moved to Pointe-Noire, processed into pellets, and shipped to steel mills of the Wabush partners.

In the 1960s the population of Labrador City was over 8500, with a work force of 1850; Wabush had 3000 for 900 miners. All were skilled labour – their educational levels were far above the Newfoundland average, and each person was required to upgrade continually. At that time, two-thirds had been born within the province, though not that many were from Labrador itself. While some Labradorians did come seeking work and some of them settled, there was never the influx from the coast to Labrador West that there had been during the construction of Goose Bay.

A young and vigorous entrepreneur class was growing up, seizing initiatives in both wholesale and retail. In Labrador City, Charlie Jubber was the first with a bakery and a drug store; Cyril Fleming began an investment business; Gerry Bailey from Deer Lake started garbage and snow removal. As well, competent law offices were established, notably by the firm of Arthur Miller and Edward Hearn, which has been successfully practising law there for many years. These energetic and enthusiastic young professionals and businessmen, mostly from the Island, built lives for themselves and their communities and gave the area a strong organizational base on which to build.

Gordon Manstan had been in the North before, with the Bay at St-Augustine on the Quebec North Shore. Hired by Bowrings in 1960 for its store at Carol Lake, he later joined IOC, where he worked for twelve years. But he had begun some small businesses of his own and when the opportunity arose to buy the Jubber store, he and his partner, Doug House from Aguathuna on the west coast of the Island, created Houseman Enterprises to operate it. Later, when the Crosbies encountered financial difficulties in 1975, Manstan and House bought their importing and distributing business. Thereafter, they added a retail food business. Manstan and House were both able to provide for their comfortable early retirement with the profits they made.

What had helped Manstan in his decision to leave IOC was a fundamental change in the housing market. Until 1974 the company had owned the houses in Labrador City and had disposed of them to new workers when former employees moved out. But a court case developed when an occupant in the service industry refused to leave. That year, lawyer Ed Hearn discovered that legally, if an occupant had paid rent for a house for seven years, it was possible to offer the bank payment in full and acquire ownership of the house. It was a major breakthrough in public housing and in the life of the town. The court judgment meant that those who lived in company housing could buy their houses rather than building new ones – a prohibitively costly expenditure. The judgment cost the company millions of dollars, and Hearn was for some time persona non grata. But it meant that an entrepreneur class could more easily develop. It also meant that the community was becoming less dependent on the company and more dependent on itself.

Other Newfoundlanders had come to work for IOC. Lester "Ghandi" Coombs was the first personnel manager. Many of the Newfoundlanders were from former American bases on the Island, where jobs had disappeared with the withdrawal of the armed forces. Greg Shepherd from the Stephenville area bought the movie theatre; Ron Whitten operated a gas and oil distribution business; Gerry Hunt from Conche and Roy Hunt from Bonavista Bay began H. and H. Construction. Pat Tarrant left the purchasing office of IOC to start Carol Auto and later had other successful businesses. Most of these entrepreneurs were English-speaking tradesmen of one kind or another who, of necessity, had to deal with Sept-Îles, a predominantly francophone community. But this never seemed to be a drawback; by and large, the two language groups got on well together. Quebec businessmen thrived as well. The St-Maries, who had been there almost from the beginning, expanded into Goose Bay as a result of the announcement in the 1990s that the rich nickel deposits at Voisey,s Bay were to be mined. Flip Dawson from the Eastern Townships had a number of successful enterprises, including a travel agency which had the arresting slogan "Please Go Away."

From the outset, the companies provided almost everything, as well as setting the policies for both the mines and the towns. Even the early local improvement districts were made up of company employees, such as Art Rendell and Bill Campbell or, in Wabush, Mac Moss. In fact, the companies were the government. As they withdrew and as new services were required, the people turned to the provincial government. But the response was not always what they expected. Like many northern hinterlands, Labrador was far from the province's centre of power. For those who usually thought of the island and the province as one and the same, the northern territory was too often out of sight and out of mind as Walter Rockwood in another part of Labrador had pointed out. Moreover, the requirements (for instance, a road to the outside) were now very expensive and would involve a substantial financial investment by the government. Nevertheless, the residents of Labrador West knew that they were contributing substantially to the provincial coffers – more than any other enterprise. Like the fish being taken from the Labrador coast and the wood shipped from Goose Bay, the ore they dug from the ground was, in their view, being shipped out in a relatively raw state primarily for the benefit of someone other than themselves and with too little return to the area.

Even those who had come from the island sensed the gulf that existed between Labrador and Newfoundland – a gulf much wider than the Strait of Belle Isle. Smallwood must have realized this problem, for in 1964 the name "Government of Newfoundland" was changed to "Government of Newfoundland and Labrador," and in the fall of 1966 the premier announced the results of an aerial survey on a proposed 880-kilometre road across Labrador. That same year he created the Department of Labrador Affairs, whose minister, Charles Granger, showed great imagination by calling not only for a road but for a tunnel under the Strait of Belle Isle. Granger had served faithfully and well as the second MP for Grand Falls–White Bay–Labrador and was well respected in the area. Understanding the prickly relationship between the two parts of the province, he acknowledged in a speech to the legislature that "Labrador does not exist for the benefit of Newfoundland and this province does not exist for the benefit of Labrador. We have to work together for this one great task."

Closing the gap in infrastructure was formidable. The task of bridging the psychological gulf was even less easy, as was pointed out in a letter to the editor of the *Evening Telegram* (21 January 1966) from Martin and Fowlow of Labrador City. One of the writers, Bob Martin, later filled with great distinction the position of superintendent of education for Labrador West. The writers charged that for too many people on the Island, Labrador was just a "rich status symbol ... off there somewhere – nice to point to and marvel at the apparently limitless resources there for the taking." The real need, they pointed out, was communications. True, Eastern Provincial Airways provided the best possible service from Labrador to the Island, though the promised fare subsidies had not been forthcoming. But with regard to electronic communications, the English station originated from the Maritimes and rarely covered Newfoundland events: "We know every local event from Nova Scotia, New Brunswick, Prince Edward Island and the Gaspé area – but nothing of the part of Canada to which we are supposed to belong. We do not know if our fellow Newfoundlanders are basking in sunshine or deluged with rain, we get no legislature report – nothing. Is this the way to weld a province together?"

They might have added that the newspaper of choice, because it was so readily available, was the Montreal *Gazette*, not the St John's *Evening Telegram*. Only improvements in communication, they said, could truly make Labrador feel part of the province. "To put 'Province of Newfoundland and Labrador' on licence plates is a proper gesture but has not the same unifying force as communications among people. Let us not accentuate the 'and Labrador' too much but truly make the Province of Newfoundland all embracing." Smallwood knew the problem and tried to assuage feelings, but mostly with gestures that he felt he could afford. More expensive demands would take longer to fulfill, and some clearly could not be accomplished without the will and cooperation of the Government of Canada.

Labrador West had always been of an independent mind. Well educated and with some of the highest salaries anywhere in Canada, with the best facilities and amenities provided by the companies, and within reach of Montreal, it had a mind of its own. This was evident from the beginning. When Smallwood tried to parachute Ted Henley into the new riding for the 1962 election, the locals would have none of it. One evening in the beer hall it was discovered that Charlie Devine had had some experience with politics, so then and there the miners selected him as their man to run against Henley. Out of 1000 votes cast, Devine captured 600 and Henley 400. (The Tories, sensing that discretion was the better part of valour, had not run a candidate.) For the next four years Devine sat in the legislature as an Independent, doing his best to bring Labrador West to the attention of the seat of power.

Some of the issues he dealt with, such as motor vehicle registration, persisted into the 1990s. Private vehicles had been coming into Labrador West since 1963, but obtaining licences from St John's was a costly and agonizingly slow process. Devine finally persuaded the province to send the RCMP a hundred licences for sale in the community. It took him two years to get Magistrate Lloyd Wicks posted to the area so that court cases could be tried efficiently. But his attempt to get a representative of the Department of Mines stationed in the area met with an astonishing lack of success – astonishing because 92 per cent of the minerals exported from the province were coming from Labrador West. In addition, Devine thought there should be a provincial building to show the government presence and to provide convenience for those who had business with it. He was told that the government could not afford it. Not until 1970 was such a building erected. Devine served until 1966, when he was eclipsed by the meteoric rise of Tom Burgess, a charismatic Irishman. Running initially for the Liberal Party, Burgess was destined to flash briefly if uniquely across the political sky.

CHURCHILL FALLS

The next major development that caused a population movement in and to Labrador was the construction of the great power project at Churchill Falls. Foretold for some time by far-sighted Labradorians such as Harry Paddon, an area that had for some time been the preserve of hunters and trappers was harnessed for industrial purposes in the latter part of the twentieth century.

John McLean had been the first non-aboriginal to record seeing the Grand Falls, though obviously the Innu had known of them for centuries. "The noise of the fall has a stunning effect, and ... can be heard for more than 10 miles away, as a deep booming sound," wrote A.P. Low after an arduous voyage inland in 1894. He told a committee of the Canadian Senate that the cataract would generate "several millions of horse-power, and in addition to mechanical horsepower it would also furnish the heat whereby by an electrical process, the reduction of the ore by electricity might be performed. Transportation might also be provided by electric power."

Other explorers included Bryant and Kenaston from the United States, who arrived at North West River in 1891 and persuaded pioneer John Montague to guide them. The journey took them more than four weeks of poling and portaging. But it was worth it, Bryant wrote, for "a single glance showed that we had before us one of the greatest waterfalls in the world." To Bryant's chagrin, Cary and Cole, two recent graduates of Bowdoin College in Maine, had reached the falls before him.[19] As we have seen, the trappers of Lake Melville knew the falls well, particularly Arch Goudie, Henry Baikie, and others who had traplines in the area. Byron Chaulk of Happy Valley, in his song "Sons of Labrador," paid tribute to his father's generation in connection with the falls:

They climbed the highest mountain,
They faced the bitter cold,
To lay another trap line.
The fur it was their gold.
It seemed that nothing stopped them
Bold hearts one and all,
Not raging river, nor rapids
Nor the mighty waterfall.

You ask them why they'd gone there,
Where no one went before.
'Tis easy to explain, sir,
We're sons of Labrador.
Now we don't take the credit
For those men brave and bold.
Their names are stamped upon this land,
Their story has been told.
These men they are our fathers
And we can't ask for more.
Their heritage we proudly claim,
We sons of Labrador.

Smallwood, who had flown over the falls on a return visit from Labrador West, had been struck by their awesome magnitude and was determined to harness them. He included them as a major bargaining chip in his attempt to get British industry to invest in Labrador and exploit its potential. In 1952 he spoke to the British Federation of Industries, calling publicly for a consortium to develop Labrador in the tradition of the Hudson's Bay Company. His timing was right. The headlines he received backed the idea and heralded such a concept as the beginning of the "New Elizabethan Age." Lord Beaverbrook and Sir Eric Bowater helped Smallwood gain access to Sir Winston Churchill, who also liked the concept and put the premier in touch with his financial adviser, Lord Leathers. Smallwood was invited to lunch with the Rothschilds, whose imagination also was stirred by the idea. A consortium was coming together.

Back in Newfoundland, Smallwood passed through the legislature a bill to incorporate the British Newfoundland Development Corporation, which included the Rothschilds, Rio Tinto, Anglo-American of South Africa, and English Electric. Thus Brinco was born, with the rights to some 130,000 square kilometres of Labrador and 26,000 on the Island, including two major power sites and 50 million cords of wood. The consortium committed itself to spend $250,000 per year and to pay the Newfoundland government royalties of 8 per cent. Powerful corporate interests were beginning to exert an influence on the future of Labrador and its people. But twelve years later there was only the Whalesback Mine near Springdale on the Island to show for their efforts. Yet Smallwood never gave up hope. He pushed Brinco and pounded on the doors of New York and London as well as New England. The breakthrough came in 1962. The Diefenbaker government suddenly reversed the long-standing ban on the export of power, while in Sweden technology had conquered the problems of transmitting energy over long distances. At the same time, Consolidated Edison appeared as a customer for half the output of the upper river.

In 1963 Robert Winters, the newly appointed chair of Brinco, assembled a competent managerial team and persuaded some of the top U.S. and Canadian firms to form Acres Canadian Bethel and open negotiations with Newfoundland and Quebec. This was to be the largest industrial project in Canada since construction of the Canadian Pacific Railway, and at the time it was the largest hydroelectric project in the world. In keeping with its stature, Smallwood, to the consternation of many Labradorians, decided to rename the falls and the river after Churchill, who had been his first benefactor.

Brinco wanted to develop the power, reserve a small amount to serve Newfoundland's needs, and sell the remainder to Hydro-

Québec, which would offer its surplus power to Consolidated Edison. By far the hardest part of the negotiations was the relationship between Premier Lesage of Quebec and Smallwood. Smallwood was well aware of the battle that had preceded the 1927 boundary decision and knew very well the recalcitrant attitude of Quebec during the Confederation discussions. The battle over the pellet plant in Wabush only added fuel to a fire already burning well. Earlier, Quebec had nationalized its power, including Shawinigan Engineering, which was a 20 per cent shareholder in Churchill Falls Labrador Corporation, Brinco's operating subsidiary. By this act, Quebec had become a one-fifth shareholder in Newfoundland's most valuable asset. Now Lesage proposed joint development, with the use of Quebec men and materials – a redundant ploy, in view of the future dictates of economics. Later the two met again, and this time the offer was 10,000 square miles (25,900 km²) of northern Quebec territory to Newfoundland in exchange for 10,000 square miles in southern Labrador, which included the headwaters of the five rivers that flowed into the St Lawrence. The offers got nowhere.

When negotiations with Quebec broke off, Smallwood tried to get Quebec to allow the power to flow over transmission lines directly to New York. Again he was denied. Smallwood considered approaching Prime Minister Pearson, with a view to having the federal government intervene to ensure the wheeling of Labrador power through Quebec, but he was dissuaded from doing so, as Philip Smith has noted in *Brinco*:

At around this time, the idea that the federal government might build the transmission line across Quebec was revived and there was discussion in Ottawa as to whether the Prime Minister should write to Lesage on the subject. After consultation with Joey, Jack Pickersgill drafted a letter in which, he suggested, Pearson should say he was "greatly disturbed" at the possible abandonment of the Hamilton Falls scheme, since it was "important to the economic and financial progress of the country as a whole," and should offer to build the line with or without the partnership of Hydro-Québec. "We would not seek," the draft said, "to do this under the constitution by declaring the line a work for the general advantage of Canada, but only by agreement with the government of Quebec." Shown the draft for his comment, Gordon Robertson, Clerk to the Privy Council and Secretary to the Cabinet, objected to this last sentence in particular. "It seems to me," he wrote, "that at this stage, this reminder that the federal government could take constitutional power for this work would be regarded as a threat; moreover, it is a device the government might eventually have to turn to as a last resort and therefore should not be given away in advance ..." Also,

Robertson said, the letter as a whole implied that Pearson was taking Smallwood's side and trying to put pressure on Lesage. Pearson apparently
agreed, because it was never sent.[20]

While the federal government was aware of the needs of Newfoundland and Labrador, it was even more aware of the political influence
of Quebec. Other commodities, such as oil, flow between provinces
with no hindrance. But Churchill Falls was developed in the context
of a national energy policy that allowed Quebec to be the sole dealer
in the export of Labrador energy to the United States. Had Churchill
Falls been an oil project, Canada's energy policy would have permitted the building of an oil pipeline corridor through Quebec, allowing
the benefits to flow to the resource owner. But Hydro-Québec
exported the power to the United States at returns estimated to be in
the order of $400 to $600 million a year.

Next, Smallwood tried to sell the idea that became known as the
"Anglo-Saxon route" – wheeling power across the Strait of Belle Isle
and then across Cabot Strait through the Maritimes and thence to
Consolidated Edison. The cost was prohibitive. In 1964 Smallwood
was sending a signal to Quebec as much as to Labrador when he
changed the name of the government to Newfoundland and Labrador.
"We want the world to know that Labrador belongs to us," he said,
as he continued to taunt Quebec. The war of words continued, with
Smallwood now publicly contemplating the idea of nationalization.
But by now Quebec's power needs had changed. Officials warned
their government that without Labrador power, Quebec would be
rationing electricity by the early 1970s. Consequently, talks resumed.
The price gap was narrowed when the federal government introduced the Public Utilities Income Tax Transfer Act in 1965. It specifically put in place a series of tax rebates that significantly enhanced
the viability of the project.

However, the boundary was still a problem. Lesage announced
that there would be no deal without "a rectification of the Quebec
Labrador boundary." Although Smallwood had, during the course of
negotiations, discussed changing the boundary in an attitude that he
described as "from the lips out," his response at this time was
unprintable. The year 1966 saw the election in Quebec of the Union
National government of Daniel Johnson, which threatened to be even
more difficult than the Liberals had been. Still, Quebec had to have
the electricity, and that same year the Quebec government approved
the purchase of Churchill Falls power. Smallwood had won, though
it would turn out to be a phyrric victory. In any case, for Newfoundland this meant $20 million per year in royalties (one-tenth of the

provincial revenue at that time), a chance to compete for seven thousand jobs a year, and a chance to develop exclusively for the province more than 3 million horsepower on the Lower Churchill.

On 17 July 1967 four hundred and fifty guests were airlifted from Montreal and St John's to witness Smallwood officially opening construction of the project. But, aware that Quebec claimed it had priority on the project for men and materials, Smallwood dispensed with the usual platitudes and in no uncertain terms told all present – and the entire world – where he thought Labrador belonged and whom it would benefit. But the reality was very different. Try as he might, with special training programs and with government officials such as Tom Conway to see to it that Newfoundlanders had a fair chance, in the end few Newfoundland companies were able to handle jobs there. The two-thirds of the workforce that were from Newfoundland were mostly in unskilled jobs. Quebecers held all the supervisory posts and the positions of power. Part of the problem was the desire of Newfoundlanders to go home. Smallwood himself said in 1966: "Newfoundlanders must stop this miserable business of working in Labrador only for the summer." To make it easier for those on the Island to travel to and from Labrador, Smallwood inaugurated a subsidy on Eastern Provincial Airways.

Whether the subsidy was available to Labradorians is open to question. Hiring was done through a central office in St John's, and the round-trip subsidy was available for those who "originated" there. Dick Budgell of North West River claims he did not get subsidized for travelling back to Goose from Churchill Falls, nor did Clayton Montague. The royal commission dealt in its report with the issue of hiring Labradorians, although not with the question of subsidy. It contended that the absence of any Manpower (the name of the Department of Human Resources in the 1970s) office in central Labrador, and the consequent lack of information about employment opportunities in Labrador West, was reflected in the very small number of people from central and coastal Labrador who found employment in the mines and at Churchill Falls. Following establishment of the Manpower offices, the needs of the people in Happy Valley–Goose Bay were met in a limited way, while people living on the coast were virtually as badly off as before. Evidently, the people who lived closest to the development – some of whom had an association with the area going back generations, if not centuries – had great difficulty accessing the new jobs.

The situation had been different in 1961 during construction of Twin Falls, near Arch Goudie's trapline on the Unknown River. The purpose of the project was to supply power to the iron mines.

Brinco's recruiting officer, Arthur Cockrill, had been convinced that if he hired local people, they would stay around for a long time as permanent residents. Consequently, his assistant Sel Delehey had asked Terry Corbett, the magistrate in Goose Bay, to recommend prospective workers. Corbett's neighbour Barbara Budgell suggested he contact Dr Paddon in North West River. As a result, the first workers were from that community. They included Barbara's husband Dick, as well as Stanley Baikie, Winston White (son of Dick White, the northern trader), Max McLean from the family of Malcolm, Harvey Montague and his son Clayton, Treadway Baikie, and Morris Chaulk. Andy Chatwood, who had been the Bay manager in North West River (and later became the MP for Grand Falls–White Bay–Labrador), was in Twin Falls briefly before moving to Wabush. Later, with the closedown of Twin, most of these men moved to Churchill, where many of them lived and worked until retirement. Clearly, the hiring at Twin and the hiring at Churchill were done differently, with different results.

Smallwood's intent to benefit the Island was clear in his statements: "If we are not big enough, if we are not imaginative enough, if we are not daring enough to colonize Labrador, someone else will do it," he said in March 1966. The emphasis was clearly on the Island, though there were people in Labrador who were skilled through working at Goose Bay and the other defence sites on the coast. The question is, Were those in Labrador who wanted jobs treated the same as those on the Island?

In May 1969, three years after the first agreement in principle had been reached, Hydro-Québec signed a final agreement with Brinco. The purchaser of the power and the provider of the completion guarantee, which allowed Brinco to bond-finance over a forty-year period, reserved the right to buy all the electricity produced by Churchill Falls for a period of sixty-five years and committed itself to doing so. The contract provided for a fixed price of three cents per kilowatt hour for the first forty years. But thereafter, the contract required a slightly lower price for the remaining twenty-five years. This provision was beyond anything called for by the bond financing. In fact, it would lead inevitably to the insolvency of the project and the necessity for cash infusions by Hydro-Québec, which in turn would result in the takeover of Churchill Falls. Brinco felt that it had no choice but to agree to the demands of the twenty-five-year extension to the year 2041. For the people of the province, this issue, more than any other, symbolizes the unfairness of the contract.

Newfoundland did retain the right to use up to 300 of the 5200 megawatts, a provision that eventually saw the power from Churchill

Falls lighting the streets and homes of Happy Valley–Goose Bay and North West River. But apart from the jobs they obtained, this was really the only benefit that Labradorians saw from the development of a river that some of them had known and used for generations. Four years later, the oil crisis completely changed the situation and the price of hydroelectric power started to climb. The return to Quebec escalated while, because of the dictates of the agreement, the return to Newfoundland remained the same. As a result, Quebec took in something like eighty times what Newfoundland did. And for the latter part of the contract, Newfoundland would take in even less. Moreover, the contract could not be changed. Any change to it would allow Hydro-Québec to take over the development.

In the following years a number of attempts were made to redress the inequity. In 1976 a dispute between Quebec and Newfoundland over the recall of power was decided in Quebec's favour. Later, the provincial and federal governments set up the Lower Churchill Development Corporation, with an investment of $15 million, but failed to trigger action at Gull Island or Muskrat Falls because of the inability to strike a deal with Quebec for the wheeling of power. In 1980 the government of Brian Peckford passed the Upper Churchill Reversion Act in an attempt to give Newfoundland complete ownership and control of the waters of the Churchill River by cancelling the 1961 lease to Brinco. But the Supreme Court of Canada ruled it ultra vires on appeal.

In 1996 Premier Brian Tobin rekindled the controversy by demanding, yet again, that the contract be reopened. When the Quebec government refused, Tobin chastised Premier Lucien Bouchard for recognizing the legitimacy of the Canadian courts when it suited him. Declaring that he was cornered, Tobin began a media blitz across Canada, denouncing the contract as unjust and threatening to cut off the power of Hydro-Québec from Churchill Falls. He was not, he vehemently declared, going to borrow, tax, or close down hospitals and schools for the privilege of pumping power to Quebec so that they could make a billion dollars a year. In 1998, after intense negotiation, Tobin reached an agreement with Bouchard on the development of the Lower Churchill. Ostensibly, the terms would see the injustice rectified. The two met at Churchill Falls where the new agreement, a $12 billion enterprise straddling the border, gave Newfoundland the compensation it looked for to make up the shortfall on the Upper Churchill.

But unlike the situation in the 1960s, this time the Innu were organized and ready to assert their presence and their rights. The 14,500 Innu of Quebec lived in nine communities along the North

Shore and were represented by two organizations: Mamit Unnuat (Innu of the East) and Mamuitun (Together). The Labrador Innu of Sheshashiu and Utshimassit (Davis Inlet) were represented by the Innu Nation. After the Innu disrupted the original plans for the press conference, forcing proceedings to be held elsewhere, there were assurances that they would be consulted from now on. In the meantime, they had captured the media's attention. The relationship between the Innu and the government had changed. By this time, the government realized that it must include the Innu as an integral part of negotiations, and Tobin followed through on this commitment.

The new proposal involved, as before, the waters of the St John and Romaine rivers that were to be diverted and rerouted north into the Smallwood Reservoir to produce more electricity. Feasibility studies were undertaken for another dam on the Churchill, at Muskrat Falls, and for a $2.2 billion undersea cable to carry power to the Island. But the project came at an uncertain time in the energy field. The deregulation of the U.S. electricity market opened the door to many competing power companies in New England and New York State. Moreover, new efficient gas turbines were replacing nuclear generators. In addition, the Lower Churchill project needed a long-term agreement.

Subsequently, in the spring of 2000, it became clear that Quebec would no longer be a partner in the development but would merely be a purchaser of power at Gull Island. Since the plan to divert the rivers had been scrapped because of environmental problems and land claims, Quebec would not be an investor. The Quebec minister pointed out that Newfoundland would have no choice but to use Hydro-Québec lines to wheel power to market. Nothing much had changed. Still, at present – in 2003 – talks are proceeding with the Government of Quebec. Indeed, the two sides have indicated that they have reached an agreement in principle to harness the Lower Churchill.

While modern communities had grown up in Labrador, particularly in the centre and the west, they were single-industry towns, vulnerable to the vicissitudes of distant markets – just as the fishing villages of the coast had been in earlier times. In the absence of rural economic development on the Island and on the coast of Labrador, men and women, mostly from the Island, had flocked to Labrador, attracted by the opportunities it presented for a new start. But the economic security they began to enjoy did not blind them to the vulnerability of the communities they had come to; or to the fact that they had moved even farther from the centre of power to a territory that had an identity all its own. Over time, they would absorb this identity, and their demands would grow for the elimination of vulnerability and isolation, both through the provision of alternate means of employment and also through improvements to transportation and communications. While satellites and the Internet eventually linked them electronically to the outside world, their objective in transportation focused more and more on an asset almost all parts of Labrador would share: a highway across Labrador, from Quebec through Labrador West and Goose Bay to the Strait of Belle Isle, connecting them with distant neighbours and enabling the free flow of goods and materials to and from Labrador.

CHAPTER SIX

Then and Now

There's not much more to say,
But I know we're here to stay,
To live and hunt and trap on this great land,
But most of all to me,
Is to have the liberty,
To be a son of Northern Labrador.

Song by Sid Dicker, Nain

When the cool autumn moonlight shines down through the trees,
No place under heaven would I rather be.
Where the wild birds are flying and the caribou roam,
Many places I've rambled, but this is my home.

Song by Harry Martin, Cartwright

By the 1970s the town of Churchill Falls was a modern community in the middle of a vast, largely uninhabited plateau, with all the amenities of any Canadian community of its size. Its population consisted of a mixture of Labradorians, Newfoundlanders, and others. Few Innu were ever employed there, though they had for centuries used Ossokmanuan and Michikamau lakes. The company provided houses, schools, recreation facilities, medical evacuations, and modern working conditions. Yet the wilderness was at their door. Max McLean, who had grown up in North West River in the family of Malcolm, and Stanley Baikie, who had trapped alone in the area of Churchill Falls since his early teens, were able to set their rabbit snares and hunt and fish almost as well as they could have done if they had stayed home. It was a comfortable community, where the only politics were company politics, for the government was the company, and the company was the government.

By the time Churchill Falls came into being, the modern people of Labrador had settled in communities, most of which lasted into the new millennium. The Innu had been settled more or less permanently

in Davis Inlet and Sheshatshiu, though the problems of the formerly
nomadic people in adapting to these new communities escalated over
time almost to the point of collapse. But in the 1970s it still was not
clear which government, federal or provincial, had what responsibility for aboriginal people. It was clear that the Innu did not have
charge of their own affairs or control over their own lives. The Inuit,
who were not without their own problems of adaptation but were
better prepared because of the presence of the Moravians, were
largely situated on the north coast in Nain, Hopedale, Postville,
Makkovik, and Rigolet, apart from those whose forebears had moved
to Lake Melville during and after the war.

In the south, from Cartwright to Mary's Harbour, where the Labrador
Metis established their presence in the 1970s and 1980s, and where
there are still traces of Inuit ancestry, the life of the people had not
changed a great deal from what it had been in the nineteenth century
(apart from the advances in technology). The Labradorians of this part
of the coast had somehow brought themselves through the hard times
of the 1930s. With the coming of the base, some moved to Goose Bay
for employment and then settled there permanently, leaving behind
the "gently rolling hills, pine trees, rocky shore, gray water ... exactly
like all the Grenfell hooked rugs," as Anne Lindbergh had described
it when she and her husband Charles had landed at Cartwright in
1933. The coming of Confederation brought the social safety net to
those who remained on the south coast and allowed entrepreneurs
such as Ben Powell of Charlottetown, the Penneys and Parrs of Port
Hope Simpson, and the Acremans and Rumbolts of Mary's Harbour
to build local enterprises.

As part of the resettlement policy, some communities were closed
and the people shifted to "growth centres." Families from Batteau
and Spotted Island were moved to Cartwright, and farther south
there was movement from the bays to Charlottetown, Port Hope
Simpson, and Mary's Harbour. This movement put further pressure
on these communities, particularly after downturns in the Atlantic
ground fishery. People felt there was pressure on them to move, and
there was discontent after the move because facilities usually lagged
behind. Fishing was the mainstay of most communities, with the
exception of some wood harvesting at Port Hope Simpson, and when
fishing failed there was really nothing to fall back on except unemployment insurance or make-work programs. Schools and hospital
services had improved and most communities were served by diesel
generators, but in too many communities on this section of the coast
in 1970 there were still no water and sewer services.

More importantly, there was no alternative economic base. In the
1950s Ben Powell, whose father was from Carbonear and whose

mother was a descendant of the earliest Campbells of Lake Melville, settled in the community of Charlottetown. Beginning with a sawmill and store, he expanded into boat building and, later, sports fishing. His activities are well documented in his fascinating account of life on the Labrador in the middle of the twentieth century. But Powell was an exception.

In the Straits after the 1870s, the English merchant firms and Jersey houses had been taken over by Job Brothers of St John's who, with the exception of Red Bay Stores, monopolized the Newfoundland shore fishery in the Straits well into the twentieth century. From Red Bay to L'Anse-au-Clair near the Quebec border, the descendants of local settlers from such places as the Channel Islands and Conception Bay considered themselves Labradorians. But linked as they were to each other by road in the 1950s and by ferry to the Newfoundland Straits after 1967, they had perhaps the closest connection with the Island, certainly in terms of transportation and commerce. On the other hand, they were geographically and socially close to their Quebec neighbours on the North Shore who, in an ironic twist to the Quiet Revolution, came to have reasonably close ties in commerce and communications with the Island.

At the far end of Lake Melville, life in North West River and Mud Lake was tied more and more to Goose Bay. Mud Lake had changed very little from the time Harry Paddon had arrived to set up a medical headquarters; transportation to Goose was still by boat in summer and by snowmobile in winter. A road had connected Goose Bay and North West River since 1955, and a cable car had been strung in 1959 at the end of that road. In Goose Bay and Happy Valley the livelihood of most of the residents was dependent on the base, whose role was changing and would continue to change for the next twenty years. In 1957 the U.S. side of the base became part of the Strategic Air Command, whose task during the Cold War was to refuel planes that were mounting surveillance over the pole and providing the potential counterattack to the Russian threat. In the sixties the Royal Air Force arrived to practise low-level flying over the vast spaces of Labrador. Later the Germans, the Dutch, and later still the Italians joined the British in training the pilots of jet bombers.

By this time Happy Valley was well established. It had been incorporated in 1961, an event followed by the election of the first town council in Labrador. Reflecting the cosmopolitan nature of the town, the first mayor, Leon Cooper, was neither a Labradorian nor a Newfoundlander but a Jewish trader and hotel owner from Montreal. The rest of the council was made up of a Cape Bretoner (Vic White), three Newfoundlanders (Gerry Hiscock, Pat Vickers, and Jim Ryan), and two Labradorians (Frank Saunders from Davis Inlet and Dave Brown from the Cartwright area). Here, too, an entrepreneurial class was emerging – men who seized the opportunities to provide services for the base and those who lived near it. George Shepperd from Conception Bay began a dry-cleaning business that flourishes to this day. Reg Snelgrove built a strong retail business. Pat Vickers was successful in insurance and other ventures. Ed Battcock was an early farmer in Goose Bay, as was George Crawford. Of course, the Hudson's Bay Company maintained its retail presence for some time until a consumers cooperative was begun. Charlie Warr and his brothers Bert and Bob began a pharmacy but soon diversified into other enterprises.

First-class fish camps for trout and salmon had for some years been operating nearby, run by such people as Peter Paor, a Montrealer, and Jackie Cooper, a descendant of Raoul Thevenet of Reveillon Frères in North West River. But clearly the most successful was Mel Woodward from Boat Harbour on the Great Northern Peninsula, where many of the residents of Happy Valley originated. Beginning with a single oil truck, he and his sons built a business that is now among the top five in the province. It includes shipping along the Labrador coast and north to Baffin Island, trucking, automobile sales in Labrador and on the Island, and the servicing of both domestic and international aircraft at Goose Bay. Woodward's first oil truck brought in $150,000 one year in the 1960s; in 2001 the Woodward Group turned over $200 million. That same year Mel Woodward Sr was inducted into the Newfoundland and Labrador Business Hall of Fame. Later he was awarded an honorary doctorate by Memorial University. His son Peter, an outstanding business executive in his own right, was chosen to head the premier's Advisory Council on the Economy.

In 1969 the economy of Goose Bay was diversified with the coming of the Melville Pulp and Paper Company, a subsidiary of John Doyle's Canadian Javelin. But Smallwood's original promise to build a chip mill in Goose was dropped in favour of a linerboard mill at Stephenville. Goose would simply be a supplier of pulpwood. This turn of events infuriated the population, confirming their conviction that their future was hostage to that of the Island, and Smallwood in a public meeting was faced with one of the most hostile audiences of his career.

Javelin was generally seen as temporary, unreliable, and uninterested in the local economy. As far as the public was concerned, Javelin was in Goose Bay to make a quick profit and get out. Nearly all the workforce was imported, cutting practices were shoddy and untidy, and several hundred thousand dollars' worth of equipment was left in the woods to rot. Eventually, Javelin was replaced by the government-owned Labrador Linerboard, but in time this too faded and died.

All along, the economic foundation of Goose Bay had remained the base. But in 1968 the RCAF closed its station, leaving only fifty personnel to handle air traffic control, while the Department of Transport stepped in to fill the gap in administration. The reduction in the Canadian military and the subsequent transfer of federally leased land to the province gave rise to a Local Improvement District for the civilian area outside of Happy Valley. Mel Woodward was appointed to head the new administration, but it had a short life because in 1973 Happy Valley and Goose Bay amalgamated. The new town had all the modern facilities, including police, fire department, hotels, and television. Modern schools were operated by the Roman Catholic School Board and the Labrador East Integrated School Board. After a great deal of public and political pressure, a district vocational school was opened in 1973.

All this was put in jeopardy in 1978 with the withdrawal of the U.S. Air Force. The departure of one of the "founders" of Goose Bay – a familiar and generous employer and benefactor – was not only traumatic for the community but threatened its very survival. Fortunately, the Government of Canada ordered the Department of Public Works to fill the huge void left by the Americans and preserve the jobs. It also funded the Goose Bay Project Group, tasked by the federal Department of Regional Economic Expansion with seeking economic alternatives. Relief came in the 1980s when agreements were signed with the German and Dutch air forces to practice low-level flying.

THE LOW-LEVEL FLYING CONTROVERSY

While the Innu had been unorganized and did not protest during the construction of the Quebec North Shore and Labrador Railway or Churchill Falls, it was another story when the presence of the armed forces in Goose Bay reached its zenith with a proposal to establish a full-scale NATO training base. This would mean that beyond the four countries already training at Goose Bay, more NATO nations would do so. Even those who defended the presence of the military on the basis that it was the mainstay of the economy were apprehensive of such a massive build-up.

In *Nitassinan*, Marie Wadden has said that the events that occurred between 1985 and 1990 were "unparalleled in Innu history and in the history of aboriginal resistance in Canada." In 1978, the year after the formation of the Naskapi-Montagnais Innu Association (NMIA), the Innu began to submit complaints to authorities in Goose Bay about low-level flying. By 1983 they had travelled to what was then West

Germany to find allies for their cause. In 1984 Peter Penashue, who later became president of the Innu Nation (successor to the NMIA), held a press conference in Ottawa to demand cancellation of the agreements. The lobbying intensified. The people of Sheshatshiu established ties with the peace movement and certain churches, and in June 1989 the Anglican Church of Canada officially opposed low-level flying and supported civil disobedience in defence of ancestral lands, calling on the federal government to stop the flying. Anglicans in Goose Bay were outraged. Unlike members of the NMIA and other First Nations, they were not permitted to address the Synod. Bishop Martin Mate charged that the native people were the captives of the peace movement. Many believed that low-level flying would become like the seal hunt – a target for the environmental movement. The news media began to take interest.

In April 1987 the Innu organized their first direct protest, setting up tents just beyond one of the runways. Five of them were arrested, along with their priest, Father Jim Roche. Later, more than seventy-five Innu men, women, and children stormed the airfield and threatened to occupy it until they were granted a meeting with the visiting NATO assessment team. The Innu went onto the runway seven times during the fall of 1988. By the end of March, twenty-six Innu were in jail. The court case about it witnessed an historic judgment when Judge James Igloliorte, himself a Labrador Inuk, dismissed the charges on the grounds that the Innu honestly believed the land to be their own. Robert Michelin, whose berry patch it was, would have believed the territory around the airport to be his. Whose land was it anyway, and how could it be shared? The trial received extensive coverage and the ruling, even though it was overturned later, was considered to have a major impact on native claims.

More protests followed and more court cases. Meanwhile, outside support for the Innu continued to grow both in Canada and overseas. The Department of National Defence launched a major public relations campaign. The Innu countered with an application for an injunction to stop the low-level flying. It was denied by Madame Justice Reed, who ruled that such an order would result in "extensive disruption, dislocation and prejudice against the community of Happy Valley–Goose Bay." It would put about seventeen hundred direct and indirect civilian jobs at risk. On the other hand the Innu would lose no rights, she said. As well, she noted the refusal of the Innu to cooperate in any way to mitigate the effects of low-level flying. With an annual total of less than two hundred Innu being flown into the training area and a military policy that allowed a three-mile radius around any known Innu location, Reed saw ample latitude for both sides to

live in relatively peaceful coexistence. Moreover, she pointed out that
there was not clear evidence of damaging environmental effects. She
alluded to the point made by Hank Shouse, a longtime resident of
Labrador and a former mayor of Happy Valley–Goose Bay (who had
married Bella, a daughter of Malcolm McLean). He had stated, "Indians have told us ... they don't care about low-level flying. They want
to settle land claims so they can get the benefits of it – either money
today or money forever."[1]

But the protests had mobilized the entire community of Sheshatshiu.
And the powerful images of protestors walking across the military
airfield not only struck a chord with the national media but provided
the Innu themselves with a bond that had eluded them previously.
Said Daniel Ashini, "The protests had an effect, we interrupted the
flying, and the people found out that if they were united and if their
efforts were concentrated they could do a lot of things they wouldn't
be able to do by themselves. There has been a lot of unity created by
the Innu."[2] Martha Hurley, one of the women arrested after a demon-
stration organized by Rose Gregoire, said, "I always used to think that
I was a useless Innu. I felt that non-natives always beat the Innu. But
now everything has changed since our protest has begun. I feel we
are stronger and our frustration feelings are being let out ... It feels
like trying to get out the years and years of being stamped under."[3]

However, in an indication of north-south differences that would
recur, the Davis Inlet people, also part of the NMIA, were not as
interested in the protest and felt that the association should be dealing with land claims and not only low-level flying. Farther north and
surrounded by Inuit communities, they were not so affected by the
military activity. In 1988 the northern band threatened to leave the
association and form one of its own. For its part, the Labrador Inuit
Association (LIA) took a more moderate position on flight training,
saying that there should be no increase until the environmental studies
had been completed.

While the Innu opposed the NATO base, the people from the north
and south coasts, from North West River and Mud Lake, as well as
a substantial number of people from parts of the Island defended it
just as vehemently. Second and third generations of the original
settlers were building new homes and jobs. They realized that in the
short term there was no alternative economy, and they were determined to hold onto what they had built. Mayor Harry Baikie, himself
a product of the Lake Melville Orkney-Inuit heritage and a member
of the LIA, defended the base: "The base is the only industry we've
ever had at Goose Bay. Others have been tried but none of them have
lasted. Goose Bay was a good northern location for the military in

the '40s and it still is today. It's our industry. We're a single industry town."[4] Doris Saunders, another longtime resident of Happy Valley who had both European and Inuit ancestry (and was editor of the award-winning historical magazine *Them Days*), agreed:

The West Germans say they don't want the jets because they make too much noise. And it shouldn't matter whether it's one person or a lot of people bothered by the noise. But I want Happy Valley–Goose Bay to last forever, and I don't want to be living on welfare. I want to always be able to provide for myself, and I would like that to be possible for all the people here and their children. Whoever wants to stay here should be able to stay here and work. But not at any cost. We should have some say in how it's developed, how far to go. It shouldn't be done to line somebody's pockets. And it shouldn't be done with Newfoundland taking everything out and putting nothing back. And that's been the trend up to now.[5]

Since the 1940s, flying had been the mainstay of Goose Bay, and in spite of strong protests against it, so it remained, for better or for worse. Ironically, the NATO base as conceived was not established; both Goose Bay and Konya, Turkey, lost. But Goose retained those NATO nations already training there and later added the Italians. But the divisions between those who occupied the land first and those who came later were sharpened and widened by the controversy over low-level flying. It provided a strong measure of solidarity both for the community of Happy Valley–Goose Bay and for the community of Sheshatshiu – if not the Innu Nation – making it all the more difficult for the two communities to live together. Different aspirations, which had been dormant but growing since the beginning of the military presence, had flared into the open.

LABRADOR CITY AND WABUSH

In Labrador City, after construction of the IOC concentrating plant in 1962, the workforce had stabilized. Strong unions emerged to ensure fair wages – among the highest in the country – and superior training and working conditions. In Wabush, too, private businesses had grown as well as modern schools and community facilities. Soon there was a fully serviced hospital and a TV station, which broadcast taped programs in English and French until full satellite transmission became available in 1974. Wabush airport was opened to serve both communities as well as the nearby community of Fermont in Quebec. The latter was connected to Labrador West by road in 1976, and in the mid-eighties Alex Snow (at one time the MHA for western Labrador),

Flip Dawson, Gordon Parsons, and Gary Peckham became the first to drive to Baie Comeau over the rough road that in time became the western end of the Trans-Labrador Highway.

The communities of Labrador City and Wabush were unique in the province. Better linked to Quebec than to Newfoundland, their population was nevertheless 20 per cent French and 10 per cent foreign born. It was not unusual for residents to take a ski holiday in the Laurentians, though Labrador City itself eventually boasted a fine ski hill as well as world-class cross-country trails. Similarly, it was common for people to plan a weekend around a game of the Montreal Canadiens. The exceptional educational institutions were operated in both English and French; social and recreational facilities were far ahead of most of the rest of the province. Both towns had been well planned and laid out. In 1971 Labrador City had a population of 7500, with another 3500 in Wabush, the majority from the Island but some from other parts of Labrador as well. By this time there were probably more Lettos and Dumaresques in Labrador West than there were in L'Anse-au-Clair.

As IOC withdrew some of its support for the town, the provincial government became all the more important. But the province was not wealthy, and apart from the fact that it had other demands, there was a feeling that Labrador West already had better facilities and a higher standard of living and therefore needed less government support. Later attempts to establish the government presence, such as stationing the Royal Newfoundland Constabulary there or building the Arts and Culture Centre, did not assuage the feeling of neglect and alienation. The local residents believed that, far too often, Labrador was out of sight and out of mind.

Yet if western Labrador lived in splendid isolation from the Island, it was not much closer to Happy Valley–Goose Bay and had virtually nothing in common and virtually no intercourse with coastal Labrador. From time to time, sports and other activities brought the westerners in touch with central Labrador, but for the most part the two areas continued to lead separate lives – one a northern mining community, the other a northern air force base. The expense of air travel was a big impediment to greater social interaction, and it was only with the coming of the Trans-Labrador Highway in the 1980s that the two communities began to see more of each other.

LABRADOR ATTRACTS ATTENTION

"Attention," says Arthur Miller of Willie Loman in *Death of a Salesman*, "attention must be paid." The late sixties and early seventies brought attention to Labrador, and they brought change. In February 1970 the first pan-Labrador conference was held in Goose Bay, sponsored by the Labrador North Chamber of Commerce and organized by the Extension Department of Memorial University. For the first time, representatives from all over Labrador met to discuss the issues of the day with invited guests from the outside. For the first time, the parts were coming together to examine Labrador as a whole, to assess where it was and where it was going. Making an attempt to overcome centuries of outside influence, the Labrador Inuit Association was just in the process of being born under its first president, Sam Andersen of Nain. Taking advantage of the changing attitudes of the late sixties and early seventies, the Labrador Inuit were beginning to build a political and cultural organization that would, by the nineties, be one of the most powerful organizations in the whole of Labrador. But they were not key actors at the conference. As the Innu and Metis were not yet organized, there was little if any representation from the aboriginal community.

At the conference, which was entitled "Labrador in the Seventies," it was clear that the different areas did not know much about each other.[6] However, the expected grievances were raised and recommendations made, many of which were later reflected in the report of the Royal Commission on Labrador and helped form a blueprint for change. It was obvious that change could come about only with the help of the federal government, and federal Transport Minister Don Jamieson, the keynote speaker at the conference, was prescient in his analysis and observations of what was wrong and what needed to be done. He acknowledged that improvements to infrastructure and quality of life would only be accomplished with the assistance of federal funds and that in addressing the needs of Labrador, even for those within provincial responsibility such as roads, a substantial federal expenditure would be required. He pointed out that DREE (the federal Department of Regional Economic Expansion) had been created for the purpose of responding to the needs of areas like Labrador. Earlier, Labrador had made use of the Atlantic Development Board, the forerunner of DREE, to construct, for example, the bridge across Goose River. Jamieson was convinced that DREE could help Labrador, and he said that the federal government would provide "constant help to the provincial government in order to get these road networks built."

Jamieson made an incredible number of commitments. He supported a roll-on, roll-off ferry from the Island to Goose Bay, a highway across Labrador, a series of airstrips, and an ice-free port for Goose. He also called for some sort of pan-Labrador organization so that the federal government would have a specific body to work with.

The emphasis, he urged, should be on government by the people rather than for the people. In what may have been his most prescient pronouncement, he mused whether there was "value for dollar spent" in the subsidies provided to ferries, including those across the Gulf of St Lawrence. This argument, made more than thirty years ago – that ferry subsidies should be redirected to surface transportation – was, as things turned out, the one used to obtain the funding for the current construction phases of the Trans–Labrador Highway.

THE NEW LABRADOR PARTY

In tandem with changing attitudes all across the country, during the 1970s there was social and political change in Labrador, helped by scheduled air service and progress in electronic communications. Perhaps the most dramatic change was the birth of the New Labrador Party. The feeling of alienation from and dissatisfaction with the government in St John's that had been present in both old and new Labrador came to a head in February 1969 in the Wabush Recreation Centre. There Tom Burgess, an Irish union leader who had left the Liberal Party two years after his election in 1966, fired the resentment of an audience of about a hundred with his passionate denunciation of the provincial government, which was ignoring him and his Labrador agenda. Catching the mood for change, Nelson Sherren nominated Mac Moss to be the first president of the Labrador Rights Party, which eventually became the New Labrador Party. The party proclaimed it would fight to put Labrador "on a co-equal basis with the rest of the province."

The movement for change was not confined to the New Labrador Party. In 1971 Premier Smallwood, now convinced of the necessity of getting local residents elected – people who could speak forcefully and with knowledge of their areas – appointed Mel Woodward in Goose Bay and Roy Legge in Labrador West to his cabinet. Both had lived in Labrador for some time, both understood it, and Woodward had made it his home. These local men who ran for the Liberals in the election of 1971 gave voters the expectation of change within the ruling party. This approach carried the day, as the Liberals held two of the three seats in Labrador. Evidently, more people chose to effect change within the government rather than by removing it from power (though in fact the Liberals' tenure proved to be short lived).

At the time the New Labrador Party (NLP) was formed, Mac Moss was only twenty-eight, a young man in a young community, with a great deal of ability, energy, and enthusiasm, not to mention dissatisfaction. The group tried as best it could to support Burgess and his family (he had married Rhyna McLean, the granddaughter of Malcolm and one of the first nurses in Labrador West). For a group that had very little political experience apart from at the municipal level, it made the "After Dark" section of *Playboy* magazine when 104 per cent of the voters of Labrador West turned out to vote in the election of 1971. While the other NLP candidates in Labrador – Herb Brett in Labrador North and Mike Martin in Labrador South – lost in their contests with Mel Woodward and Joe Harvey, respectively, Burgess received 80 per cent of the vote over Roy Legge in Labrador West. And after a dramatic provincial contest that ended in a tie between the Liberals and conservatives, he became the lone NLP representative in the House of Assembly.

During the feverish last days of the Smallwood administration, as the premier fought to hold onto power, Burgess was courted from all sides. John Doyle tracked him down outside a club in Labrador City and took him to the Wabush Hotel to woo him back to the Liberal Party. Later, he flew Burgess and other members of the NLP (including Herb Brett and Josiah Normore from the Straits) to St John's and the Holiday Inn, where Liberal sympathizers were also staying. The offers to the NLP were many and various, not only from the Liberals but also from the Conservatives. After the Conservatives won the 1972 election, Richard Cashin, Mike Martin's employer at the Fishermen's Union, arranged a dinner at his house between Burgess and the new premier, Frank Moores. Cashin's low regard for Burgess was sealed when at one point he found him in the kitchen mixing fine cognac with Coke.

The outcome of the meeting was no more satisfying. The negotiations came to naught. Tired, frustrated, and out of money, the delegation returned to Labrador. Burgess then tried to get his supporters in Labrador West to help him rejoin the Liberals, but they had had enough of his vacillating. It was Burgess himself, they knew, who had scuttled their efforts to bring Labrador greater public attention and get it fair treatment. The sudden rush of potential power had gone to his head, and his tacking from side to side destroyed his party's credibility as well as his own. He yearned for microphones and cameras, but when they appeared in front of him he usually failed to get the message right. As Mac Moss put it, "Tom lost it in front of the mikes." Burgess eventually ran for the leadership of the provincial Liberal Party, but his procrastination and his inability to bargain successfully finished his political career, and soon afterwards he left the province.

After Smallwood resigned in January 1972, he was replaced as Liberal leader by Ed Roberts, who went on to take "Smallwood's defeat" against Frank Moores in the March 1972 election. In the subsequent election Roberts, who by then was representing a new Strait of Belle Isle riding that included the Labrador Straits, was denied a fair chance to attain power when Smallwood formed the Liberal Reform Party and split the Liberal vote. Later, after the Liberals regained power, he become the MHA for Naskaupi district and the most effective minister in the government of Clyde Wells. Roberts gave outstanding service to Labrador, particularly in realizing the economic contribution that the base at Goose Bay made to the provincial economy, and by finding maintenance funds to keep the Trans-Labrador Highway open during the winter and helping find construction funds for its completion. His sterling service to the province was acknowledged by his appointment as lieutenant-governor in 2002 and by an honorary doctorate in 2003.

Meanwhile Mike Martin, in March 1972, had become the first native-born Labradorian elected to the provincial legislature. But the New Labrador Party was unable to survive in the long run. Reflecting on its legacy, Mac Moss believes that it succeeded in attracting the attention of the Island, particularly those in government, and it articulated in a most dramatic way the feelings and needs of Labrador. But it was never the NLP's intention to create a separate area (though the separatist label was affixed to it by some, and in fact the option was explored). Its objective was simply fair treatment – that the people of Labrador should be treated like people on the Island. Many of the NLP members in Labrador West and Goose Bay had come from the Island but felt disowned once they settled in Labrador. Indeed, whether it was the population of the coast or central Labrador or the affluent west, all felt unfairly treated. The idea that Labrador was a territory to be exploited for the benefit of those on the Island, as often expressed in the columns of the St John's daily newspapers, was anathema to them.

The emergence of the NLP and the new policies espoused by Labrador's new MHAs had an effect, especially among those who held the reins of power. The message was that the people of Labrador were no longer prepared to be taken for granted and no longer willing to be quiet, whether they expressed themselves through the Liberal Party, the New Labrador Party, or the Conservative Party.

OTHER DEVELOPMENTS

The political ferment was symptomatic of the change that was occurring. Between 1970 and 1975, many of Labrador's communities were incorporated, regional development associations were formed, heritage societies were founded, and in 1974 a new Labrador flag was sewn together by Mike Martin's wife, Pat. Martin, who was the New

Labrador Party MHA for Labrador South at the time, spearheaded the creation of the flag as part of the twenty-fifth anniversary celebrations of the province. His group looked for symbols that represented the heritage of Labrador. The white for the snow was easy to find; the blue for the water was also historically important; the green was for the land that all had come to love whether or not they were born there. Black spruce, growing in almost all parts of Labrador, provided three branches on its twigs representing the Inuit, the Innu, and the settlers. Another section was added, the two twigs representing the past and the future. Flags were sent to all towns and villages in Labrador, and soon it was flying. It has been flown all over Labrador – on municipal buildings, on toques and sweaters, on letterheads – the green, white, and blue colours appearing on fences and even garbage cans, in fact, anywhere that colours can be affixed. For all the people of Labrador it is their flag, and they fly it proudly.

Although Labrador Services Division, virtually "the government" on the Labrador coast, had been absorbed within Rural Development, the provincial government placed an assistant deputy minister, John McGrath, in Goose Bay "to accelerate the delivery of government services and to encourage economic opportunity." Later, Cyril Good-year – who had been a Ranger in Nain and, after his retirement from the RCMP, was a magistrate in Goose Bay – was appointed deputy minister of rural development in St John's. The government funded the Labrador Resources Advisory Council as well as the Labrador Craft Producers Association, and last but by no means least, the Combined Councils. This body had begun on the north coast with the strong leadership of Bill Andersen and the Makkovik Town Council. But it soon spread to all of Labrador and is still in existence today, a forum and clearing house for all the municipal councils of Labrador.

The Royal Commission on Labrador

The 1970s was also the decade that saw the creation of the Royal Commission on Labrador. Chaired by Donald Snowden, the former head of Memorial University's Extension Service, and including Cyril Goodyear, Renée Snell of Labrador City, and Freida Hettasch of the north coast, it was an inquiry into "the economic and social conditions of life in Labrador." It was quite critical of government attitudes towards Labrador, noting "the shabby presence of Government in some parts of Labrador and the lack of presence in others," and it concluded: "It is not that government has vacated the field in Labrador, it has never occupied it." The commission found that the industrialization of Labrador since Confederation had not brought a proportionate increase in the availability of wage labour for longtime Labrador residents.

The report confirmed what Labrador residents had been saying about the Island's indifference to and neglect of their area. The government, it said, must take some decisions, including more effective use of federal funds and expertise, greater familiarity with the programs of other governments in other northern areas, a readiness to heed local advice in all phases of planning, and steps to move some of the basic functions and responsibilities of government out of St Johns and into the regions affected.

Fred Rowe, in his memoirs, challenged the findings of the commission. He claimed that in its charge of neglect, it failed to distinguish between the pre-Confederation and post-Confederation periods. He pointed to the excellent facilities in Labrador West, Churchill Falls, and Goose Bay. But in the first two cases, the companies had provided the lion's share of the infrastructure and amenities. It is true that the province made major improvements to Happy Valley and to a lesser extent to North West River: land title, housing, water and sewer systems, a hospital, a vocational school, electricity, schools and bridges (with federal assistance), an air ambulance service, and an air mail service for the coast. And it is true that Rowe took up the cause of the civilians at Goose Bay and made a substantial contribution to the building of the community. But his contention that the coast received adequate attention in the early years after Confederation does not stand up to scrutiny.

While electricity was provided to the coastal communities, the roads were inadequate at best, and no water and sewer systems were provided until the 1980s. The same was true of proper medical facilities in those communities, other than the ones the Grenfell organization had served historically. Economic development was not seriously attacked until the 1980s, when DREE programs and the Canadian Saltfish Corporation provided infrastructure and marketing expertise to communities that had hitherto been occupied solely by summer satellites of Newfoundland fishing interests, who took most of their product away to the Island. The fact is that Labrador was not on the Island. It was far away and expensive. With a short shipping season and tough terrain, services were difficult to install and maintain.

But the real problem lay deeper. In the nineteenth and early twentieth centuries. Labrador had been a place to go to temporarily, a northern Eldorado where resources could be scooped up quickly before heading home to the south. Even in the middle of the twentieth century, the two solitudes did not really communicate with each other or keep in touch. Newspapers, if they did happen to reflect a Labrador point of view (which in the view of Labradorians was not often) arrived late. And for decades Newfoundland radio and television was unheard in Labrador, and Labradorians had no way of talking back even if they had received the transmission.

The response to Labrador continued to manifest itself. Tony Paddon, the highly respected administrator of medical services in northern Labrador (and son of the man who composed the "Ode to Labrador"), became the first Labradorian lieutenant-governor in 1981. Several years earlier, as the recipient of the Royal Bank Award, he had noted the disparities between the two parts of the province: "Far more than salt water, the Strait of Belle Isle is also a barrier between two points of view, two standards of living and two attitudes. On the entire Labrador coast there is not a single community water supply or safe method of sewage disposal ... It is no argument that essential services are more expensive to provide in Labrador than on the Island. If they are essential, they should be provided ... but even more, a sense of belonging, of being respected and of having a place in the Province." His appointment was as much a recognition that attitudes to Labrador must change as it was to honour the man and his achievements. James Igloliorte, a teacher born in Hopedale, who had attended high school while at the Grenfell Mission dormitory in North West River, was appointed the first Inuk judge in Canada and stationed in Labrador. Later, after a hard fight, Labrador obtained its own federal seat in the Parliament of Canada, and I became the first MP for Labrador.

The Labrador Resources Advisory Council

During the 1970s, while the iron mines flourished and while Goose Bay reeled from the pullout of the Americans and the closure of Labrador Linerboard, several ideas that had been recommended by the royal commission came to pass. One of these was a planning and advisory council made up of representatives from the federal, provincial, and local levels for the development of the fisheries. But the focus soon switched from fish to oil, as the energy crisis of 1973 encouraged petroleum exploration off the Labrador coast. Eastcan Exploration is said to have spent $100 million on Labrador exploration in the early seventies. After the Company of Young Canadians conducted a survey in Labrador and presented the concerns of the people about oil and gas development, the government proposed that a body be formed to act as a liaison for local Labradorians. Thus, the Labrador Resources Advisory Council (LRAC) was born in 1976. It was made up of one member for each of the regions of Labrador, as well as the Sheshatshiu Band Council and the Labrador Inuit Association. The executive was elected, and paid staff were appointed, including Bill Flowers of Rigolet.

But the council constantly struggled against debilitating weaknesses. It was funded by government, but in its policy recommendations it was often forced to bite the hand that fed it, making it suspect, particularly with those who saw it as a collection of closet Labrador separatists. Moreover, the desires and expectations of the various regions and ethnic groups were often antithetical. Nevertheless, it did bring the diverse regions of Labrador together as never before.

Although the LRAC never advocated separatism, suspicions in St John's continued to grow. Two emotional debates on the topic took place in the House of Assembly, one in 1977 and one in 1980. In 1981 the LRAC expanded its membership to take in chambers of commerce, the development associations, the Labrador West District Labour Council, and the various regional fisheries committees. This compounded the conflicting regional interests at a time when the aboriginal bodies were developing their own agendas and strengths. As well, the focus of public attention had shifted from gas and oil back to fish and transportation. After the election of 1979, it was clear that the government wanted to change the LRAC mandate. Finally, in 1982, it discontinued funding the council, arguing that other bodies, particularly those of the aboriginal people, had made it redundant.

The Labrador Metis Association

Another organization that made its appearance during the 1970s and 1980s was the Labrador Metis Association. It was formed in 1986 to protect the traditional, constitutional, and aboriginal rights of the Inuit descendants in southeastern and central Labrador. These people were unable to join the Inuit and part-Inuit of the north because they did not come from within the Labrador Inuit Association's land claims area. Although they had just as much Inuit blood and shared a similar way of life, save for the Moravian influence, because of their geographic circumstances they could not obtain the health and education benefits their northern counterparts enjoyed. Initially rejected by the provincial government, the organization was able to secure certain federal funds outside the land claims process from, for example, the Native Economic Development Program and its successor, the Canadian Aboriginal Economic Development Strategy. As well, the Labrador Metis Association fought for and obtained its share of job-creation funding for aboriginal people from the federal Department of Human Resources, and through its economic development arm it initiated projects in central and southern Labrador. Ottawa has recognized the potential aboriginal right of the Metis to harvest certain species of fish and game. But land claim negotiations proceed at a snail's pace, and the Metis (now the Metis Nation) have resorted to public protest of one form or another from time to time to maintain their presence and affirm their rights.

Transportation and Communications

Attention still continued to be paid to Labrador. By 1980 there was a roll-on, roll-off ferry operating from St John's and Lewisporte to Goose Bay, as Don Jamieson had proposed at the "Labrador in the Seventies" conference. The first, the MV *William Carson*, met the same fate as the *Titanic*. Although there was no loss of life, the ship sits on the bottom of the Atlantic with the first Labrador load of the season – beer – and Fred Brett's grand piano. Undeterred, CN Marine replaced her with others, such as the *Sir Robert Bond* and later the *Northern Ranger*. As well a year-round mail service was begun to the coast. Docking facilities were improved, fish plants were constructed, and an airstrip program was started that eventually spread to thirteen communities.

Meanwhile, the CBC expanded its services. In fact, once it finally established itself in the Labrador region, the CBC was the one medium that drew all of Labrador together and made its voice heard on the outside. CBC-TV and, more importantly, CBC Radio developed a real consciousness of Labrador, its identity and sense of alienation, and genuinely tried to be inclusive. A loyal band of broadcasters and technicians, including Joe Smith, constantly sought to improve services and to broadcast and preserve local stories and culture. Many Labradorians of the 1960s will remember the humorous and heart-warming episodes of Gordie Rendell and Joe Goudie's "Mokami Mountaineer," a program about "them days" in Lake Melville. With Rendell as the straight man, Goudie recreated in local dialect the follies and foibles of those early settlers. Goudie went on to a career in provincial politics and later to a career in ecotourism, but he will probably be best remembered for the character of "Unk," an aging Inuit-Orkney trapper, that he played so well on Labrador CBC. Unfortunately, the federal cutbacks to CBC funding in the 1990s and the corporation's subsequent decision to reduce and eliminate certain regional services stymied such local efforts. The fight to maintain the CBC, the only pan-Labrador media outlet, failed; it became another victim of federal budget balancing and deficit cutting, and staff and equipment were carted away, leaving it a shell of its former self.

Yet Labrador was becoming part of the global village. The people adapted well, not only to the review panels put in place to assess the various proposals, but to the communications revolution itself. Indeed, Smart Labrador, an electronic net that allows any community in Labrador to talk to any other, was chosen over all other proposals from the province for federal funding. This initiative not only connects the parts of Labrador with one another, but it connects people to the information they need and establishes a link with the rest of the world. In 2002 it reported that 21,000 kilograms of equipment had arrived by boat, plane, and skidoo. Forty-one sites were fully functional and Smart Labrador was offering a Heritage Mall, an e-commerce pilot project where craftspeople would be able to sell on-line. As well, Broadband will provide the foundation for a virtual courtroom and mental health assessments. Face-to-face meetings have become commonplace. The new technology can open up exciting possibilities for educational institutions such as the College of the North Atlantic and Memorial University, which had already used the Labrador coast in its pioneering work with telemedecine.

Another educational development had been taking place in the Lake Melville area. To complement the regional school boards that had been created and led by such outstanding educators as Frank Roberts, Ron Sparkes, Bob Martin, Pat Hanrahan, and Pat Furlong, a vocational school had been built at Goose Bay that developed into Labrador College. In answer to demands that had arisen at the "Labrador in the Eighties" conference, educators like Beatrice Watts and Tim Borlase led the way in developing local curricula and putting in place unique linguistic and cultural programs to meet the special needs of Labrador children, both aboriginal and non-aboriginal.

FROM THE 1980S INTO THE 1990S

A paramount issue that had been attracting increasing attention was the environment. Labradorians are natural environmentalists; the relationship of the early people to the land established a respectful bond with the rest of nature. During the development of the iron mines in the west and the construction of Churchill Falls, little thought had been given to environmental effects. Some lakes were polluted and others enlarged, flooding large tracts of forest area, including Innu gravesites. By the 1980s and 1990s there was an acknowledgment that development could not come at any cost and that there must be safeguards against destructive environmental degradation. Yet conflict over the environment versus jobs often divided rather than united Labradorians. At the "Labrador in the Nineties" conference, the chair, Carol Brice-Bennett, noted in her opening remarks: "The process of environmental assessments, reviews and studies has brought conflict, and polarized individuals, families, organizations and communities in Labrador more than any other single issue in the 80s."[7]

Because of the opposing viewpoints, rather than working together on pan-Labrador development that all groups could agree on, the various regions ploughed ahead with their separate plans. They were aided by a number of federal-provincial cost-shared programs; the native peoples' agreement, several DREE programs culminating in the Comprehensive Labrador Agreement, Labrador Venture Capital, Labrador Community Futures, and the Canadian Aboriginal Economic Development Strategy. Indeed, threading through government programs and filling out forms threatened to become a cottage industry. Yet while government programs were still not perfect, at least there were government programs that purported to be targeted at Labrador needs. It can be argued that these very programs created a new dependency. But at least, attention was being paid to Labrador.

In the north the Inuit were growing stronger and speaking with one voice, especially through their award-winning broadcasting arm, the OK (OkalaKatiget) Society. Like other aboriginal groups across the country, they had received organizational funding in the 1970s and had grown steadily in strength and influence. Strong leaders such as Bill Edmunds, president of the Labrador Inuit Association, gave the northern communities a new voice and initiated a political revival. Through the Labrador Inuit Development Corporation the Inuit engaged in a commercial caribou hunt, not unlike the earlier program for the Innu that Max Budgell had proposed to Walter Rockwood. More significantly, they began mining anorthosite, a bluish grey form of Labradorite, for the Italian market and beyond. (By 2002, almost a hundred local people were employed at the quarry at Ten Mile Bay and other sites.) Already in the 1990s Gilbert Hay and John Terriak were becoming two of the best soapstone carvers in Canada, while John Goudie achieved great success with the excellence of his Labradorite jewellery and carving. Similarly, Madeline Michelin in Sheshashiu was becoming known for her Innu tea dolls.

Musicians were also making their mark, performing a blend of Labrador songs old and new. They came from all areas: the Flummies in the east, Black Spruce in the west, Tipatshimun in Sheshashiu, Harry Martin in Cartwright, and Shirley Montague from North West River. As well, Labrador theatre developed, led by Edmund McLean and Lorne Pardy. *Them Days*, the magazine devoted to recording and preserving the history of Labrador in the words of its people, was good enough to win an honorary degree from Memorial University and the Order of Canada for its founder, Doris Saunders. Newspapers such as the *Labradorian* in Goose Bay and the *Aurora* in Labrador West helped to tie their communities together. But the media were still regional, and there was not (nor has there ever been, with the exception of CBC Labrador) an effective pan-Labrador communications vehicle.

A renewed interest in local history and culture provided the incentive for the eventual establishment of the Parks Canada Basque Whaling Centre at Red Bay. Farther north, the original "capital" at Battle Harbour is still being recreated. It is a unique tourist attraction made all the more accessible by the new road running north from Red Bay to Mary's Harbour and on to Cartwright, which will emerge as a transshipment centre for the north coast. In the Lake Melville area, through the efforts of the Heritage Society, not only was the Labrador Interpretation Centre born, but the old Hudson's Bay Company store that Donald Smith had managed in the last century has been turned into the Labrador Museum. Farther north, work is underway for the revival of the historic Moravian buildings and artifacts at Hebron and Hopedale, with their priceless heritage.

Largely as a result of tourism, increased traffic in the Straits led to demands for ever-larger ferries and culminated in the provision of the *Apollo*, owned by the Woodward Group. Many hope it will be the forerunner of a fixed link to the Island – a tunnel under the Strait of Belle Isle to carry trucks and people and possibly even a power line from the Lower Churchill. A tunnel would allow the two sister sections of Newfoundland and Labrador to be joined together and physically linked to the rest of the nation.

The Straits are also the site of the Labrador Shrimp Company, probably Labrador's greatest success story. The company grew and prospered, extending its reach in shrimp and crab all along the coast to Cartwright. Where for centuries Newfoundland and British companies had taken out the raw product for processing elsewhere, a local company owned and operated by local people invested in secondary processing of high-value species and, in doing so, brought coastal communities new life. From Cartwright to L'Anse-au-Clair, it is the Labrador Shrimp Company that owns and operates the fish plants that keep local people employed and their communities alive. Formed at the instigation of Richard Cashin, president of the Fishermen, Food, and Allied Workers' Union, and assisted by Max Short, this co-operative of fishermen grew and thrived under the leadership of its first president, Frank Flynn, and its managers, Gilbert Linstead and Ken Fowler. In partnership with established Scandanavian fish companies and using the latest Faroese technology, the proceeds from deep-sea shrimp have been used to develop other ventures, most notably in crab. As well, the company has produced the roe of sea urchins and welk for the lucrative Japanese market. Its child prodigy, the Labrador Credit Union, spawned when the Bank of Montreal pulled out its services, had grown to have assets of $8 million by 1990.

In the west, although the companies had retrenched and retooled, their populations had stabilized. With company order books full, retirees were inclined to stay in Labrador West and help create a permanent community where the Carol Project had started its bush operation in the 1960s. The completion of the road between Labrador West and Goose Bay in the 1980s meant that these two industrial centres were more often in contact with each other. They shared the goods and services that came to them over the road from Montreal, substantially lowering their cost of living. As well, the road provided them with a way out for themselves and their products, and also brought more tourists to both areas.

There were increasing demands for further roadwork. These demands were acceded to in the 1990s with the announcement of the transfer of the federal ferry services to the province, along with $345 million to improve the road from Labrador West to Goose and to build the road up from the Straits to Cartwright. As noted before, the rationale for obtaining these federal funds emerged from the refinements some of us were able to make on the idea that Don Jamieson had mused about at the "Labrador in the Seventies" conference – whether there was value for money in all the subsidies that were being provided for ferry services. The answer that came back was no. The funds could be used more effectively to provide surface transportation within Labrador. This was, and is, an entirely valid concept and one that has been accepted by the federal government. Its application is perhaps still not finished. With the construction of the road north from the Straits, the pre-eminent issue on which all of Labrador agreed, and which had been fought for since the 1970s, took a giant leap forward. In 2002 the provincial government announced that it would find the funds to complete the section between Cartwright and Goose Bay, thus linking Labrador by road from the Strait of Belle Isle to Quebec. However, on the north coast, sea service is still not entirely satisfactory to the local population, and the highest costs in the area continue to escalate.

During the 1980s and 1990s a strong private sector emerged in almost all regions of Labrador. In Labrador West, names from the 1960s such as St Marie and Hunt in construction, Manstan, House, and Cornick in the wholesale and retail trade, and Hodge in trucking and transportation had come to the fore in the business sector that had grown up serving IOC and the other resource development companies, as well as the local communities. Indeed, the names of some of these same Labradorians are found among the shareholders of the Shabogamo Company that is successfully mining and shipping silica to Quebec and overseas. In the Lake Melville area the Woodward Group ranks as one of the most successful businesses in the province, particularly in aircraft servicing, shipping, transportation, and automobiles. Both the Inuit and the Innu have entered joint ventures with non-aboriginal companies in food and security services. Some businesses, like Barney Powers's Labrador Construction, began partnering with aboriginal groups, as did Provincial Airlines, while Air Labrador and other regional carriers had occupied the transportation market since the 1970s. The Burdens successfully pursued enterprises in sanitary products and fast food. Others, like Lloyd Montague in North West River, built solid businesses in adventure tourism, as Ed Blake did in the sale and care of snowmobiles in the Lake Melville area and along the coast.

On the north and south coasts, while co-operatives were the largest operators, other business people continued to thrive: the Lettos, the Lethbridges, and the Penneys in hospitality; the legendary Ben Powell in sawmilling and boat building; Jim Jones in transport; and Stelman Flynn in the production of local Labrador products. It was this strong and growing private sector that saw the advantages of the development of natural resources and the great potential that Labrador could offer both to themselves and to the people among whom they lived. Most importantly, it was these people who created the long-term jobs. By the 1990s, Labrador had a private sector ready to meet the challenges of both resource development and environmental protection.

There was a growing consensus that if development was to take place, everybody had to be included. Notwithstanding the fight over low-level flying, Peter Penashue of the Innu Nation recognized this at the "Labrador in the Nineties" conference. "Sometimes," he said, "it may seem in the media as if we would like the Euro-Canadians to move away, but that's not possible. We have to find a way in which we can live together, but not in a way where one is dominant over the other as it has been."[8] Toby Andersen, the articulate land claims director of the Labrador Inuit Association (who was a descendant of Torsten from Makkovik), echoed the same sentiments: "We hope there will be benefits in the land claims settlements for non-aboriginal as well as for aboriginal people."[9]

Voisey's Bay

Near where the Innu had trod for many years, near where Amos Voisey had established a trading post, and near where, in the twentieth century, Dick White had bartered furs, the richest nickel deposit in the world was discovered. It fuelled the expectations of Newfoundland and Labrador, and especially the land claims of both the Inuit and the Innu, giving them a new cause around which to rally their communities. Several kilometres inland, the mineral zone was drilled on 22 October 1994, turning Newfoundland prospectors Chris Verbiski and Al Chislett into millionaires overnight. The zone proved to be the centre of a massive sulphide deposit right on the surface, now known as the Ovoid. Subsequent drilling revealed that it contained 28.7 million tonnes of ore, nickel, copper, and cobalt. Further drilling revealed a second huge ore body, the Eastern Deeps, estimated at 43.3 million tonnes of ore, although at a greater depth and therefore more expensive to extract. Yet another high-grade mineralization has been discovered at the Western Deeps. Clearly, there is enough valuable ore in the area for decades to come and for all to share.

Although an environmental hearing was held and the project given approval by a panel, the mine is right at the overlap of land claimed by both the Inuit and Innu of Labrador. But this common interest in nickel helped to bring closer together the two aboriginal groups, whose relationship historically had not been warm. The project also whetted the appetite of the business people of Goose Bay, many of whom invested in anticipation of opportunities ahead.

But the biggest problem for Inco, the owner, was the negotiation with the provincial government. As Premier Joey Smallwood had done in the case of Labrador West, Premier Brian Tobin took the position that the mine could not be developed unless there was complete processing in the province. In fact, the jobs that secondary processing would bring were the only advantage for Tobin. Federal policies would ensure that 80 cents of every dollar were returned to Ottawa, either in the clawback of equalization payments or in federal taxes. New money, therefore, was really of very little benefit to the province; most of it would be used to pay back the federal government for past transfers.

So Tobin, to the chagrin of some in Labrador, insisted on a smelter in the province. But market forces and the availability of smelter capacity elsewhere in the country convinced the company not to go ahead with a conventional smelter. It did offer to construct an experimental smelter using a new hydromet method, but Tobin would have none of it unless there were firm guarantees in place. Stalemate ensued. Both aboriginal groups continued discussions with the company that would see them benefit in revenues, royalties, training, and jobs, but nothing happened. Although the Inuit passed the milestone of a land claims agreement in principle, the stalemate over Voisey's Bay halted all progress with the company.

But following the election of Roger Grimes's government in 2001, talks resumed. Grimes was a strong and skilful negotiator who had shone in the onerous health, education, and energy portfolios of the Tobin administration. Not only did he understand the smouldering resentment over past resource exploitation and the challenge to retain money and jobs in the province, but he appreciated the emerging rights and growing strength of the aboriginal organizations while also being aware of the need for flexibility if a deal was to be reached. By allowing some ore to be shipped out of the province in the early stages of the mine but insisting that jobs and processing had to be done locally, Grimes and his energy minister, Lloyd Matthews, won landmark concessions from Inco to return a like amount of ore to the province for processing after the nickel at Voisey's Bay had been exhausted. As well, the company agreed that over the next several decades it would invest nearly $3 billion and create two thousand jobs in Labrador and at Argentia, the abandoned U.S. naval base on the Island. Inco promised to build a mine and mill at the site of the northern Labrador discovery, and research facilities and a processing plant at Argentia. The project is expected to add $11 billion to provincial GDP.

A jubilant Grimes and Inco CEO Scott Hand revealed the details of the agreement to an enthusiastic crowd at the Hotel Newfoundland in June 2002 and, later the same day, to an enthusiastic gathering of Labradorians at the Aurora Hotel in Happy Valley–Goose Bay. Later in the month the agreement in principle was approved easily by the legislature. But would the members of the Labrador Inuit Association approve the agreements that their negotiators had struck with Inco? On 24 June both the Innu and the Inuit voted overwhelmingly to approve the impact benefit agreements negotiated with Inco. That night, the crowd that had gathered at Bentley's on Hamilton River Road in Happy Valley for the start of the seventh "Voisey's Bay and Beyond" conference felt an electric current run through their midst as the news was announced. They knew that the last hurdle to the development of Voisey's Bay had been cleared. They knew that the moment was historic and that life in their area of Labrador would never be the same.

For the first time, all racial groups and all areas of Labrador had supported a project from which they could all see benefits, as had their partners on the Island. A deal had been made of which all approved and in which all would share. Now, perhaps, the resentment built up by the power that went to Quebec, the fish that went to the United States, and the iron ore that went all over the world could be finally assuaged. A Labrador resource would be developed from which the people of the province would get maximum benefits.

While both Labrador and the Island would benefit from the mine, clearly the big winners were the aboriginal groups. In contrast to the paltry $7000 which Mathieu André had received in the middle of the twentieth century for leading Joe Retty to the first marketable iron ore deposits, the Innu and Inuit early in the twenty-first century would receive hundreds of millions of dollars. Not only had the negotiations for the mine driven land claims negotiations much more rapidly, but both aboriginal groups had negotiated separate impact benefit agreements with Inco. Land claims will eventually give both groups self-government, substantial control over resource development, along with traditional hunting and fishing rights, and, most importantly, control over their own lives and their own future. The impact benefits agreements with Inco will ensure that the Innu and Inuit will have priority in securing jobs and training for them. Negotiators for both groups had been persistent and persuasive, knowing that even though secure well-paying jobs might not by themselves overcome the dependency and social dislocation of the past decades, they would be a key weapon in the arsenal to improve quality of life.

In the long run, Grimes's greatest achievement may not have been negotiating the development of the largest sulphide deposit in the western World and the largest mining project in Canada. It may prove to have been the presence with him, at the head table, of representatives of the various peoples of Labrador. William Barbour, president of the Labrador Inuit Association, was there and gave all due credit to the benefits negotiator, Isabella Payne of Nain. Peter Penashue, president of the Innu Nation was there. The Honourable ernest McLean, the provincial minister of aboriginal and Labrador affairs (and the grandson of Malcolm) was there. Wally Andersen, parliamentary secretary to the minister of aboriginal and Labrador affairs, was there. (A descendant of Thorsten and a member of the Labrador Inuit Association, he had for some years been assiduously defending the rights of the people of the north coast.) Lawrence O'Brien, originally from L'Anse-au-Loup, a descendant of the Irish immigrants into the Strait of Belle Isle, was there as the member of parliament for Labrador, and I was there as the Labrador senator. Gerry Byrne, provincial representative in the Canadian cabinet was there, as was Scott Hand, the president of Inco, whose patience, persistence, and flexibility had been a key factor in finalizing the deal. And so was Stewart Gendron, the president of Voisey's Bay Nickel.

What made the occasion truly historic was that aboriginal and non-aboriginal Labradorians and Newfoundlanders sat at a table with both levels of government and a powerful multinational company, where all declared themselves winners. This had never happened before. If it could be done for nickel, why not for fish or wood or tourism or oil and gas? For some years, parts of the private sector had recognized the wisdom of acquiring aboriginal partners. Labrador, the land of parts, was coming together. Perhaps there was an acknowledgement that a co-operative effort, practised for centuries by aboriginal people, would work for the whole of Labrador. As the provincial forest management plan is being drawn up, Innu are part of the planning and writing team, and much of the data was collected by Innu Forest Guardians.

NEW HORIZONS

Although aboriginal organizations had gained a great measure of influence and control over events that threatened to change their people's lives, a strong and influential pan-Labrador organization had not developed. While it had been talked about from the 1970s onwards, nothing satisfactory had materialized. Perhaps this was because there was no consensus on what shape it should take. To the Innu, it had earlier meant a separate state based on land control and resources negotiated through land claims; to non-aboriginals, it had meant regional government representing all of Labrador.

Of course, the Combined Councils continued to exist, but on a shoestring and without sustained influence. Various governments had created new structures, such as the Department of Labrador Affairs. But until recently, the management had largely been in St John's, near the centre of power and away from the people it served. Labrador was still a land of parts. Even the north and south coasts had little in common with each other, while the road had only brought closer contact with the centre and the west. At the conference "Labrador in the Nineties," Sharon Edmunds, the daughter of former LIA president Bill Edmunds, summed up her workshop thus: "People identified of utmost importance the 'unification' and 'solidarity' of the five different regions, to form a common voice for Labrador. Most people said if this were not done, Labradorians would never gain the kind of control over their lives they would like to achieve."[10]

Recently, the provincial government announced the latest incarnation of the Department of Labrador Affairs with several innovations.

The minister, Wally Andersen, is now located in Labrador, and the key portfolio of aboriginal affairs has been added to his responsibilities. Many hope that the new department will help achieve the goal of pan-Labrador cooperation.

The regions do unite from time to time around certain issues. In 2001 a pan-Labrador conference was hosted by the two towns in Labrador West to discuss the completion of the Trans-Labrador Highway and the building of a fixed link under the Strait of Belle Isle. But meetings such as this have not been the rule. Perhaps only in the Labrador Winter Games, which are held every three years, has the pan-Labrador spirit been witnessed. As the teams from all the Labrador communities march onto the arena in Happy Valley – their uniforms being variations on the theme of the Labrador flag – it is clear that there is a spirit emanating from the land itself and the people who call it home. Only then is Labrador greater than the sum of its parts. And all are more or less equal because of the very nature of the games, which include unique arctic competitions, ensuring that athletes from Nain and Davis Inlet can excel every bit as much as those from Goose Bay or Labrador West. Here is a pan-Labrador that works. But for the political equivalent, the call has echoed every ten years from the voice of Don Jamieson in the 1970s to the voice of Sharon Edmunds in the 1990s.

Until the nineties, the push for influence in policy making was directed south to the island of Newfoundland and its government. For decades if not centuries, Labrador and Newfoundland have been uneasy stepsisters occupying the same semi-detached neo-British house. Geographically separate, and with different economic and cultural histories, the people of Labrador – whether they came from the frozen Arctic, the Orkney Islands, Quebec, or even the island of Newfoundland – believed over the years that the resources around them had been exploited for the benefit of someone else and that their needs were seldom considered and were certainly not paramount. So in relation to the Island, they constantly tried to get recognized as an integral part of the province and to gain more control over their own lives and their own place. Perhaps, with the creation of the new Department of Labrador Affairs, it has become clear that Labrador is different, that it is not just another peninsula of the Island, and that it cannot be run effectively from St John's with old and erroneous attitudes.

Even before the founding of Nunavut in 1999, Labradorians understood that they could have a meaningful relationship with those to the north as well the south. Indeed, for some years the federal Department of Revenue had designated Labrador as part of the North. This was an issue brought to public attention very forcibly in the 1980s during the debate on the federal taxation of northern benefits. As a result of winning that debate, Labradorians have been able, like all other northerners, to deduct from income tax certain subsidies for transportation and housing. And in the 1990s the federal Department of Foreign Affairs designated Labrador as part of the defined North for federal purposes. The Labrador Inuit Association had for some time been a part of the Inuit Circumpolar Conference, and since the creation of the Arctic Council the bonds between countries and territories around the pole, including Labrador, have strengthened.

In Goose Bay, Perry Trimper of Jacques Whitford, the environmental engineers, noticed that Labrador had more in common with the Komi Republic of Russia than just in the colours of their respective flags. Harry Baikie, who at the time was mayor of Goose Bay, led a delegation to Russia, and the relationship started to build. In the late 1990s, members of the chambers of commerce from the two regions met to examine business opportunities between Labrador and the regions of Yamal-Nenets and Khanty Mansyisk in Russia. Meanwhile, cruise ships from the Scandinavian countries were taking the arctic route to Labrador. It was becoming clear that while Labrador had a relationship with its western neighbour, Quebec, it might equally have a relationship with its northern neighbour, Russia – and, indeed, with its eastern neighbour, Greenland.

But it was the founding of Nunavut that opened new horizons for that new territory's southern neighbour. Many skilled people moved from the province to work in Nunavut. Also, if goods and services were coming over the road from Quebec to Goose Bay, why couldn't they go on from there by sea or air to Iqaluit? Could connections be made not only in trade and commerce but also in education and research? With the coming of Smart Labrador, some are thinking of a unique postsecondary institution that as well as serving the educational needs of Labrador young people could also reach out to the Arctic and the Near North. The Smithsonian Institution in Washington has for some years had a close connection with Labrador, particularly with the aboriginal people, and so has Bowdoin College of Maine. There are those who are excited about the idea of links between institutions in the south and a new postsecondary creation in Labrador, led by Memorial University, to serve the needs of the Arctic.

Conclusion

Labrador is still a land of promise, still a land rich in resources. There is wood to be harvested with care, water power to be harnessed after environmental protection is assured, minerals to be processed, largely unexplored territory to be enjoyed by ecotourists, marine resources to be caught and processed, and offshore oil and gas to be exploited. But the greatest resource, as always, is the skill and ability of its people. Sadly, there is still net emigration. Can technological advance, wired communities, and a reorganized education system stem the flow? Already young people, both aboriginal and non-aboriginal, are training in fields such as archaeology that were hitherto not part of their consciousness. Can enough jobs be created quickly? Can educational institutions and training centres be upgraded to meet the needs of young people? This is the challenge.

Can the necessary capital be attracted and the necessary markets found? They were found for iron ore and Churchill Falls, though there was a heavy price paid by the province. While investment did not happen in the case of uranium or for substantial forestry development, Inco has invested in the rich nickel deposits. As for the fishery, it has really only developed with the growth of fishermen's co-ops. As well, the Labrador Inuit Association, through the Labrador Inuit Development Association, has exploited the deposits of anorthosite stone in the north with the help of Italian businessmen. Tourism is still a fledgling industry, though it clearly has great potential.

In order to develop Labrador's potential and create jobs we need infrastructure. Now that funds have been promised to complete the Trans-Labrador Highway between Goose Bay and Cartwright, there will be a first-class gravel road from the Quebec North Shore all the way across Labrador to the Strait of Belle Isle, with a connection to the Island. This is perhaps the most important asset in developing

Labrador's economy and knitting together its parts. There are also airstrips in place, adequate health-care facilities, and water and sewer services in most communities. Most settlements are plugged in and switched on, though their systems may not be as fast as they might like.

But while there has been investment in facilities and connections, there has not been the concomitant investment in education, either secondary or postsecondary. This is perhaps the most important investment, for without it the emigration will continue, in spite of capital and infrastructure. Some help will come with the finalizing of land claims agreements and the Voisey's Bay impact benefit agreements between the aboriginal groups and Inco. But to be fair, effective resources need to be applied in non-aboriginal as well as aboriginal communities.

Wilfred Grenfell, in the introduction to his book *Labrador: The Country and the People*, dreamed about the future:

To us here, away out of the world's hum and bustle, it seems only a question of time. Some day a railway will come to export our stores of mineral wealth, to tap our sources of more than Niagaran power, to bring visitors to scenery of Norwegian quality yet made peculiarly attractive by the entrancing colour plays of Arctic auroras over the fantastic architecture of mountains the like of which can seldom be matched on the earth. Surely it will come to pass that one day another Atlantic City will rise amidst these unexplored but invigorating wilds to lure men and women tired of heat and exhausted by the nerve stress of overcrowded centres.[1]

Some of the vision of Paddon and Grenfell has materialized. Changes have come, and no doubt more lie ahead. The difference in the new century is that Labrador's people must be consulted, must be partners, and must share in the wealth in a way they did not in earlier decades. Although no regional organization has been put in place and there is no one body that effectively brings the parts together, Labrador is represented by local politicians who know their constituencies and can speak for them from personal experience. As well, the entrepreneur class that grew up during the 1960s, 1970s, and 1980s is well placed to take advantage of economic opportunities. And the Government of Newfoundland and Labrador – as it is now rightly and officially called – will continue to be aware that Labrador is not just another peninsula of the province but a place geographically, historically, and culturally different. There are Newfoundlanders, and there are Labradorians, and most people now have come to accept this reality. Even before the official name change, more and more Newfoundlanders were calling the province "Newfoundland

and Labrador," recognizing the identity of Labrador and the need for the two to be partners and not just fellow travellers.

At the present time – in 2003 – there are about 30,000 people in Labrador spread over 300,000 square kilometres of sometimes rocky and sometimes forested, sometimes cold and sometimes warm, often rich and always beautiful challenging land. They came from different places and had different origins. They brought different skills and different expectations. They came for different reasons. They had common obstacles to overcome. They settled in different places, and Labrador is still a land of parts that needs putting together. But they are all Labradorians, which Patty Way and Richard Budgell defined at the "Labrador in the Nineties" conference as those who have chosen to make it their home. Phyllis Moore, a pioneer business-woman in Labrador West, contends that "being a Labradorian is a matter of mind, heart, and soul, not exclusively a circumstance of birth." For as Rilke has said, "One composes within oneself one's true place of origin." None of these people is going home; this is home for all of them. They have felt its magnetic pull, witnessed its beauty, experienced its bounty. And more will come. There is room for many more.

The challenge of the future, as in the past, is how these different people in different places with different skills and different expecta-tions can find a way of living together. It was the challenge of the Inuit and Innu; and only recently, because of the overlap of land claims and the realization that both could share in the good fortune ahead, did they improve their dialogue.[2] It was the challenge for the ancestors of today's aboriginal people when they encountered the Europeans. The two cultures learned from each other, it is true, but the Europeans were the dominant society. It was the challenge of the early Labradorians who encountered the Newfoundland fishermen on their shores in the eighteenth and nineteenth centuries. It was the challenge of Canadians and people from other parts of the world as they came to work side by side with the settlers. It was the challenge of the French and English workers in Churchill Falls and Labrador West. Today, in the wired world and the global economy, Labra-dorians are better informed and confident of their ability to articulate their needs and aspirations.

Elizabeth Goudie in her memoirs spoke of her hope for the future. Perhaps she speaks for many in Labrador:

Now things are changed, even the name of Grand River to Churchill River. Many of us didn't like it when we heard of the change because Grand River was its name since the 1800s and to the trappers it was their home and I would say their birthright. I have nothing against the name Churchill – he was a good man too – but no one asked us if we were satisfied having it changed. If Joe Smallwood had seen the trappers return from Grand River with their frostbitten faces, half-starved and exhausted, he might have thought twice before he changed it, but that is beside the point now. For many old timers it still is Grand River, but for the younger generation it will be Churchill River and I hope they treat it with respect. I hope the younger people will take pride in Labrador because it's a country of beauty and wealth. Its people were a *people* in the past. The trappers made their own laws, they respected each other's laws and they carried them out to the best of their ability. I will never change deep within my heart and I hope I can be a friend to people. We should all strive to live in peace with one another. That's the only way to live right.[3]

Notes

INTRODUCTION

1 Tanner, "Outlines of the Geography, Life and Customs of Newfoundland-Labrador," 61
2 Stewart, *Labrador*, 120
3 Boilieu, *Recollections of Labrador Life*, 26

CHAPTER ONE

1 Gosling, *Labrador*, 76

CHAPTER TWO

1 Magnusson, *The Vinland Sagas*, 55
2 Munn, *Wineland Voyages*, 13
3 Gosling, *Labrador*, 123
4 The term Naskapi was borrowed originally by the French from the Saguenay River Innu. In the Innu language the word meant "people of the place where it fades out of sight" and referred to groups that lived beyond the horizon. The earliest occurrence of the name Naskapi comes from Father Laure in 1731, who identified a group north of Lake Ashuanipi, at the head of the Moisie River. At first it was used simply to describe one group of Innu, but later it became an epithet meaning "uncivilized people" or "those who have no religion," or simply "the most primitive." By the late nineteenth century it referred to the Innu living farthest from trading posts and missions. These Innu call themselves Mushuau, meaning "the barren ground people." In reality, of course, the Montagnais and Naskapi are all one people, speaking Innu Aimun, a Cree dialect, and are part of the Algonkian linguistic family.

5 The name was altered in 1820 to honour Charles Hamilton, governor of Newfoundland 1818–24; the inner arm was called Lake Melville after Viscount Melville, a lord of the British Admiralty.

6 Winston White, "Living on the Land," St John's *Evening Telegram*, 2 Feb. 1997

7 Maggo, and Brice-Bennett, *Remembering the Years of My Life*, 20

8 Campbell, *Sketches of Labrador Life*, 26

9 Poole, *Catucto*, 15

10 Townsend, *Captain Cartwright and His Labrador Journal*, 15

11 Ibid., 7

12 One Rigolet family adopted the name Palliser, either out of gratitude or because of a close relationship that one of its members had with Sir Hugh Palliser. The descendants of Inuit families, including the Pallisers, remain at Rigolet to this day.

CHAPTER THREE

1 Gosling, *Labrador*, 257

2 William Tuglavina became a chapel servant in Nain. William's sister Regina and her daughter Sophia were also chapel servants, and after William's death in 1852 his son Frederick was appointed to assume his position. During the twentieth century, William Barbour was replaced as chief elder of Nain in 1924 by his relative and friend Martin Martin, who was succeeded by his son-in-law Jeremiah Sillett. A modern-day William Barbour is president of the Labrador Inuit Association (LIA). But there were no Inuit ordained ministers until late in the twentieth century.

3 Memorial University Library, Centre for Newfoundland Studies, unpublished diary of Mr Moss, a planter at Battle Harbour in the 1830s.

4 The practice of instruction in Inuktitut was discontinued after Confederation. But in 1978, with the leadership of Beatrice Watts (the former Beatrice Ford of Nain), the Labrador East Integrated School Board, in partnership with the LIA, introduced Inuktitut as a second language from kindergarten to nine. In 1986 the teaching of Inuktitut as a first language was introduced from kindergarten to grade three. Today both these programs are offered in varying degrees along the coast according to interest and the availability of teachers.

5 Harry Paddon, *Labrador Memoir*, 217

6 Harry Paddon, *Daily News* Labrador souvenir supplement, 19 Oct. 1938

7 Winston White, "Living on the Land," St John's *Evening Telegram*, 2 Feb. 1997, 12

8 Maggo and Brice-Bennett, *Remembering the Years of My Life*

9 Peacock, *Reflections from a Snowhouse*

10 Williamson, "Population Movement ... of Northern Labrador"

11 Wallace, *John McLean's Notes of a Twenty-Five-Year Service*, 229

12 McDonald, *Lord Strathcona*, 63

13 Smith was transferred to Montreal in 1869 after twenty years in Labrador. At this time the federal government had just completed negotiations in London for the purchase of most of the Hudson's Bay Company's territory for $1.5 million. But the Metis of the West resented the company's disregard for their rights through settlement and feared the domination of a centralized English-speaking Protestant government. Prime Minister John A. Macdonald appointed Smith to investigate the insurrection that occurred.

Smith continued to have a remarkable career. From being a major force in the evolution of the economy of Lake Melville, he became a major force in Canadian economics and politics. His skill as a financier made possible the construction of the Canadian Pacific Railway, for which he drove in the last spike. During his years with the Hudson's Bay Company he transformed, as Peter Newman put it, "a dominion of wilderness into a commercial enterprise." As president of the Bank of Montreal for twenty-seven years he made it the largest financial institution in the country. His diplomacy settled the first Riel rebellion, and his dramatic political turnabout while he was MP for Selkirk toppled the government of Sir John A. Macdonald.

14 Merrick, *True North*, 7

15 Hudson's Bay Company Archives, North West River journal, 10 Jan. 1890

16 Ibid., 4 Oct. 1890

17 The film is being made by Ken Pittman of Red Ochre Productions, St John's

18 Borlase, *The Labrador Settlers*, 103

19 Bella Shouse, interview with Wallace J. McLean, 7 Jan. 2002

20 Richard Budgell, "People as Good as You"

21 Merrick, "S.S. *Kyle*," 36

22 Rompkey, *Grenfell of Labrador*, 40

23 Poole, *Catucto*, 40

24 Anthony Paddon, *Labrador Doctor*, 11

25 Harold, Paddon, Jr. *Green Woods and Blue Waters*, 12

26 Yale School was so named because it was built by student volunteers from Yale University, led by Varrick Frissell. He later lost his life, off Newfoundland, when the sealing ship *Viking* was destroyed by explosives during the shooting of the first Hollywood movie made on location.

27 Harry Paddon, *Labrador Memoir*, 207

28 Buckle, *The Anglican Church in Labrador*, 80

29 Ibid., 81
30 Anthony Paddon, *Labrador Doctor,* 68
31 Manteskueu, in Innu Nation, *Gathering Voices,* 27
32 Young, *A Methodist Missionary in Labrador,* 14
33 The descendants of Lydia Brooks Campbell still carry on the story of
Labrador life that she began. Doris Saunders, who traces her lineage
back to Lydia, has received the Order of Canada and an honorary
degree from Memorial for her publication of *Them Days,* a magazine of
early Labrador life in which the people tell their own stories in their
own words.
34 Buckle, *The Anglican Church in Labrador,* 71
35 Ibid., 102
36 The Rev. Joyce operated an airplane out of Red Bay serving the
Plymouth Brethren congregation, and Pastor Morrison of the
Pentecostal Church later operated a plane out of Postville and then out
of Fox Harbour.

CHAPTER FOUR

1 Boilieu, *Recollections of Labrador Life,* 30
2 However, Grenfell took a different position later when the bad times
hit. Then he urged Mackenzie King to take over Labrador.
3 Budgell and Stavely. *The Labrador Boundary,* 10
4 Neary, "Newfoundland and Quebec," 47
5 Ibid., 35
6 Smith, *Brinco,* 22
7 Horwood, *Newfoundland Ranger Force,* 39
8 Archives of Newfoundland and Labrador, letter from Gower Rabbitts
to Sam Broomfield, Feb. 1920
9 Ibid., petition from northern Labrador to governor of Newfoundland,
1921
10 Ibid., petition from northern Labrador to governor of Newfoundland,
1924
11 Dick White, letter to Prime Minister Alderdice, in McGrath, "Life in
Voisey's Bay," 132

CHAPTER FIVE

1 CBC Goose Bay Archives, Gordon Rendell, taped interview
2 Neary, *The Political Economy of Newfoundland, 1929–1972,* 102
3 Carr, *Checkmate in the North,* 94
4 McGrath, "On the Goose," 31
5 Perrault, *History of Happy Valley,* 2

6 Jamieson, *No Place for Fools*, 63

7 William Keough, speech in Hiller and Harrington, *The Newfoundland National Convention 1946–1948*, 599

8 Archives of Newfoundland and Labrador, letter from R. Harris to H.L. Pottle, 1953

9 Ibid., letter from J.R. Smallwood to L.B. Pearson, 1964

10 Ibid., letter from Walter Rockwood to the deputy minister of welfare, 1968

11 Ibid.

12 Ibid.

13 Archives of Newfoundland and Labrador, letter from Max Budgell to Walter Rockwood, 1958

14 Rich, *Struggling with My Soul*, 22

15 Letto, *In Cain's Footsteps*, 84

16 Ibid., 87

17 The original participants in the company were Hollinger Consolidated Gold Mines, Hollinger North Shore Exploration Company, Labrador Mining and Exploration Company, M.A. Hanna Company, Hanna Coal and Ore Company, Armco Steel Corporation, National Steel Corporation, Republic Steel Corporation, Wheeling Steel Corporation and Youngstown Sheet and Tube Company.

18 Young's father was Armenius, the author of *A Methodist Missionary in Labrador*, who had served on the Labrador coast in the early part of the century. Ewart Young himself taught for some time on the coast. He had been a confidant of Joe Smallwood and was one of the first of those who convinced Smallwood to start the movement for confederation with Canada.

19 John Montague, from the Orkneys, drowned some time later while tracking a canoe through Gull Island rapids. His grandson, Harvey Montague, who used to be a trapper in the same area, later became a janitor at Churchill Falls. Two of Harvey's sons also worked at Churchill: Ed as project geologist, and Clayton as an equipment operator.

20 Smith, *Brinco*, 191

CHAPTER SIX

1 Linda Strowbridge, "Innu Protest Sparking Resentment from Some Local Whites," *Sunday Express*, 13 Nov. 1988

2 "Labrador Innu to Resume NATO Protests," *Evening Telegram*, 8 Mar. 1989

3 Ibid.

4 "The Message Was Clear ... But No One Came to Listen," *Northern Reporter*, 1 Jan. 1990

5 Stephen Maher, "Fifteen Years of Recording Labradorian Lives," *Labradorian*, 10 Oct. 1989

6 An organization that had tried to do something about this was the Extension Service of Memorial University. Earlier, Tony Williamson had spent some years on the Labrador coast, using film as a tool in community consciousness-raising and community development. This method, the Fogo Process, which in effect held up a mirror to individuals and to the whole community, was highly regarded at the time as an innovation in learning and was showcased in the National Film Board's *Challenge for Change* series.

7 *Labrador in the Nineties*, 9

8 Ibid., 23

9 Ibid.

10 Ibid., 53

CONCLUSION

1 Grenfell, *Labrador*, vi

2 It was a proud Sheshatshiu band chief, Paul Rich, who announced in November 2002 that the Innu Nation had become status Indians, a development that will enable them to manage their own affairs.

3 Goudie, *Woman of Labrador*, 197

Bibliography

Abbott, Louise. *The Coast Way: A Portrait of the English on the Lower North Shore of the St. Lawrence*. Montreal: McGill-Queen's University Press, 1988

Andersen, Joan. *Makkovik: 100 Years Plus*. St John's: RB Books, 1996

Armitage, Peter. *The Innu*. New York: Chelsea House, 1991

Baikie, L.D. "*Up and Down the Bay*." Unpublished, 1989

Boilieu, Lambert de. *Recollections of Labrador Life*. London: Saunders, Otley, 1861

Borlase, Tim. *The Labrador Inuit*. Happy Valley–Goose Bay: Labrador East Integrated School Board, 1993

– *The Labrador Settlers, Metis and Kablunangajuit*. Happy Valley–Goose Bay: Labrador East Integrated School Board, 1994

Brice-Bennett, Carol. *Reconciling with Memories: Hebron Forty Years after Relocation*. Nain: Labrador Inuit Association, 2000

– *Two Opinions: Inuit and Moravian Missionaries in Labrador*. St John's: Memorial University of Newfoundland, 1981

Buckle, Francis. *The Anglican Church in Labrador*. Labrador City: Archdeaconry of Labrador, 1998

Budgell, Richard. "People as Good as You: Mixed-Ancestry Labradorians and Cultural Identity in Central Labrador 1836–1941." MA thesis, Carleton University, 1997

Budgell, Richard, and Michael Stavely. *The Labrador Boundary*. St John's: Labrador Institute of Northern Studies, Memorial University of Newfoundland, 1987

Cabot, William Brooks. *In Northern Labrador*. Boston: Gorham Press, 1912

Campbell, Lydia. *Sketches of Labrador Life*. St Johns: Killick Press and Them Days, 1980

Canadian Environmental Assessment Agency. *Military Flying Activities in Labrador and Quebec*. Ottawa: Ministry of Supply and Services, 1995

Carr, W.G. *Checkmate in the North*. Toronto: Macmillan, 1945

Cooke, Alan. *A History of the Naskapi of Schefferville*. Ottawa: Indian and Northern Affairs, 1976

Davies, K.G., ed. *Northern Quebec and Labrador Journals and Correspondence*. London: Hudson's Bay Record Society, 1963

Davies, W.H.A. "Esquimaux Bay and the Surrounding Country." Literary and Historical Society of Quebec *Transactions* 4(1842)

Dutton, Sean Patrick. "Flying the North: The Controversy over Low-Level Tactical Fighter Training in Labrador." BA (hons) thesis, Acadia University, 1990

Dyer, Gwynne. *Full Circle: First Contact*. St John's: Newfoundland Museum, 2000

Dyke, A. Prince. "Population Distribution and Movement in Coastal Labrador, 1950–66." Thesis, Faculty of Graduate Studies, McGill University, Montreal, 1968

Economic Council of Canada. *Newfoundland: From Dependency to Self-Reliance*. Ottawa: Economic Council of Canada, 1980

Fitzhugh, Lynn. *The Labradorians*. St John's: Breakwater Books, 1999

Fitzhugh, William. *Environmental Archaeology and Cultural Systems in Hamilton Inlet, Labrador*. Washington: Smithsonian Institution, 1972

Forbes, Alexander. *Quest for a Northern Air Route*. Boston: Harvard University Press, 1953

Geren, Richard, and Blake McCullogh. *Cain's Legacy*. Sept-Îles: Iron Ore Company, 1990

Goodyear, Cyril. *Nunatsuak*. St John's: Creative Publishers, 2000

Gordon, Henry. *The Labrador Parson*. St John's: Newfoundland Archives, 1972

Gosling, W.G. *Labrador*. London: Alston Rivers, 1910

Goudie, Elizabeth. *Woman of Labrador*. Toronto: Peter Martin, 1973

Government of Canada. *Economic Prospects for the Goose Bay Area*. Ottawa: Bureau of Management Consulting, 1973

Grenfell, Wilfred. *Labrador: The Country and the People*. New York: Macmillan, 1909

Grenier, Robert. "Excavating a 400-Year-Old Basque Whaling Galleon." *National Geographic*, July 1985, 58–68

Gwyn, Richard. *Smallwood: The Unlikely Revolutionary*. Toronto: McClelland and Stewart, 1968

Gwyn, Sandra. "The Future Comes to Labrador." *Saturday Night*, Dec. 1978, 16–32

Henriksen, George. *Hunters in the Barrens*. St John's: Institute for Social and Economic Research, Memorial University of Newfoundland, 1975

Hiller, J.K. *The Foundation and the Early Years of the Moravian Mission in Labrador, 1752–1805*. St John's: Memorial University of Newfoundland, 1967

Hiller, J.K., and M.F. Harrington. *The Newfoundland National Convention, 1946–1948*. Montreal: McGill-Queen's University Press, 1995

Hind, Henry Youle. *Explorations in the Interior of the Labrador Peninsula: The Country of the Montagnais and Nasquapee Indians*. Vols. 1 and 2. London: Longmans, Green, 1863

Horwood, Harold. *The Newfoundland Ranger Force*. St John's: Breakwater Books, 1986

– *White Eskimo*. Toronto: Doubleday, 1972

Hubbard, Mrs Leonidas. *A Woman's Way through Trackless Labrador*. New York: McClure, 1908

Innis, H.A. *The Cod Fisheries*. Toronto: University of Toronto Press, 1954

Innu Nation and Mushuau Innu Band Council. *Gathering Voices: The People's Inquiry*. Ntesinan: Innu Nation, 1992

Jackson, Lawrence. *Bounty of a Barren Coast: Resource Harvest and Settlement in Southern Labrador*. St John's: Institute for Social and Economic Research, Memorial University of Newfoundland, 1982

Jamieson, Donald. *No Place for Fools*. St John's: Breakwater Books, 1989

Jenness, Diamond. *Eskimo Administration in Labrador*. Montreal: Arctic Institute of North America, 1965

Kennedy, John C. *Holding the Line*. St John's: Institute for Social and Economic Research, Memorial University of Newfoundland, 1982

– *People of the Bays and Headlands*. Toronto: University of Toronto Press, 1995

Kurlansky, Mark. *The Basque History of the World*. Toronto: Knopf, 1999

Labrador in the Eighties. Happy Valley–Goose Bay: Labrador Institute of Northern Studies, 1980

Labrador in the Nineties. Happy Valley–Goose Bay: Combined Councils of Labrador and Institute of Northern Studies, 1990

Labrador in the Seventies. St John's: Labrador North Chamber of Commerce and Memorial University of Newfoundland Extension Service, 1970

Labrador Inuit Association. *Our Footprints Are Everywhere*. Nain: LIA, 1978

Leacock, Eleanor, and Nan Rothschild. *Labrador Winter: The Ethnographic Journals of William Duncan Strong, 1927–28*. Washington: Smithsonian Institution Press, 1994

Letto, Douglas. *In Cain's Footsteps: People of the Labrador Straits*, Paradise, Nfld: Blue Hill, 2000

Loring, Stephen. "Keeping Things Whole: Nearly Two Thousand Years of Indian Occupation in Northern Labrador." *Boreal Forest and Subarctic Archaeology*, no. 6. London: Ontario Archaeological Society, 1988

– "O Darkly Bright: The Journeys of William Brooks Cabot, 1889–1910." *Appalachia*, Winter 1986–87, 29

Low, A.P. "Report on a Traverse of the Northern Part of Labrador from Richmond Gulf to Ungava Bay." *Annual Report of the Geological and Natural History Survey of Canada: 1896* 9, no. 658 (Reports A, F, I, L, M, R, S), 1898

McDonald, Donna. *Lord Strathcona*. Toronto: Dundurn Press, 1996

McGee, John T. *Cultural Stability and Change among the Montagnais Indians of the Lake Melville Region of Labrador.* Washington: Catholic University of America Press, 1961

McGrath, Judy, ed. "Life in Voisey's Bay." *Them Days* 22 (Winter 1997)

– "On the Goose: The Story of Goose Bay," *Them Days* 12 (June 1987)

McLean, John. *Notes of a Twenty-Five Years' Service in the Hudson's Bay Territory.* London: Richard Bentley, 1849

MacLeod, Malcolm. *Kindred Countries: Canada and Newfoundland before Confederation.* Ottawa: Canadian Historical Association, 1994

McNish, Jacquie. *The Big Score: Robert Friedland, Inco and the Voisey's Bay Hustle.* Toronto: Doubleday, 1998

Maggo, Paulus, and Carol Brice-Bennett. *Remembering the Years of My Life.* St John's: Institute for Social and Economic Research, Memorial University of Newfoundland, 1999

Magnusson, Magnus. *The Vinland Sagas.* Harmondsworth: Penguin, 1965

Mailhot, José. *The People of Sheshashit.* St John's: Institute for Social and Economic Research, Memorial University of Newfoundland, 1997

Merrick, Elliot. *Northern Nurse.* New York: Scribner, 1942

– "S.S. Kyle." *Them Days* 9 (June 1984)

– *True North.* New York: Scribner, 1933

Munn, W.A. *Wineland Voyages.* St John's: Evening Telegram, 1946

Neary, Peter. "Newfoundland and Quebec: Provincial Neighbours across an Uneasy Frontier." *Bulletin of Canadian Studies* 2, no. 2 (1978): 35–51

– *Newfoundland in the North Atlantic World, 1929–1949.* Montreal: McGill-Queen's University Press, 1988

– *The Political Economy of Newfoundland, 1929–1972.* Vancouver: Copp Clark, 1973

– *White Tie and Decorations.* Toronto: University of Toronto Press, 1996

Newman, Peter C. *Flame of Power.* Toronto: Longmans, Green, 1959

Paddon, Anthony. *Labrador Doctor.* Toronto: Lorimer, 1989

Paddon, Harold. *Green Woods and Blue Water.* St John's: Breakwater Books, 1989

– *The Labrador Memoir of Dr Harry Paddon, 1912–1938,* ed. Ronald Rompkey. Montreal: McGill-Queen's University Press, 2003

Paine, Robert. *The White Arctic: Labrador.* St. John's: Institute for Social and Economic Research, Memorial University of Newfoundland, 1985

Peacock, F.W. *Reflections from a Snowhouse.* St. John's: Jesperson, 1986

Perrault, Alice. *History of Happy Valley.* Grand Falls: Robinson-Blackmore, 1967

Plaice, Evelyn. *The Native Game.* St John's: Institute for Social and Economic Research, Memorial University of Newfoundland, 1990

Poole, C.J. *Catucto, Battle Harbour, Labrador.* St Lewis, Nfld: Catal, 1996

Powell, Ben. *Labrador by Choice.* St John's: Good Tidings Press, 1979

Proulx, Jean-Pierre. *Basque Whaling in Labrador in the Sixteenth Century.* Ottawa: Parks Canada, 1993

Rich, George. *Struggling with My Soul.* St John's: Harrish Press, 2000

Rompkey, Ronald. *Grenfell of Labrador.* Toronto: University of Toronto Press, 1991

Rowe, Frederick W. *A History of Newfoundland and Labrador.* Toronto: McGraw-Hill Ryerson, 1980

– *The Smallwood Era.* Toronto: McGraw-Hill Ryerson, 1985

Smith, Philip. *Brinco: The Story of Churchill Falls.* Toronto: McClelland and Stewart, 1975

Sparkes, Adam. "Flurry: A Case Study of the New Labrador Party." BA thesis, Acadia University, 1994

Stewart, Robert. *Labrador.* Amsterdam: Time-Life International, 1977

Tanner, V. "Outline of the Geography, Life and Customs of Newfoundland-Labrador." *Acta Geographica* (Helsinki), 8, no.1 and 2 (1944)

Taylor, J. Garth. "Historical Ethnography of the Labrador Coast." In *Handbook of American Indians.* Vol. 5. Washington: Smithsonian Institution Press, 1984

Thornton, Patricia. "The Democratic and Mercantile Bases of Initial Settlement in the Strait of Belle Isle." In Manion, J.J., *The Peopling of Newfoundland.* St John's: Institute for Social and Economic Research, Memorial University of Newfoundland, 1977

Townsend, Charles Wendell. *Captain Cartwright and His Labrador Journal.* Boston: Dana Estes, 1911

Tuck, James A. *Newfoundland and Labrador Prehistory.* Ottawa: National Museums of Canada, 1976

Tuck, James, and Robert Grenier. *Red Bay, Labrador.* Ottawa: National Museums of Canada, 1976

Wadden, Marie. *Nitassinan.* Vancouver: Douglas & McIntyre, 1991

Wallace, Dillon. *The Long Labrador Trail.* New York: Outing Publishers, 1906

– *The Lure of the Labrador Wild.* New York: Revell, 1905

Wallace, W.S. *John McLean's Notes of a Twenty-Five-Year Service in the Hudson Bay Territory.* Toronto: Champlain Society, 1932

Whiteley, George. *Northern Seas, Hardy Sailors.* New York: Norton, 1982

Williamson, H. Anthony. "Population Movement and the Food Gathering Economy of Northern Labrador." MA thesis, Faculty of Graduate Studies, Department of Geography, McGill University, April 1964

Young, Armenius. *A Methodist Missionary in Labrador.* Toronto: S. and A. Young, 1916

Zimmerley, David. *Cain's Land Revisited.* St John's: Institute for Social and Economic Research, Memorial University of Newfoundland, 1975

Index